THE IRON CIRCLE

THE IRON CIRCLE

THE TRUE LIFE STORY OF DOMINIQUIE VANDENBERG

DOMINIQUIE VANDENBERG

AS TOLD TO

RICK REVER

Volt Press

Los Angeles

09   08   07   06   05   5   4   3   2   1

Library of Congress Cataloging-in-Publication Data

Vandenberg, Dominiquie.
    The iron circle : the true life story of Dominiquie Vandenberg /
Dominiquie Vandenberg, as told to Rick Rever.
        p. cm.
    ISBN 1-56625-226-1
    1. Vandenberg, Dominiquie. 2. Martial artists—Belgium—
Biography. I. Rever, Rick. II. Title.
    GV1113.V36A3 2004
    796.8′092—dc22

                                                    2004010585

Volt Press
A division of Bonus Books
1223 Wilshire Bl., #597
Santa Monica, CA 90403
volt-press.com

Printed in the United States of America

To Sabine & Pierre

Shiko

The foot-stamping ritual performed by sumo
wrestlers to drive away evil spirits before a bout.

I am the best. There is no other like me. I have won glory. I have earned honor. I am remorseless. These things are mine and I will defend them to the death, for I am a warrior and this is my way. If you wish to travel with me on this path, read on. I will tell you honestly and plainly how I came to be what it is I am.

This, then, is the start.

Soot! Ta-nohn!

A Thai phrase meaning "the end of the road."

I'd come to Thailand to train, not to fight, but in the small frontier towns near the border with Laos there wasn't much difference between training and fighting. Either way you got bloody. Either way you got hurt. I figured I might as well collect on the pain in hard cash. Besides, thirty grand was tough to pass up for a few minutes' work. Thirty grand, that is, if you won. If you lost, well, I didn't want to think about that. I'd already beat one Thai fighter in a freestyle match. He'd crawled out of the ring on his belly. I knew he'd never walk again. Not after what I'd done to his legs. But at least he'd live. It could have been worse. Much worse.

White fighters in this part of Thailand were more rare than gemstones and the Thai fought them hard. When word got out that I was looking for matches, the offers poured in. Everybody wanted to fight a "round-eye" from a wealthy Western country, and not just for the cash. Thai pride was on the line. To the Thai who came to watch and bet, my bouts were more than fights; they were geopolitical struggles. Defeat me and for a brief shining moment the Third World could claim victory over the First.

I didn't begrudge the Thai their feelings. If I'd been forced to live like them—squatting my life away in poverty, coerced by corrupt officials into selling my girls into prostitution, watching my boys die of diseases for which the West held a cure—I too would be angry. I too would gloat over the body of the white Western fighter as he lay broken-boned in the dirt.

A year before, that's exactly what had happened. An American fighter had come to this province looking to make a name for himself as a fighter. Like me, he'd hooked up with Daniel, a Frenchmen who ran a local bar. Like me, he'd won his first few bouts, and then he made the mistake of fighting Kran.

In these parts Kran was a fighting legend. Six years undefeated. Six years of fighting at least one freestyle bout a month, and no one could touch him. To me it sounded impossible and I told Daniel as much.

"I don't want to hear that cocksucker's name in my bar," Daniel exploded as he slid another beer into my hand and moved off down the bar.

I knocked back the beer and looked around. The bar was crawling with the usual rabble. A few stools down, two Thai cops were in the middle of a drunken argument. Across the room, a soldier in uniform was too busy tweaking the nipples of the teenage whore on his lap to notice that the girl sitting next to him was picking his pocket, while on stage a Thai gangster in an oversized cowboy hat crooned in accented English to an Elvis tune that blared from the speakers: "Ruv me tenda. Ruv me true. Neva ret me gro." Just another night in Thailand at Daniel's Wild West Karaoke Bar.

I didn't know how Daniel was able to hold the place

together, what with all the fights and the guns and the booze and the girls. But I guess Daniel was used to all that. He'd opened bars and sold girls, drinks, and drugs in cities across France. After doing time in a French prison, Daniel had come to Thailand to build his own little kingdom in a country that still respected his particular brand of chaos.

At least he did chaos with style. In his cowboy boots, motorcycle jacket, and faded jeans, the tattooed Daniel was a walking pastiche of every modern American renegade tradition. With a Frenchman's flair he mixed and matched them all, and the Thai loved him for it, and feared him too, for Daniel was dangerously well connected. Those he couldn't strong-arm he bribed; those he couldn't bribe he blackmailed; and those who still made trouble for him, he disappeared. And all for the sake of his bar.

Me, I had my own dream. I wanted to be the best freestyle fighter in the world. Freestyle fighting, for those of you who don't know, is what the martial arts used to be before the blood got tamed out of them. In freestyle fighting everything is permitted. You can kick, bite, wrestle, eye-gouge; you use whatever works. The only rule in freestyle is that there are no rules. There're no strict forms, no formal katas, no points, no belts, no grading, no mercy. It's war plain and simple, fought with bare hands. "Bujutsu," the Japanese call it—the practical art of deadly combat.

Practical if you won, deadly if you lost, freestyle fighting as practiced in Thailand was an all-or-nothing game, and since I was determined to have it all I knew that sooner or later I'd have to face Kran—a truly great fighter. What an honor it would be to finally beat him. Yes, this was the fight I'd been born to. I'd defeat Kran or be defeated myself, which was just fine with me, because if I couldn't be the best at what I did there was no point in living; it would be better to die. In fact, I'd consider it an honor to hand up my life to any man skilled enough to take it from me in the ring.

"Set me up against Kran," I demanded of Daniel as he slid another beer across the bar.

"Why? You in a hurry to die? I told you what happened to the American."

"Hey, I'm not the American."

"Well neither is he anymore."

"That's a chance I'm willing to take."

"But I'm not."

"Why?"

"Well, for starters there's no money in it. Nobody in their right mind would lay odds on you to beat Kran."

"I would."

"Yeah, but you're worth a lot more to me alive and fighting than dead after one match."

"Fuck you, Daniel."

"Look, before you get all pissed off, let me tell you about Kran. He was raised in the fighting schools here and in Laos. No parents. No relatives. Nothing but fighting since the day he was born. That's all he knows. That's all he's done. You know what a cage fight is?"

"No."

"It's when they put you in a cage with a gate in the middle. On one side is a wild dog. On the other side you. Then they open the gate."

"No weapons?"

"No nothing. Just bare hands against a fucking wild dog."

"Shit."

"Kran fought his first cage fight when he was ten. You don't even want to see what he can do now."

"Yes I do."

"Dominiquie, look, I'm telling you as a friend, if you know what's good for you you'll stay out of his shit."

"I'll find the guy myself if I have to."

"Even if you did, he wouldn't give you a fight."

"Why not?"

"Because nobody goes to Kran and gets a fight. His people have to come to you."

"And how do you get them to do that?"

"You beat enough locals and eventually Kran'll show up to defend Thai honor."

"To Thai honor then." I raised my bottle and drained it off in a swallow.

Daniel shook his head. "Anybody ever tell you you're insane?"

"All the time."

"By the way, a couple guys came in today and said their fighter is better than you."

"That's what they all say. How much did they offer?"

"The usual. Thirty thousand to win. Six to the loser."

"Who's their fighter?"

"We find out tomorrow. Another beer?"

"Nah, I'm hitting it."

I trudged upstairs and fell into bed. Though the racket downstairs was appalling, I blinked off pretty quick; you would've too if you'd spent the day like I had—jogging twenty miles, sparring nine rounds full out, practicing knee and elbow strikes till they sailed fast as comets into flesh. Get tagged by one of those babies and it would reshape your world forever.

The next day, Daniel pulled up to me on his Harley as I was shadowboxing behind the bar.

"Hop on—a new shipment just came in."

"A new shipment of what?"

"Hop on. You'll see"

"What about the fight you were going to set up?"

"First pleasure, then pain. Now hop on."

I climbed onto the back of Daniel's Harley and we

roared off down the road. A half-hour later we pulled up in front of an unmarked tin-roofed warehouse. A couple of dusty military trucks sat out front. Two armed Thai gangsters stood guard at the door.

"So what's in there? Drugs? Weapons?" I asked as we dismounted.

"Nah, a lot nicer than that."

I followed Daniel past the guards, though as soon as I did I'd wished I hadn't. Inside the warehouse at least a hundred frightened girls sat on rows of benches while Thai men wandered among them. The warehouse, as Daniel explained, was a transit point where girls bought or kidnapped from up north were brought to be watered, rested, and fucked before being delivered to the brothels of Bangkok.

"It's a slave market, Daniel. Let's get the fuck out of here."

"You kidding me? And leave all this young pussy?"

I let my gaze wander over the girls. In the half-light of the warehouse, their broad Pacific faces looked like tombstones. One of the girls was praying. While she sat counting beads, a man leaned behind her and slowly trailed his tongue up from her neck to her ear. When he swished the greasy muscle inside her lobe, the girl gave up her prayer and started crying.

"Look at that one," Daniel pointed toward a girl who couldn't have been more than twelve. "Think she's a virgin? Not bad looking either. You want her?"

"You out of your mind? She's a kid."

"Yeah, so's my wife, but she's not a virgin anymore."

"Jesus, Daniel."

"Hey, don't you know that every time you fuck a virgin you add a month to your life?"

"What?"

"It's part of the ancient wisdom, my friend. The Egyptians, the Sumerians, all those motherfuckers knew it."

"Yeah, sure."

"I'm telling you, it's true, man. You should try it."

"I don't think so."

"You don't know what you're missing."

"And you don't know what you're doing. This is sick."

"What are you worried about? Them?" Daniel gestured toward the girls. "Believe me, we're doing them a favor. Go in-country sometime. See where they came from. Next to that, this is paradise."

"No, this is hell."

"You know what your problem is, Dominiquie? You're looking at this through Western eyes. You got to look at it through Thai eyes. You know what I'm saying?"

But through any eyes it was obscene.

"I'll be outside."

"Suit yourself," Daniel said as he hoisted his pants up over his belly and advanced on one of the girls.

While Daniel fucked his extra month of life out of the girl, I stood out front and kicked at the dirt like a shamed animal. What I'd seen in that warehouse had made me want to kill every man in the joint, including myself. Especially myself. I'd stood witness to evil and done nothing. That made me as guilty as any of them, in fact, guiltier, because I alone among them knew better. Right then, I swore to myself that I'd never sleep with another prostitute. No matter how horny I got, better my own hand round my dick than the mouths and cunts of little children, and what prostitute wasn't at one time in her life a little child— frightened, degraded—just like the girls I'd abandoned in the warehouse.

A few hours later, Daniel and I were out shooting pistols on a range reserved for the upper echelons of the local Thai police force.

"Good shot," one of the cops said to Daniel after I'd emptied my clip. Though he'd spoken in Thai I knew what he said even before Daniel translated. It's what people always said after they saw me put twelve rounds, tightly spaced, through the heart of a target. If the Thai cop had known it was his heart I was thinking of as I squeezed off those rounds, I don't think he would have been quite so complimentary. But after what I'd seen at the warehouse, his heart, and the hearts of all the other corrupt bastards who ran this country would forever be in my sights.

We'd come to the range to work the deal on my fight. The cops represented the fighter Daniel had mentioned last night in the bar. Before the deal could be closed, the cops wanted to check out my stuff. While they squeezed my arms and slapped my back I stood for it and smiled. "Go ahead, look me over, you pencil-dicked, scumbag, rice-farting fucks," I said to them in Flemish, a language I knew they wouldn't understand.

While the cops tittered in Thai about how their fighter was going to take me apart, I got all the details I needed from Daniel.

"Who's their man?"

"Name's Chiao Pran. A Laotian with training in Naban and Bando."

In Northern Thailand, Laos, and Burma, Naban and Bando were more than just the local fighting styles. Like football in America, or soccer to the Brits, Naban and Bando were how the boys here became men, and how the men here became legends. Known in the West as Submission Fighting, Naban and Bando both use a mixture of striking and grappling techniques. Both are bare-knuckle fighting styles, and, except for biting, eye gouging, and fish hooking an opponent's mouth, everything is allowed.

In the camps where I trained and at festivals and fairs, the Naban bouts would often take place inside an iron circle that had been sunk into the ground and filled with soft earth. Inside that circle, in an area a little smaller than a boxing ring, the champions would meet and fight in matches more ferocious than any I had ever seen.

"What's Pran's record?" I asked Daniel.

"A hundred freestyle bouts with fifteen losses. Before that, two hundred boxing bouts."

"Size?"

"Five-six, one fifty-five."

"Bet the farm."

Daniel nodded. "By the way, they want a five-round fight. Four minutes each."

"What? No way."

"That's how they want it, Dom."

"Well that's not how I want it. You tell them freestyle doesn't have rounds. We fight till it's over and that's that. I'm not going to let the bastard out of a hold just 'cause they decide it's the end of a round."

"It's the only way they'll do it."

"Then fuck 'em. Tell 'em no."

"Hey, I already bet two hundred thousand bahts on you. They gave me three to one."

"Goddammit, Daniel, I don't give a shit about the money."

"You want that shot at Kran or don't you?"

"All right then. Tell them I'll take their fight."

"I already have, Dominiquie; I already have."

Three days later, Daniel and I drove out to some flyspeck village on the border with Laos. It was the ass end of nowhere, down a long stretch of dirt roads. No electricity, no running water. Just ramshackle huts, a broken-down Buddhist temple, some fallow fields, and a gaggle of weathered Issan natives who crowded around our pickup truck as soon as we pulled to a stop.

I climbed out of the truck and did some stretches. In a

few hours I'd be facing Chiao Pran. Not that I cared if it was him or another. To me they were all just shadows cast on the wall of a tunnel—a tunnel I'd have to pass through to reach Kran. I would fight and beat Chiao and a dozen more like him if that's what it took to get to Kran. I didn't care about the money. I didn't care about the men. All I cared about was Kran. The invincible Kran. Until I faced him all my fights would be joyless. Each one nothing more than a mechanical act, as straightforward as sex between long-married couples. Chiao and I would meet, greet, and fight until one of us tapped out, couldn't get up, or was dead.

While Daniel went off to announce our arrival, I sat down and tried to psych myself up for the fight, which was next to impossible with all the Thai villagers crowding around me. *"Farang. Farang,"* the village men shouted to get my attention. Then they pointed to the girls they'd dragged along behind them—their daughters, I guessed—and launched into an obscene peddler's pantomime of what I might expect if I shelled out some cash. I waved them away, but the act only seemed to encourage them. Toothless and smiling, the men pressed ever closer with their trembling cargoes of flesh.

"For a few thousand bahts you could buy the whole lot." It was Daniel returned from the old temple where the fights were going to be staged.

"Get 'em off me, would you?"

"I told you we were doing them a favor by fucking them, didn't I? You sure you don't want one?"

I shot Daniel a look and he shouted in Thai at the villagers. They scurried away, kicking at the dogs, goats, and chickens that fluttered among them as they went.

"Come with me."

I followed Daniel to an empty hut where he told me I could wait until the time came to fight. After he left, I sat on the dirt floor and tried to put my head into fighting mode. Usually that was easy enough. All I had to do was redirect the river of fear I usually felt before a fight into an inner channel I'd carved into my psyche specifically for this purpose. A quick flip of a mental switch and my all my anxiety would instantly become a rushing torrent of impersonal rage.

But this time when I flipped the switch nothing happened. I tried again. Still nothing. Not good. In a fight, rage was my sword and my shield. Rage completed the fighting beast within me, leaving me immune to pain, free of doubt, and capable of anything. Without rage I could fight; it would be hard, but I could do it. Harder still would be the waiting. Without rage I would have to spend the next few hours wallowing in a rising tide of fear. Fear of dying. Fear of being maimed. Fear of killing, of damaging another human being just to satisfy my own terrible pride.

I crammed my head with static to try to prevent myself from hearing what my own thoughts were shouting, but the words came through anyway: Why? Why was I doing this? Why had I been burdened with this lethal gift, this maddening will to fight that defined me in my essence and sent me rushing to the far corners of the Earth to prove myself in blood? Was this, as the local Buddhists insisted, my karma? Could reincarnation explain it? Had the spirit of some long-dead warrior really possessed me in my crib? Or was it, as my mother sometimes thought after another long talk with the local parish priest, a possession of a more demonic stripe? Maybe I was just a thrill-seeker with a talent for fighting and a death wish to boot. Maybe I was a control freak. A vicious sadist. A Neanderthal throwback. Or just a fool. I'd heard it all said before, but no matter how I worried the questions the answers never satisfied. Only fighting did, and then only fighting all-out with everything on the line and nothing held back.

I knew that eventually everything would fall apart. My skill, my power, my strength—in the end they would betray me. In a final meeting I would be defeated, and the "I" that I was would be no more. Would that day be today? Perhaps it would. Perhaps it should. I didn't know anymore. I couldn't tell. Without the certainty of rage to guide me on my path, my fears rolled in and swallowed me up.

"You all right?" Daniel said as he stepped into the hut.

"Yeah, fine," I answered, but we both knew I was lying.

"You're up soon."

"Good."

While Daniel looked on, I rubbed my legs with liniment and went through my warmup exercises. The familiar routine calmed me some; still, when I stepped into the circle of dirt that served as a ring for the human cockfight to come, I felt like I'd already gone fifteen rounds.

As soon as the crowd saw me enter the temple, they came to life in a many-voiced shout. Arms pumping, thick packets of bahts held high, they parted to let me pass. There were forty or fifty of them. Tough hombres all. Heavy-hitters from the Thai mobs, high-ranking cops, soldiers, and others who lived for the fight game. Many had driven hundreds of miles to be here. Now they stood shouting catcalls, their well-dressed whores laughing, drinking, snorting coke straight from vials clutched in red-nailed fingers.

I was surprised to see four white men in the crowd. Mercenaries from the looks of them. They sure as hell weren't tourists, not in these parts. As I passed by the mercs they stared at me with the dead eyes of men who killed for the dollar. I knew the look well. For a time I'd worn it myself.

Inside the circle Chiao Pran was waiting. I took him in at a glance. He was just as Daniel described: a tough, mean little scrapper with a scarred upper body and fists and feet hard as stones. When I stepped into the ring he darted cat-like away from me while his eyes followed my every move.

"Chiao Pran! Chiao Pran!" the crowd began to chant. I circled the fighting field, uncertain for a moment of just who the real enemy was, Chiao Pran, or the crowd that thought to use and shame me for their pleasure. And all at once I felt a hot rage rise from deep within and scorch me with comforting fire. At last, I was ready for war.

I rushed at Chiao, caught him with a low front kick, and followed up with a knee strike to his stomach. He countered with an elbow to my chin, which if I hadn't seen it coming would have taken my head off for sure. I moved with the blow, down and away, and dropped to one knee. The drop was a ploy. If Chiao thought he'd hurt me, he might just relax his guard and give me an opening; all I'd need would be a fraction of a second. And suddenly, there it was—the opening! I jumped up and snapped out a foot that smashed into Chiao's right temple. He stumbled backward, flailing his arms, trying to shake his head clear, but I never gave him the chance. In an instant I was on him. We grappled and I took him down hard. Crack! The sound was his back breaking over my knee.

Chiao dropped to the dirt and I leapt on top of him, ready to continue, but there was no need. Chiao's body was limp. For a moment his eyes fluttered, then he lay still.

I stood up, raised my hands over my head and glared at the crowd. The bastards couldn't believe it. They couldn't believe it was over. They couldn't believe that I'd won. They were angry and hungry for more. But I wasn't. Even though the fight had taken just a few seconds, I was completely exhausted.

While two men carried Chiao off, I looked around for Daniel.

"Hey, you. That was bullshit! You got lucky," one of the mercenaries shouted in English as he stepped into the ring.

"You want a real fight? Come on, fight me! Come on, put up your hands, asshole."

What the hell was this? I glanced over at Daniel thinking maybe he knew, but Daniel just shrugged.

The merc pushed my shoulder, knocking me back. I didn't know who this guy was, but he was strong, and big too, well over six feet. "What's the matter, tough guy? You afraid of me? You a coward?" he said and pushed me again.

I didn't know if the merc was drunk and trying to show off for his friends, or if he knew Chiao and had stepped in to avenge him, but either way it looked bad. The merc was so full of himself that there was no way he was going to back off, not unless somebody pulled him off, and nobody in the crowd would do that. The crowd wanted this fight. Even Daniel was too busy taking bets to respond to my glances for help.

"Come on, you little chickenshit. I'm going to rip you a new asshole." The merc lifted his arms in a fighting pose and motioned me in with his fists.

I felt a new wave of rage wash over me. If the merc wanted a fight, now he'd get one. The idiot. He thought he would take me because he was big. He didn't know that fighting freestyle is not about size. It's about spirit and skill and the mad will to win. I put up my fists and nodded to let him know I was ready.

The Thai were in heaven—a white-on-white fight. As the merc and I circled, they shouted and screamed for our blood. I knew in a battle of straight kicks and punches that the merc would hold all the cards. Given his size and strength, all he'd have to do was catch me with one good shot and I'd be history. Under normal circumstances I'd play a skilled fighter of his size for time. As long as I controlled the fighting range I could wait and wear the man down. But I was already worn down and the merc was fresh. That meant I'd have to find another, faster way to finish him.

The merc opened by rushing straight at me. I slipped sideways and let him pass. Then, before he could turn, I jumped on his back, grabbed the front of his throat and sunk my teeth into the side of his neck like a vampire. While the merc tried to claw me loose, I slipped my free hand to his face and pushed a thumb knuckle-deep into his eye. The merc screamed as the eye popped out of its socket. Then he bent forward, throwing me to the dirt. I came spinning to my feet, ready to fight.

It was a clear sign, and if the merc were sane he would have tapped out then and there, tapped out and lived to tell with his eye-patch and his scar. Instead he attacked. Even though blood was streaming from his neck, even though the eye that I'd gouged was dangling from its socket like a bloody ornament, he attacked.

We fought toe to toe now, clawing and screaming like beasts in a pit. We were locked in a death struggle and everyone knew it. The merc. Me. The crowd. I kicked at the merc's legs, slipped past his withering defenses and head-butted him hard in the face. He staggered. The hole I'd bitten in his neck was large—large enough for me to force four fingers into the wound and close my hand around his inner pipes and arteries, so that when the merc finally pushed me off him, I fell to the ground with a hunk of his throat still clutched in my fist. Choking and gurgling, the merc sank to his knees. With his one good eye, he looked at me pleadingly. I got up and gave him what he wanted. A quick strike to the bridge of his nose and it was over.

Nobody talked, nobody moved as I walked out of the temple. Covered in blood, I returned to the pickup truck, where I sat and waited for Daniel. A few minutes later he slid into the driver seat and handed me a thick wad of bills. I took the money without looking and dropped it in my lap.

"You okay?"

I nodded.

"You sure? You want a drink or something?"

I stared straight ahead. I had nothing to say, not to Daniel or any man. Daniel started the truck and slipped it into gear.

"I got some news for you, Dominiquie. Kran's promoter was here."

"And?" I asked in spite of myself.

He asked me if you'd fight Kran."

"What'd you say?"

Daniel took the cigarette out of his mouth and smiled. "What the hell do you think I said?"

I stared into Daniel's eyes but they were unreadable.

"I said yes, you crazy son of a bitch! Goddamn, Dom, you know I actually think you can take the bastard. I swear I've never seen anybody fight like you just did. You're a fucking animal, man. You know that? A goddamned, fucking wild animal!"

"I know," I said and closed my eyes to the world.

Wildebras

Flemish for "wild child."

I was born with a shout in a spasm of blood, the third child of a woman whom doctors had warned to have no more children. But my mother was devout, a practicing Catholic, and when she found herself pregnant she insisted on carrying through with a birth that almost killed us both.

Before my first birthday I dropped into a coma with water on the brain. If I lived, the doctors said, I'd be slow; for the rest of my life I would have trouble learning, trouble walking, my balance would be off; I wouldn't ever be normal. At least the doctors were right about one thing, because normal is the last thing in the world I was.

Born with a warrior's spirit, I did what came naturally— I fought. First against death that tried to snatch me from the cradle, then against the disabilities that were supposed to be my lot. By the age of four I'd defied all the doctor's predictions. I was active, agile, alert, and strong. So much so that my parents took me to the doctor again. "Where's

At the family dinner table; I'm in the center.

he getting all this energy?" they wanted to know. "He's a whirlwind nonstop."

"He's hyperactive," the doctor answered, and he gave my parents a choice. Either drug me with Ritalin, or get me involved in lots of physical activity. My parents chose activity, and enrolled me straightaway in a Judo class that my older brother Rudy was taking. Looking back, I'm sure my parents cursed that decision a thousand times; if only they'd sent me to gymnastic classes, swim instruction, or the like, things might have gone differently, their worries might have been less. But it was Judo they chose, and it was a martial artist I became, because as soon as I stepped into that dojo it was love at first flip.

For the next four years I tumbled, rolled, and threw myself through childhood. Around me, the world went on as usual. Each morning, my father bundled off to the railway yard where he worked as a mechanic. My mother rushed to open her tiny grocery store, and I went off to school, though I barely noticed. Thanks to Judo I lived in a state of dizzy transcendence.

When the Judo school closed for lack of students my excess energy sought other outlets. At the time I loved Spider-Man, the comic-book hero with the powers of a spider. What a fighter he was. He could jump, cling to walls, defeat supervillains, and still make it home in time for dinner. When the older kids learned of my passion for the comic-book hero there was no stopping them:

"Hey, Dominiquie, bet you can't make that jump."

"I dunno, it looks awfully far."

"Spider-Man could do it."

So I jumped. I jumped off a crane into the water-filled cellar of a house under construction and laughed when a piece of rusty pipe sliced open my stomach. After all, what's a couple dozen stitches compared to the thrill of gliding through the air like a human spider? I jumped from the tops of barns and once, on a bet, ran without stopping through three plate-glass windows at school. I jumped from the roof of a three-story building, breaking my ankles in the process. When the ankles healed up, I jumped again, this time off a chimney and onto the roof of someone's house. Unfortunately, the roof wasn't as strong as it looked, and I crashed right through it, landing on a kitchen table where a family had just sat down to dinner.

To me, my high-flying antics were fun, but to the people of the village of Waasmont they were a sign of the devil. Less than eight hundred people called Waasmont home, farmers mostly—simple souls who lived by the land, the seasons, and the teachings of the Church. In Waasmont everyone knew his or her neighbors' business. In fact, after cattle and feed grain, gossip was the town's major crop, and in that I provided a bumper harvest.

After one jump too many, the priest was called in. "The boy should be brought to church every day," he advised my mother. "The martial arts have put violence in his soul. They've possessed his mind and made him want to punish his own body."

It's true that, when I wasn't out leaping, all I ever talked about were martial arts. For months I'd been pestering my dad to let me enroll in the Tang Soo Do class that was being offered in a nearby village. "No. No. No," had been my dad's constant refrain, not because he thought there was anything wrong with Tang Soo Do, but because after a hard day's work the last thing he wanted to do was drive me all the way to the next village and then sit and wait while I took the class. Still, until the priest placed a holy injunction against my plans, I thought my dad would come around. Now I knew that, unless I did something drastic, he never would.

For the next five days I didn't speak a word. Not at breakfast. Not at dinner. Not at school or church. No matter how they punished or cajoled I wouldn't give in. On the sixth day, my father finally broke.

"Get your *gi*. We're going to that damn karate school."

"It's not Karate. It's Tang Soo Do."

The whole ride there, I lectured him on the difference. Not that he cared, but after five days of silence I was happy just to hear my own voice.

In the Tang Soo Do class I faced the triple whammy of being the youngest, the newest, and the only kid from my village. Naturally, I got the shit kicked out of me. Every time the instructor turned his back the older boys used me as a punching bag. But I didn't mind. I was exactly where I wanted to be. With fists and feet flying I met my attackers head on.

It was around this time that the dreams began. Strange, impossible dreams of fighting using martial arts styles that I wouldn't encounter for years in my waking life. The roughness of Seidokan, the shock of Bojutsu, the liquid grace of Kung Fu, the power kicks of Muay Thai all came to me in my dreams. At night, while I slept, the door that the body wears by day was unlatched and I was set free to wander the great training halls of history. From samurai, vikings, ronin, and mountain warriors I learned how to live and to fight.

In my dreams I was brought to my true self, and just as I'd once been pushed from the womb now I was pushed again, this time into a new world of violence and war. For me, the ordinary waking world was finished. I no longer cared about work, play, or school. All I wanted from life was to realize in flesh what my etheric body already knew. I was nine years old and the great change had begun. The path of the warrior stretched out before me. To walk it, I would have to grow hard as a diamond.

I didn't know yet the mountains of pressure it takes to make a diamond. I had no idea that I'd have to be buried, that the weight of the Earth would have to be piled on top of me. It started with the death of my brother Eddy. Eddy was ten years older than me. At eighteen he looked like the picture of health—tall, strong, and muscular from his daily work as a farmhand. But, a year later, the muscles were gone. His body was rotting, stinking, his eyes yellow, his tongue black from the cancer that riddled his body.

When he died, just three months after his first complaint of pain, the loss spread through our family, making its impossible claim on us all. My father wandered between work and home like a ghost. My other brother, Rudy, who was twenty at the time, started drinking and didn't stop. My mother, never a physically strong woman, weakened and grew sicker. None of us knew at the time that the cancer was in her too, and it would be another dozen years before the leukemia that was now taking root in her bones finally claimed her.

As for me, I poured all my feelings into the cold cup of

the martial arts. By day, I kicked, wheeled, and punched like a fighting machine, endlessly churning in a deep well of pain. Practice. Practice and more practice. Training to perfect the imperfectible. Fighting against loneliness. Boxing with the grief that shadowed my every move. At night, I moved through my blackened dreamscapes like a spinning constellation of quicksilvered violence dealing death with a shout to all the monsters of the world.

Soon I had bested every kid in my Tang Soo Do class and none of them would spar with me anymore. Even kids five years my senior were afraid. I quit the gym and joined another.

At the SGF Sint-Truden gym I studied contact Karate and began entering amateur bouts. By the time I was eleven, I'd won my first title—a Belgian Junior Championship—by fighting and beating all comers in the up-to-fourteen-years-old age category.

I no longer lived at home. Between Eddy's death and Rudy's drinking my parents were up to their necks in trouble, so I was sent to live a few doors down, at my grandmother Sabine's house. Grandma Sabine was my mother's mother, and she was stubborn in a way that made me proud. During World War II, she and her husband, Joseph, had hidden Jewish families from the Nazis. While everyone else in the village had turned their backs, she and Joseph had followed their conscience and done what was right. They paid a heavy price. When a Nazi collaborator in the village turned my grandparents in, Joseph was sent off to labor as a slave in the German mines. After the war Joseph returned home, but the mines had broken his health, and shortly after being reunited with my grandmother he died. My grandmother swore that neither she nor Joseph ever regretted the act that had cost them so much. When she showed me the letters she was still getting from the children and grandchildren of one of the

Jewish families they had saved from the ovens, I suddenly realized that there are more ways to be a warrior than to be a man-at-arms. Though they'd never lifted a gun or raised their fists in anger, Sabine and Joseph belonged to the élite ranks of the warrior caste.

By now my brother's drinking was completely out of control. The nights he came home at all he would stumble through the village screaming and shouting. He crashed cars, fought cops, and got locked up on a regular basis. The whole village feared him.

I would have been happy if he'd just disappeared. No one seemed able to help him, and now because of his drinking I'd lost almost all of my friends. Parents wouldn't let their kids play with the brother of the town drunk. The fact that I was a martial artist only made things worse. "Do-miniquie's going to end up killing people just like his brother. It runs in the family. Stay away from that boy," the villagers whispered wherever I went.

And so, while the other kids dated and hung out in packs, I practiced my art. At four in the morning I'd wake up and work out. At seven o'clock I would run to school, where I would sit all day like a gorilla in too small a cage reading karate magazines from behind my schoolbooks. After school I would sprint home and train until dinner. Then I would go at it again, sometimes staying up all night to work a technique until I got it right.

I started winning more and more tournaments, but Karate no longer satisfied me. The rules, the padding, the point system used to determine the winner all seemed false to me. I wasn't interested anymore in playing tag with my opponents. I wanted to fight. All out. For real. When I walked off the mat I didn't want there to be any doubt as to who the better fighter was. It was me.

My trainers all thought I was nuts. They wanted me to play the tag-and-back-away game that winning points in

Karate requires, but I wouldn't have it. In bout after bout I would crush my opponents by knocking them out of the ring, beating them senseless, or kicking them until they quit, and still I would lose on points or from technical disqualification. I can't tell you how many times I stood and watched as my opponent was declared the winner even though he was out cold on the mat and I was up dancing and ready for more.

I quit Karate and took up Muay Thai boxing. This was more like it, much closer to real fighting. In my first Muay Thai tournament, my coach, Guy Robyns, paired me against a nineteen-year-old pro with twenty fights under his belt. The pro beat me to a pulp. In the first round alone he knocked me down twice, and when the ref finally called the fight in his favor my face was a bloody mess.

Even though Guy hadn't expected me to win that bout, *I* had, and for days after the loss I cried and fretted. Guy didn't understand. He called me a baby, a quitter; he thought that I couldn't take it, that I didn't have the heart. In fact, just the opposite was true. I had so much heart that I couldn't stand to see it trampled. I couldn't tolerate losing, not to anybody, ever.

I quit training with Guy and started looking for a coach whose vision of the martial arts matched my own. When I ran into Frank Merton I knew I'd found my man. Like me, Frank believed that success in the martial arts requires total dedication. Like me, he knew that in a real fight there are no second chances, there is only winning and preserving honor, or losing and facing death. I asked Frank to be my coach.

We started with the basics, practicing punching, kicking, blocking, and striking techniques until the techniques no longer seemed like techniques at all, but like actions as natural as breathing. Unlike other fighters, I didn't train according to a program designed to make my body peak at the time of competition and relax afterward; I was always peaked, always alert and primed for action. On weekends, Frank would enter me in every competition he could find. Muay Thai boxing, full or contact Karate, freestyle wrestling, Tang Soo Do, Judo—to Frank the fighting style wasn't important. What mattered was that I learn to control my fighting energy. If I wanted to develop rhythm and timing both in the ring and in life, I had to be willing to fight as often and as hard as possible.

Frank's methods were simple and direct, and happily they worked. Of the hundreds of matches I fought under Frank's guidance, I never lost one. A year and a half after I started with Frank, I was rematched against the professional Muay Thai fighter who'd beat me when I was thirteen. This time I knocked him out in seventy seconds. Six months after that I won the European Junior Thai Boxing championship title. I was fifteen years old and on top of the world.

After regular write-ups in karate magazines and appearances on European television, suddenly everyone in the village wanted to be my best friend. It was heady stuff for a boy so shy he was afraid entirely to mix with girls, and only spoke, even to friends, in brief embarrassed sentences.

Still, I was a handy guy to have around, especially in a fight. Like the one that happened late one night at a train station in the French part of Belgium. Five of us, all about fifteen years old, all Flemish, were waiting for a train. We'd been drinking, and, as those of you who've been to Belgium know, there's no love lost between Belgium's Flemish-speakers and its French-speaking Walloons. So, when one of my drunken mates screamed out, "Dirty Walloons!" to a gang of French-speakers who were waiting at the station, I knew we were in trouble.

"Let's get out of here," I said and ran with my buddies

down a long underground tunnel that led away from the tracks. The Walloon gang followed, throwing bottles as they came. When one of the bottles caught my buddy in the head and brought him tumbling to the ground, I turned and put up my hands in a last-ditch attempt to make peace. I didn't want to fight the Walloons. For one thing, there were ten of them and they all looked to be in their twenties. For another, none of my buddies knew how to fight. If something did start it would be up to me to finish it, and I'd never been in a street fight before. Though I tried not to show it, I was scared.

"Hey, come on, you guys. You didn't have to do that," I said, stepping up to the leader of the Walloon gang.

"Fuck you, Flemish asshole."

"Look, if this is about what my friend called you, I'm really sorry. He had too much to drink. He didn't know what he was saying. I apologize for him. What do you say we call it even, huh?" I gestured toward my buddy. The back of his head was bloody from where the Walloon's bottle had struck. But when I put out my hand to shake, the Walloon leader spit in my face and pushed me backwards.

I responded instinctively with a quick spinning back kick to the face that caught the Walloon so hard that his blood splattered both walls of the tunnel. There was no fear in me now, only a feeling of irrevocable rage. It rose through my body in hot spurts that scuttled every other sense and left me feeling more alive than I think I'd ever been.

I took my fighting stance and waited for the other Walloons to charge. I didn't care that there were still nine of them. At that moment I wanted to run through them all.

The Walloons looked between their leader, groaning broken nosed in the dirt, and me standing eager and ready to fight. None of them moved. Not a muscle. They just stood there staring at me as if I were crazy, which at that moment I was.

Finally, one of my friends broke the spell by reaching his hand toward me like one might to a wild dog. "Dominiquie, enough. Let's go," he whispered. I glanced at his eyes and could see he was afraid, and not just of the Walloons, but of me. After another few prompts, I dropped out of my stance and we eased down the tunnel. The Walloons never made a move to follow.

My fight in the tunnel made me an even bigger hero with the village kids, but I didn't care. The fight had given me a clear glimpse into the inner workings of my soul and what I saw there scared me. Rage was at my center. Wild, white-hot, berserker rage. I wondered what to do. Surrender to that rage and I could easily maim or kill. Deny it and I would wither and die like a man deprived of food. Squeezed between the pincer-grips of terror and desire, I dropped to my knees and prayed for God to help me.

A few weeks later I found myself in Germany attending a demonstration of various full-contact martial art forms. When two Japanese fighters stepped on the mat and began showing off a new fighting form called Kunto, I knew that my prayer had been answered. The form was so authentic I could hardly believe it. In Kunto fighting you could kick, punch, or do stand-up grappling. There was no padding, no gloves, weight classes, or time limits. You fought bare-handed against all comers—big or small, heavy or light—because size and weight didn't matter, only ferocity did. In Kunto, fighters trained in all different martial arts styles could meet and fight without restrictions, and when it was over only the best were left standing.

Here at last was a martial arts form that didn't stifle rage but actually encouraged it. At the same time, the strict discipline of Kunto placed checks on the amount of harm you could do. Unlike street fighting, which could quickly turn deadly, in Kunto, if at any time during a match you decided you'd had enough, you could signal your surrender simply by tapping your hand.

When I learned that Kunto was also a competitive martial art and that every four years the Nikoi Takimuro Kunto Federation sponsored an international competition, I decided then and there that no matter what it took I was going to enter that competition and win.

"Japan? You want to go to Japan?" my father roared.

"The Kunto training starts in September. Master Takimuro himself said I could enroll."

"Oh, did he? Well, I don't care what he says. I say no. You're not going to Japan."

"But Dad, you don't understand. You know what an honor it is to get invited to study under Master Shihan Nikoi Takimuro? He's like a legend. He only accepts the best. They say he teaches the hardest training course in all the martial arts, and I'm the youngest kid that's ever been invited. I have to go, Dad. I have to."

"You don't have to do anything, Nicky," my mother interrupted.

"All right, I don't have to, but I want to. I need to. You know how much the martial arts mean to me. Well, this is like the ultimate martial art."

"Doesn't work mean anything to you?" my father cut in.

"Sure, it does. You know how hard I worked for this."

"That's not what I'm talking about. The martial arts are a hobby. You've got to start earning a living soon."

"Your father's right. You don't even have the money to go away."

"I'll raise the money."

"Without a job?"

"It doesn't cost that much."

"How long is this training course, anyway?"

"Six months."

Me at fifteen, getting ready for Japan.

"Six months? What about school?"

"I'm dropping out of school."

"But you can't leave school. I won't allow that."

But I could leave school, and I would, just as soon as I turned sixteen.

"I need to sit down," my mother said.

"Now look what you've done. You've upset your mother."

So I let the subject drop. To raise the money to go to Japan I cut back on my competitions and started working weekends as a nightclub bouncer. I didn't tell my parents. I was afraid they'd try to stop me, which would have been easy enough; at fifteen I was way too young to work in a bar, and I'd only landed the job because a guy I trained with in an Amsterdam gym owned the club.

The Stains of the Street, the club was called, and outside of a battlefield or maybe a prison I couldn't have picked a better place to begin my education in violence. There were fights all the time. Every night somebody was getting tossed out or knocked down. At first it was me. But then, after I learned how to handle myself in a bar, it was always the other guy.

The first thing I had to learn was how to read the clientele. I broke them down by categories according to their likelihood of causing trouble. Least dangerous was the poseur crowd: the slumming Euro-trash trendoids jazzed up on hard drugs; the weekend showoffs; the skinheads; leather boys and their cycle-slut girlfriends doing their stud-and-chain thing. Next came the lovers in an endless forlorn parade: angry lovers, jealous lovers, wretched, bitter, broken lovers; lovers who didn't know they were in love until they stepped up to the bar and had a few drinks; lovers who had never been in love and were determined to make up for it by having it out with anyone who had. After that were the weightlifters—steroidal muscle freaks on testosterone highs that you had to beat to the bone before they'd go down. And finally there were the straight-out losers, always the club's toughest customers: the out-of-work, the out-of-luck, the insufferably ugly with no hope and no chance, the short-fuse artists, criminals, crazies, and all the rest of life's rejects standing tough at the bar over one last stiff drink, looking for a reason, and, failing that, just a body to fight.

For a bouncer the rules of engagement were simple: Always be wary. Never turn your back. Try to placate whenever you could. A kind word or friendly pat often worked wonders with a belligerent customer. When it didn't, you used force, and never too much force. You didn't want to hurt or humiliate a customer; you just wanted him out, and you didn't want him coming back with a grudge. I learned that the hard way when someone I'd thrown out slipped back into the bar with a knife. When he plunged the blade into my back, all the above rules were off. I beat him senseless. Then I beat him some more. Then the other bouncers moved in and, while I yanked the knife out of my back, they beat him again.

With blood running down my back and pooling in my boots, the staff was eager to get me to a hospital, but first I asked the bartender to serve me a drink. As I stood at the bar with my cognac, everyone in the place stared at me like I was nuts. But I knew exactly what I was doing, because in no time word of my stunt had spread through the club's grapevine, and, from then on, whenever I stepped up to a troublemaker they usually backed down.

After six months I'd saved more than enough money to pay for my trip to Japan. When I told my parents I was leaving, my father shouted. My mother wept. I didn't blame them. The truth can do that. Like being born, the truth hurts. You scream and struggle, but you can't fight what's in the blood.

I packed my bags and left for Japan.

Kiai

The focusing of life force so that energy, mind,
body, and spirit come together in a shout.

The plane banked and began its descent into Okinawa. Somewhere on that rocky island lay the
Kunto training camp. For months I'd been too
busy preparing to think about anything else, but now, with
the island finally in sight and my dreams about to become
a reality, I began to worry. What if I wasn't good enough?
What if they laughed at me—or, worse, sent me home?

I tried to make my mind go blank. No anticipation. No
past. No future. Only the empty fullness of the now. That
was how I planned to succeed in the Kunto training—by
living in the moment, dissolving myself in time and becoming an empty vessel ready to be filled with Master
Takimuro's teachings.

Very Japanese of me, very Zen, I thought, causing my
concentration to collapse. So much for my becoming an
empty vessel. Who was I trying to fool anyway? I was no

Zen master. I was only a sixteen-year-old boy about to step into a fighting pit with grown men.

I thought about the Kunto training. Apart from what I'd seen and heard at the demonstration in Germany I knew almost nothing. But, then, almost nothing was known about Kunto in the West. Freestyle full-contact Karate was still illegal in most parts of Europe, and freestyle full-contact fights, when they were held, went unreported in the martial arts magazines. Traditional Karate schools didn't recognize this form of fighting either, and many masters refused to let their students fight against the Kunto stylists. But, to me, that's exactly what made Kunto so exciting. It was dangerous, forbidden.

No matter how hard it gets, I thought, I can take it; I'm tough. I was trying to psych myself up for what was to come, but I didn't know what tough was. Not really. Not yet.

The plane bit hard into the runway and shuddered to a halt. Eager to stretch my legs after what seemed like an eternity in the air, I sprang into the terminal and followed the signs to the baggage area. That's where I first saw them. Even though they were Japanese and dressed much like others in the terminal, I could tell that they were men of the Kunto school. They looked hard and lethal. They had what the Japanese call *hara*. I could see it in the way they walked, in the way they stood and addressed me with their eyes. They each had that calm and complete awareness that belongs only to men who are in total possession of themselves.

They approached me like hunters closing on prey, and instinctively I froze. As they moved toward me I wondered how I would ever learn to fight such men—men who, the longer you looked at them, the more they seemed to grow in strength and steel.

Without dropping their gaze, they stepped up to me and bowed.

"Dominiquie Vandenberg," the shorter of the two said,

straining his mouth around my name, "you will come with us, please."

I followed them into the crisp Okinawa autumn. We got into a waiting car and drove in silence through the streets of Naha. The city was a curious mixture of West and East, the gaudy and the sublime: an American fried chicken joint sat cheek by jowl next to a tiny soba shop; people had to walk under a neon billboard advertising Johnnie Walker Scotch to reach a sidewalk Buddhist shrine.

Not so long ago there had been hand-to-hand fighting in these streets. In 1944 much of the city was leveled by a massive American bombardment. One-eighth of the island's entire population had died during the bombing and ensuing land invasion. Reconstruction was swift. United States soldiers Americanized the city with bulldozers, constructing broad avenues and military bases that had been occupied by the Americans until 1972, when the island was finally ceded back to Japan.

Occupation was nothing new to the people of Okinawa. The history of the island is a history of vassalage and war. Much of what we consider modern Karate originated here, devised by farmers hundreds of years ago to combat the armed samurai who then dominated the island.

We headed into the hills above Naha. From the heights I studied the precise contours and proportions that civilization had carved upon the land below. As the city slipped out of sight, I felt as if I was shedding myself of the world, leaving behind its forms and categories. For me there was only one goal now. To graduate from the training course in the top ten—the only ten who would be guaranteed a fighting berth in the upcoming Freestyle World Championship bout. To me everything else was illusion. Pain. Humiliation. Fear. Weakness. Nothing would distract me from my goal. When I descended from this mountain I would be a new man.

Karate Ni Sente Nashi

A statement of overall self-control. Translated literally it means, "In Karate there is no first attack."

Takimuro's training compound consisted of a U-shaped wooden building enclosing a yard of dirt and rock. A Japanese bell dominated the yard. A covered veranda spanned the inner length of the building and provided access to a fully equipped dojo, a mess hall, sleeping quarters for the men, and residences for the senior instructors.

One of the instructors led me to a locker where I was told to stow my luggage. I was handed three articles of clothing—a light cotton karate *gi,* a heavy winter *gi,* and a pair of wood-soled shoes—and told to change. For the next six months these three items would be my only protection against wind, rain, cold, fists, and feet.

I was led to the students' sleeping quarters, which were nothing more than a large empty room with tatami mats laid out in rows on a wooden floor. As I made my way to the only mat that hadn't been claimed, I could tell that the other students were sizing me up. Of course, I was doing the same, eyeballing the others as I passed. All of them were older than I, some I guessed by a decade or more. All those years of martial arts training had filled these men full, and every inch of them was cinched with corded muscle just waiting to be used. They looked deadly.

"Hey, kid, what d'you think you're doing here?" a bull-necked Hungarian sneered as I passed.

"I'm taking the course, same as you," I said staring up at him. The Hungarian was huge. The top of my head barely reached the bottom of his bulging pectorals.

"Oh yeah? Who let you in? How old are you anyway, boy?"

"Old enough."

"Well, you don't look old enough. To me you look more like a baby." The Hungarian eyed me, then turned his back. "Doesn't he look like a little crybaby?" he shouted to the others.

A hush fell over the room. The words had been cruel, but turning his back on me had been the ultimate sign of disrespect.

I thought about trying to take him down, establish my rep here and now. It wouldn't even matter if I won or lost the fight, as long as I showed I had fire. But I knew the instructors wouldn't see it that way. None of us were allowed to start a fight without permission, and anyone who did would get tossed from the course. As I stood, blinking back tears, I could tell by the way the Hungarian's muscles were plaiting that he was just waiting for me to make my move, but instead of leaping up and tearing into him I turned and walked away.

As soon as I reached my tatami, everyone in the room started talking as if nothing had happened, but something had. I'd allowed myself to be caught in a trap. If I fought the Hungarian I'd get bounced from the course. If I didn't, by rights any man in the room could call me a coward. Either way I lost. I'd been defeated, not by fists, but by shadow warfare that had played against my fear of not being accepted and my uncertainty about my own skill.

I vowed never to let that happen again. From now on I would give these men wide berth. Let them press their tyranny on one another. I would practice restraint. This was my first lesson. My training as a warrior had begun.

Meijin

A great master.

I n the city he could easily be mistaken for something he was not; his balding pate, shining eyes, and friendly paunch gave the impression of one of those smiling cat figurines you often see in sushi bars. Here is a soft man, you might think, a man who could do you no harm, but let your eyes linger and you couldn't help but notice the tough yellow calluses that stained his shins and his feet, or the quail-egg-sized lumps that passed for knuckles on his hands. They stood out like beacons to those trained to see them, clear signs that this was a man of great training, a man to be reckoned with—my master, Takimuro.

We were called to assemble in the yard. The master was seated cross-legged on the ground. On either side of the master, two instructors stood ready. At a signal from the master, the instructors lifted a wooden two-by-four high above their heads. The master took a deep, even breath, then catapulted himself upside down toward the board. Almost faster than my eye could follow, he arced through the air and kicked at the board, which instantly splintered in half.

Next, the master placed his open hand on top of a stack of twenty bricks. When an assistant brought a sledgehammer down on his hand, the bricks shattered in a spray of dust. The master moved on to the next demonstration.

Two beer bottles sat balanced on a sawhorse. The master flicked his open hand at the bottles. There was a blur, a quick clip, and the tops of the bottles fell, sheared at the neck, while the lower half of the bottles remained standing on the horse.

After several more demonstrations, the master turned and faced us:

"I show you these things because it seems students have come to expect them, but now that you have seen them I tell you they are nothing. Boards and bottles do not move. Bricks do not fight back. Here you will fight against men who move without limitation. Here you will learn to inflict the most damage possible while exerting the least effort. Each of you has brought his own skills to this training, but skill is not enough. Whatever expertise you think you have, Kunto requires more."

Naturally, we were curious about the background of such a man, and whenever possible we plied the other instructors with questions. For our trouble we got little in return. We learned that Master Takimuro had been born to a samurai family. As a young man he had studied various martial arts but had found them all wanting. In his middle years he left wife and children for a time to go up into the mountains and find his true art. He returned with Kunto.

Kunto translated literally means "the way of the fist," but one look at Master Takimuro and you knew it meant more. It meant *shibumi,* the Japanese ideal of elegance refined to its austere essentials. It meant *zanshin,* the essence of alert domination. It meant *haragei,* the physical art of controlling your center and acting always with courage. But, most of all, it meant *giri,* the obligation a warrior feels for his master, and the master for his wards.

It was with a profound sense of *giri* that I bowed to the master after his demonstration was through. As I watched him walk off, I felt humbled and at the same time proud to have placed myself in the service of such a man. Already I could sense the seeds of him within me, taking root. For the next six months I would tend my garden. The harvest, when it came, would be rich.

Sakki

The intention of doing harm, the force of a killer.

The instructor clapped his hands. We bowed as Master Takimuro entered the dojo. We'd been training for several weeks now and had fallen into a routine. Every morning we rose at 6 A.M. for a one-and-a-half-hour barefoot run through the Okinawa hills. After our run we studied Judo and Jujitsu techniques. Then we had our first free sparring session of the day. After that we ate, rested, trained in Karate techniques for several hours, switched to shadowboxing, and finished with a session on a Japanese punching board called a *makiwara*. After dinner, we would usually do about an hour of intense calisthenics, there would be more free sparring, and we would finish the day with a cool-down and stretch.

Takimuro whispered to three of his training instructors. The instructors nodded and began donning protective gear. Whenever we sparred against the training instructors they wore protective gear. We, on the other hand, wore no gear at all. We had to learn to take their kicks and punches as they came—and, believe me, they came. The instructors thought nothing of punching us in the face or kicking us in the groin. Whenever they fought against us they went at it all out. It was always a serious attack done at full strength and full speed.

The instructors stood ready. Takimuro's eyes scanned the class until they came to rest on me. I stepped forward, ready to spar with one of the instructors. It wouldn't be the first time.

"You will engage all three at once," the master directed.

"What!" My mouth opened to speak a word that I knew better than to utter. I'd never fought against three at once. Up until now, I'd barely been holding my own against one.

Before I even had time to plot a strategy, the three instructors circled and charged. A low kick to the legs of the first, followed by a spinning back fist into the face of the second gave me just enough time to turn and Judo throw the third one to the floor. My moves had been reflexive, but before I could make good on my advantage the first one was up again and attacking. We got into a duel of fists and feet, which went on until the second one jumped me from the side and the two of us collapsed in a tumble. Luckily, I caught him in an arm bar and by the time we hit the mat he was already tapping out. The next thing I knew, my knees were being seized in a viselike hold that pinned me to the mat. Then, before I could even try to break free, the remaining instructor began to pelt my head and ribs with kicks. I locked my arms over my face in a defensive covering action. Not that it did me much good. Stuck face up under a barrage of kicks, I knew I was doomed. But I wouldn't submit. I wouldn't tap out. Even though the pain was incredible, I was determined to salvage at least a shred of self-respect from this fight by showing them just how much punishment I could take.

When Master Takimuro finally gave the sign to stop, my whole upper body was covered with bruises. As the four of us stood and bowed, I glanced at the master. His gaze, as usual, seemed lost in the middle distance. Still, I could tell he was unhappy.

That night I was unable to sleep. I kept thinking about what I had done wrong. My problem wasn't with my technique. My form was excellent, one of the best in the class. Even my classmates had begun to show a grudging respect for the ease with which I mastered new moves in the training drills. No, my problem lay elsewhere, deeper. It was a problem of attitude—or, more precisely, of fear. I was afraid of hurting my attackers. In sparring contests I held back even when my partners didn't. It's funny, because I wasn't afraid of being hurt. I could take punch after punch and keep coming, but when it came to dealing out the same pain I was getting I held back. That's why Master Takimuro had been unhappy. I hadn't shown enough aggression. He didn't think I had the killer instinct.

And then, like a revelation, it hit me. It wasn't that I didn't possess the killer instinct; what frightened me was that I possessed it too much. I was afraid that once I let the instinct out I wouldn't be able to recall it. I thought back to all the Norse tales I'd read as a boy. When a rage came over a Norsemen he would fight against whoever stood before him. Friend, foe, it didn't matter; there was no escape from the blind raging fury. I pictured myself giving in to a berserker's rage, going completely out of control and laying waste first to the camp, then to the whole bloody world. I remembered the rages I'd felt back in Waasmont—fearsome, overpowering things that started in my toes and rose until my whole body was white-hot and shuddering with incipient murder.

I shut my eyes while an inner river of vertigo collided with a rising tide of fear. Eventually the feeling passed, but the problem remained. What was I to do? I'd spent years constructing my martial arts form. I had the tools, the will, the discipline, the intelligence. The boat had been built, the vessel launched, but there still was no wind in my sails. If I could just find a way to let the rage in me blow without losing control, I knew I would be unstoppable. The question was how? I'd traveled thousands of miles to be made into a champion, but I still felt as far away from myself as the day I'd left home.

Ma-ai

"Distancing," an essential tactical element
of any fighting art.

While the others talked about fights they had been in or seen I sat alone. I couldn't match them in stories; I didn't want to. The less they knew about me the better. Most of them wanted nothing to do with me anyway. There was no glory in fighting a sixteen-year-old. If they won they gained nothing. If they lost they felt humiliated. So they left me alone, which was just as well because it gave me a chance to study them.

In the previous weeks I had sparred at one time or another against almost everyone in the training. Most of the fighters came from Seidokan or Kyokushinkai Karate schools. These fighters used their hands and feet to launch conventional stand-up attacks. The other fighters were trained primarily in Sambo wrestling, Krav Maga, Judo, Jujitsu, or other styles that emphasized grappling, throwing, and other ground fighting skills. Ground fighter or stand-up fighter, almost everyone was primarily one or the other.

After fighting hundreds of bouts I began to realize that, no matter what style they fought in, most of my opponents were slaves to their strategy; they fought the same fight over and over. Stand-up fighters, for example, tended to fight in one of three ways. Some were what I called robotic fighters. These men were usually tall, usually heavy. They fought like a bull coming at you, always moving forward, punching and kicking straight ahead, or, if they were Korean stylists, from the side. Their objective was to use their superior strength to bludgeon you out of the ring.

Other men were moveable fighters. The moveable fighter, usually a smaller man, fought like a mosquito. He attacked with a flurry of stinging blows then retreated. Attack. Retreat. Attack. Retreat. His objective was to infuriate his opponent, and ultimately to wear him down, and then capitalize on any mistakes his opponent might make.

The combination fighter fought more like a lion. He used a series of trained maneuvers to get you in position for the kill. His whole fight was one long setup for the knockdown.

Generally, the ground fighters fell into one of two categories: technicians or non-technicians. The technicians, the best of whom came from the Brazilian-based wrestling schools, fought like snakes. They would press and twist and lock their opponents into one hold after another. Their approach was always sequential, swift, and relaxed. If you were able to slip out of one hold, they would always follow up with another. Once they were on you it was almost impossible to get them off. Eventually, they would exhaust you, lock you in a submission hold, or get their arms or legs around your neck and choke you until you submitted.

The non-technical wrestlers were usually larger men who relied on brute strength to bring you to the ground. They fought like gorillas, moving in and overpowering you with their sheer dumb brawn. Their wrestling style was always unpredictable, usually savage, and it was precisely these qualities that made them so dangerous.

Against each of these fighters I began to develop countermeasures designed to throw them off balance and make them fight not their fight, but mine. Against ground fighting technicians I would employ low leg kicks. If they closed I would grapple, but always with the thought of getting away. Against non-technical ground fighters I played a waiting game. Because the non-technical grapplers relied so much on brute strength, they would usually exhaust themselves after just a few minutes, so I played these men for time; then, whenever possible, I would finish them off with striking techniques. Robotic fighters could usually be stymied by moving around and taking them down when they turned. Moveable fighters called for different countermeasures; you had to either smother them and bring them to the mat, or corner them and go for the quick knockout. Against combination fighters I would always try to control the fighting range. At a critical moment I would feint, close, wrestle them down, and try to choke them out.

Of course none of these methods were absolute. Sometimes I would decide to meet a man at his strengths. Other times I would practice the same solution again and again against different body types and fighting styles until I got it right. But, in the art of fighting, the principle of varying your fighting style and strategy in relation to your opponent is as near to an absolute as you can get.

Shugyo

A regimen of severe physical training
intended to harden the spirit.

As the course progressed our daily routines grew harder. Our two-mile runs turned into ten-mile runs, then into ten-mile midnight runs performed in bare feet. In the dark, my feet picked up stones and it wasn't long before the soles of both my feet were full of infected blisters. Most mornings, every step felt like an injection of fire until I could adapt myself to the pain.

To get us used to the blows we might expect in a fight, the instructors started caning us with bamboo poles. Some days they would concentrate their beatings on our backs; other days we would be called on to expose our stomachs, thighs, or forearms to the crack of the bamboo, until it got so that some part of our anatomy was always black and blue.

When they weren't running or beating us, the instructors tortured us with calisthenics. We did push-ups and sits-ups, and tossed heavy wooden medicine balls until our bodies refused to hear the message from our brains that said to keep going. To add jeopardy to the routine, sometimes the instructors would make us do our push-ups over sharpened katana swords. We did these push-ups until our instructors told us to stop, or until our arms couldn't hold us up anymore and we collapsed onto the blade. Then we would wear the wound as a bloody reminder of what it meant to fail in Kunto.

Our sparring sessions got crueler too. We didn't just fight in the dojo anymore; we fought outdoors on concrete slabs, in bombed-out, abandoned monasteries, and across broken terrain. We fought in mud, in darkness, in water and rain. We fought in the freezing cold without warming up, dressed only in our light summer *gis.* We fought from close quarters. We started fights while sitting in chairs, and raged at one another from across tabletops. We fought in simulated crowds against one, two, three, and more. We fought until we were exhausted and the effort of delivering a blow hurt almost as much as the pain of receiving one. We fought until every cell in our bodies was ready to mutiny, and then we fought more.

None of us believed a martial arts course could be this hard. Under the constant bombardment, men who had shown up with that look that says, "I'm bad. I'm an ass-kicker," suddenly began to look as if they'd lost something. In the morning it got harder and harder for them to slap on their game faces, and soon their darkest fears began to show through.

One morning we woke to find one of them gibbering in his native language. His eyes rolled in his head; ropes of snot trailed from his nose. We tried to help him shake it to no avail; he was finished, abject, insane.

He wasn't the only one. Men started disappearing from the course on a regular basis. One day they were fighting beside you, the next day they were gone. Sometimes it was their bodies that went—a broken arm or leg, a gangrenous foot—sometimes it was their minds, but whatever the cause it was always terrible to see. All those hours of kicking and punching, the years of training, lost in a second to a slip of the body or a twist of the mind. We all knew it could just as easily have been us, but we suffered the knowledge in silence, afraid of jinxing ourselves with a word.

I hung on, conserving my strength as best I could. I was sick in soul and body. Every part of me felt bruised. This was about survival now and nothing more. During the day I tramped mindlessly from one exertion to another. At night I fell over dead from exhaustion, only to rise the next morning and begin the whole process again.

I began to sneak and hide food. Meal times had been cut to fifteen minutes and no matter how fast we shoveled it in we never seemed to get enough. A hidden handful of rice, a lump of cold fish consumed alone in the dark would soothe my stomach but not my mind. As I squatted alone and ate, I couldn't help but think of how far I still had to go. There was so much yet to do that the weight of it made me want to run screaming into the night. Instead, I found solace in tears.

Through it all, Master Takimuro was everywhere, watching us with a gaze cold and still as the moon. I remember him watching me as I struggled sloppily through a practice drill. I was exhausted and despaired of ever getting it right when the master stepped up to me.

"Try again. This time against me."

I looked at the man. He'd been right there beside us the whole time, but his energy, rather than dimming, seemed almost numinous. Centering my weight low in my body, I put up my fists and moved forward, building power as I went until I lashed out with a kick that was aflame with murder. In that instant Takimuro wasn't my sensei anymore, he was simply a man who'd been torturing me, pushing me beyond what he or any man had any right to expect.

The next thing I knew I was sprawled on my back with the master's foot on my face and his voice ringing in my ears:

"Your problem is that you haven't given up yet. When you do, when you think its never going to happen and that you can't go on, when you've forgotten everything, that's when it will happen for you. But first you have to give up."

Give up? I thought to myself. What else could I possibly give up? I'd already given my strength, my mind, my heart to this cause. While other kids were out dating, dancing, and driving fast, I was here freezing and starving and fighting for my life.

Of course, I didn't understand the true meaning of the master's words, but I would. Soon his remark would lead me away from the path of defeat and onto the path of the warrior.

Mushin

Awareness without thought.

Minutes feel like hours and hours, ages when you're hungry, cold, tired, and wet. Winter had settled over the camp. An icy wind blew off the South China Sea so bitter it made us whimper as we sat outside in our light *gis* and waited. It was the middle of the night and we were squatting cross-legged in the dirt. Why, we didn't know. When the instructors had roused us and told us to get dressed, we did. When they paraded us out and commanded us to sit in silence we obeyed. That had been hours ago. Now the instructors returned carrying buckets filled with water. No one moved, no one spoke, as the instructors drenched us with the water.

"You will remain seated until your *gis* are dry," one of them shouted. Then they left. In the dark I heard teeth chattering. My own? I wasn't sure. I was shaking too hard to tell. I thought about standing and stomping my feet to get warm, but the order had been given. If I stood up I would be dismissed from the course. But if I stayed where

I sat I was sure I would faint, and they would dismiss me for that too.

What to do? Perhaps I could think myself warm. I set my teeth as best I could and tried to imagine myself in a steaming hot tub. When that didn't work I decided I would will myself to endure. Up till now, I'd made it through on the strength of my will alone. That is, after all, the Western way—heroic man battling against the elements, defeating nature, overcoming every obstacle to achieve his victory. But for the first time in my life the obstacle I faced outstripped my tenacity. This is one fight I would not win the Western way.

As I sat, sullen and shivering, the master's words drifted back into my head: give up, forget everything; that's when it will happen. Perhaps the master meant *mushin,* the meditative state of pure mindlessness where all the chatter and concerns of normal life are put aside.

Before I came to the training I had learned to meditate. I thought meditation would help make me strong. But I quickly discovered that I didn't have the patience for *mushin.* To me it felt unnatural to sit and do nothing. I would always rather do than not do, but now, after attempting to do and falling short, I decided to try to surrender myself to the silence of *mushin* once more.

I closed my eyes, let my thoughts fall away, and concentrated on my breathing, steadying it, letting it carry me further and further with each exhalation until I rode it all the way to the void.

I suppose it was the rustle of the instructors' *gis* that brought me back. I didn't know how much time had passed—hours, I supposed—because my *gi* was dry and the first hint of dawn was bluing the sky. I had done it, or, more precisely, it had been done for me, through me; I had done nothing except to give up, forget, and surrender. The master's words were true.

The instructors drew closer. No one moved. No one spoke. Then I noticed that they were carrying buckets. The water hit me with the force of an ax.

"You will remain here until your *gis* are dry."

The man next to me started to cry. Another collapsed in an unconscious heap. The instructors turned and left. The next day both these men would be gone. I closed my eyes and let my thoughts fall away. A few deep, steady breaths and the void beckoned. I leapt in joyfully.

Kokoro

The fighting spirit.

After a rib-heaving run we arrived at the waterfall. In other circumstances I might have stopped to admire the beauty of the place, but not today; today we had come here to fight.

We stripped off our *gis* and waded into the clear water at the base of the falls. The water was icy, so cold that as soon as we stepped in our bodies went numb, except of course for our balls, which shriveled and sang like a pair of caged bees. I faced off against the man with whom I'd been matched. He was a giant, six foot seven, 260 pounds. When we stood toe to toe, the water barely reached his waist while I was in up to my chest.

The giant thought that gave him the advantage. He thought he would make quick work of me. But, then, he thought he was still fighting against the boy who had started this course instead of the man I'd become.

I'd like to tell you that the change in me was the result of an act of will, that there was a definite turning point marked by some epiphany or apotheosis, but there wasn't. I cannot identify the day or the hour that I lost my fear of hurting others in a fight and surrendered myself completely to the hyperreality of combat without limits. Like many of life's miracles, it seemed to happen naturally, without my even noticing. In fact, the less I concerned myself with my fighting spirit, the more it seemed to consolidate itself as a part of my overall character until finally it became the fulcrum of my life.

The giant grinned as we waited for the signal to start. The fool. At a critical moment his overconfidence would cause him to hesitate, but I would not hesitate; when it came time to do or die, I would do, and if this fight were just a tad more real he would die.

When the instructor gave the signal to start, the giant opened just as I knew he would, by advancing behind a wall of front kicks. Because he was tall, his kicks didn't have far to travel to reach my face, and his feet shot out of the water like cannonballs. I knew I couldn't block many of those kicks without getting my arms broken so I began backing into deeper water. That suited his strategy perfectly; deep water would give him an even greater advantage. Once I was in past my shoulders, I knew he would try to close the distance between us. Then he would use his weight and strength to try to drown me.

I started slipping sideways, keeping just out of his reach. Every now and then I threw a spinning back kick at his stomach, but the water and the mud sucking at my feet blunted my kick's effectiveness and he just kept advancing, pawing and slapping at the water as he came. That's when I realized that he was fighting against the water as much as I was, and that gave me an idea. I could use the power of the water to defeat him.

Despite the cold, I willed my body to relax. Then I dipped under the water and swam the two short strokes it took to get behind him. Like a missile, I shot out of the water, grabbed onto his back, and threw a surprise choke-hold around his neck. But he was smart and strong and he tucked in his chin, making it impossible for me to close the hold. I tried head-butting the back of the head, but despite my best efforts I couldn't get him to lift his chin. He, on the other hand, had no problem lifting me. With one hand he grabbed me by the scruff of the neck and threw me through the air like a rag doll.

I came down with a splash, and before I could even rise out of the water he lashed out with a foot that caught me squarely in the forehead. Everything went silent as I slipped under the water. In the cold I lost all feeling. I knew I was drowning, but the head kick had so scrambled my mental signals that I didn't know how to save myself. So much for my theory about using the power of the water to defeat him. I had only defeated myself.

Luckily, the giant came to my rescue. He thought that by lifting me up by the throat with left hand, while punch-ing me in the face with his right, he would finish me. In-stead, it revived me, and I began to struggle again, not that it did me much good. The giant's grip around my throat had cut off my air. It seemed I'd only traded one form of suffocation for another. With only seconds of conscious-ness left to me, I kneed him in the balls and shin-kicked his face. That did the trick. He let go.

I fell back and sucked air. Then he was on me again, punching with short lefts and rights that sent me diving under the water to get away. Again he grabbed my neck, but this time instead of lifting me up out of the water, he held me down. So much for my other theory, the one about him being overconfident. My opponent was a tough and wary fighter who wouldn't make the same mistake twice. Well neither would I. With his hands still tight around my throat, I twisted my body upside down until my legs found his neck. When I locked my calves in a triangle chokehold and squeezed, I thought for sure that would make him tap out, but again I was wrong, because again he was able to tuck his chin against my hold.

It looked bad for me. My head was underwater. His hands were on my throat and I was almost out of air. In a last desperate move, I punched at his chin from my upside-down position. There was almost no power in the punch, but I wasn't looking for power. All I wanted to do was to lift his chin a fraction of an inch so I could close the leg hold. I punched him once, then again, and when his chin jerked up I closed my legs around his neck and squeezed for all I was worth.

Three seconds later he was tapping out like a madman. I let go of my hold and came up for air. The giant was already stumbling backwards, clutching his neck, gasping for breath. Our combat was over.

I strode out of the water, alert to everything, immune to pain. That's what a good fight can do for a man: it can make him feel so alive, so intimate, so at the height of his consciousness that he never wants it to end.

I don't think anyone can understand this heady mixture of ecstasy, violence, and absolute freedom unless he's experienced it for himself. Oh, you can read about it in books like this and others, but unless you are willing to reach into the ugly throat of darkness yourself, to drive arms up to elbows into all that is savage and primitive, you cannot possibly know how it feels.

Yes, sex is close—great sex, that is—but sex is not violence, at least not for me, and most people who rush to surrender to sex would never dream of throwing themselves with similar abandon into a fight. Most people fear their potential for violence and that's good. It takes years of discipline to refine the form that can express violence and shape it into something artful, even beautiful to behold. For me, that's what the Kunto training was all about.

I'm different from many highly trained martial artists in this way. Where they practice martial arts as a kind of moving Zen, or as a way of compensating for some other insecurity, I fight for the pure raging joy that combat brings. I'm not interested in money or glory. I couldn't care less about becoming one with the universe or any of the rest of that New Age crap. Nor am I one of those small-dicked punchers out to prove what a tough guy he is on the street. No, I fight for the same reason a river roils and rushes, which is to say I fight for no reason other than that fighting is the only and perfect expression of the rage that roils and rushes in me.

Among our group in the Kunto training there was only one other who I thought possessed this kind of fighting spirit. He called himself Thaiwell. Like me, Thaiwell was fast, had great stamina, and was a well-trained technician. Like me, Thaiwell lived to fight and would endure any-thing to become even better at his craft. But there the simi-larity ended, and in every other respect we were as opposite as fighting men could be. Where I was all blister-ing energy, Thaiwell was cold fire. Where I rushed in, he lingered. Where I held my tongue out of shyness and hu-mility, his silence was born of arrogance. Where I had to earn whatever respect I got, Thaiwell commanded it with-out apology, as if it was his right.

It amazed me that the same warrior spirit could inform two such different personalities, and, while I couldn't help but respect the skill and certainty that Thaiwell brought to the ring, as a man he made me sick. A patina of egotism corrupted everything he did. Even his fighting was not en-tirely pure. Before a sparring match, while most of the oth-ers paced nervously, Thaiwell would stand rooted and aloof, cultivating an air of menace. His gaunt cheeks, racehorse muscles, and bone-narrowed eyes all strained to project a sense of threat. During bouts, Thaiwell would toy with his opponents like a cat. I used to watch him moving in and out at will, humiliating his adversaries until he grew disgusted and closed in mercifully for the kill.

Many in the training course feared Thaiwell, though I was never among them. I had long since given up my fear of any man. If a fighter was better than me in a particular martial arts skill, instead of fearing him, I would step up and challenge him. I would take a beating if I had to, take many if that's what was required to learn a fighter's secrets. Whatever happened, I knew in the end that I would dominate. I always had. I always would. Against Thaiwell it was only a matter of time.

Yudansha

A martial arts student with at least a
first-degree black belt.

This was it—the final test. There were seventeen of us left. Seventeen out of twenty-seven. After the test there would be ten. The rest would be given a certificate for having completed the course and sent home. The ten would be honored with a fourth-degree *dan* black belt in Kunto Karate. The ten would be fêted and invited to fight in the next Freestyle World Championship competition.

I was determined to be the first of those ten. I felt good. My feet had healed. My mind was calm. Top to bottom I was ready to go. The first day would be the hardest. We had to fight thirty men. The men had been brought from Japan; all were black belts. We would fight each man for three minutes. We would fight them all-out, without protective gear. If any one of them beat us, we would lose points. If we dropped out due to exhaustion or injury we would lose everything.

That morning we gathered in the dojo. Master Takimuro glanced at his scorecard and called out my name. I was first up. I stepped onto the tatami. My first opponent stepped out with me. Then the signal was given and the fight that would test the logic of my life began.

I started strong. In control. I took punches when I chose and blocked others when I wished. Three minutes. Not long. My next opponent stepped in and we grappled. My technique was perfect. I was hitting on all cylinders. Sharp. I fought another, then another, then another. Forty-five minutes later I had stood my ground against fifteen black belts.

Master Takimuro called for a stop. It was time for the board-breaking test. The master asked me how many two-by-fours I wanted stacked on the breaking stand. I chose three, the minimum allowed. We were all qualified to break at least ten boards, but I didn't want anything to happen to my hand. Sprain it now and it would be impossible to go on. Besides, the whole purpose of this test was to measure whether you had the strength to continue. A person who couldn't break at least three boards after fighting fifteen men, it was felt, had exhausted himself and would likely get hurt if he continued. I broke my three boards and was allowed to go on.

I fought another six men in succession, then called a time out. Fifteen minutes. I needed it. The black belts were tough, tough as hardpan streets, tough as our callused feet that had pounded those streets for mile after mile, day after day. All that training but it wasn't enough. Not for this. My breath was coming like torn paper. My legs had gone rubbery. I glanced at the nine men I still had to fight. They stood waiting, their jaws set, their eyes burning with a lust for blood and broken teeth.

I sat down and massaged my legs with heated oil.

Sweat rolled off me like summer glacier melt. I wondered if I had the strength to go on. A quick sip of water and I started digging back. Back home. Back to Belgium. Back to my mother, her head emerging from behind our front door. She is smiling. Her teeth are perfect. "You be home before dinner now, you hear me?" she is saying. And I am off running. Further and further until I'm dressed in wolf skin and a two-horned battle helmet and I can feel the steady lurch of the boat as our oars rhythmically lift and dip, lift and dip. We're sailing into battle, me and the rest of my Viking crew. And as we draw close to the enemy I can feel my blood quickening, the berserker rage within me rising until I'm howling like a beast and there's nothing I can do but stand and fight.

I cut through the next three black belts like a scythe. The fourth went down hard. The fifth refused to go down at all but I hung on. The sixth and seventh seemed to take hours. We clinched and grappled, wet and intimate as raw meat. The eighth was obscure, like some fragment of a bad dream. I was fighting like a sleepwalker now, outside time, beyond space, from a dark place whose only measure is punishment.

I was barely able to paw at the air as the thirtieth fighter stepped onto the mat. He opened with a kick. I stood there for a blind moment, dripping blood, then the pain hit and I felt myself slipping back. There's my mother smiling her perfect smile. Could that be me racing into the kitchen in time for dinner? Where are my wolf skins and my two-horned battle helmet? My mother humiliates me with a look that says she knows better, and I collapse into my seat at the dinner table just as the black belt unleashed a vicious combination to my head. I felt myself starting to fall. I was all played out. This was the end, or would have been if the fight had been allowed to go on. But I'd made my

(Copyright 2004 by Kevin Lynch)

three minutes. The fight was over. I'd done it. Thirty fighters. Now at last I could rest.

The next day, it took all my willpower just to stumble out of bed. I dressed, ate, and dragged my aches and pains down to the dojo for another set of tests. Today, we would be fighting against four simultaneous attackers.

As soon as I walked in, Master Takimuro called my name. First up again. The adrenaline started rushing as I made my way into the center of the circle of four, but before I was even able to take a stance, one of them lashed out with a kick to my back that sent me sprawling forward. I grabbed the two in front of me and took them with me to the mat. As I fell, I head-butted one and elbowed the other in the throat. As I rose to my feet, one of the two still standing aimed a kick at my face. I blocked the kick with my forearm and threw the whole weight of my shoulder into his thigh. He tumbled over my back. It was deadly quiet in the dojo as I climbed to my feet and met my fourth opponent with a kick to the balls and a Judo throw over my shoulder.

I stepped to the outside of the mat. When one of the men on the floor grabbed my leg, I kicked him in the face until he let go. Only three now rose to face me. The one who'd taken the elbow to the throat stayed down. The three attacked simultaneously. I kicked one in the leg, turned, punched another twice in the face, then low-kicked the third so hard I could hear his leg snap as he fell to the floor.

The sound of that leg breaking stopped the other two in their tracks, giving me just enough time to execute a hard spinning back kick into one of their stomachs. When the other one charged me, I dropped onto my back and used the forward force of his attack to throw him into the crowd of spectators.

Only one black belt left. We clinched and I took him to the floor, where we grappled until I was able to follow up a well-placed head butt with a chokehold. He tapped out. I came to my knees and saw Master Takimuro nodding. I had completed the test with style and speed. One more day to go.

We started the final day with a test of our breaking techniques. We had twelve minutes to run a course in which we had to break stacks of boards with our hands, bricks with our feet, and baseball bats with our shins. I completed the course in eight minutes.

Next we had to do four hundred push-ups and two thousand sit-ups while they timed us with stopwatches. After that, we had to stand without flinching while they broke boards over our bodies. Then there were running tests for distance and speed. After all I'd been through it seemed like an easy morning.

The afternoon brought greater challenges. First, Master Takimuro had us demonstrate several fighting movements and strikes. After that, we had to fight three bouts against the black belts, only this time we were restricted to using only two techniques in each bout. The object here wasn't necessarily to win, but to show that we could at least hold off an attacker even though we'd been limited to using a simple one-two combination of strikes.

"Right leg *ushiro-geri*. Left hand *uraken*." The master called out the two striking methods I would use in my first bout.

I bowed and assumed a fighting pose. The black belt flashed in and for the next three minutes I held him at bay.

"Left leg *mae-geri*. Right hand *oi-zuki*."

Again I fought the black belt to a standstill.

For my third bout the master allowed me to pick the two techniques. I chose a left-right combination of low kicks.

"Fight!" The order was given and I waited for the black belt to advance. As soon as he moved in, I let go with a kick to his leading leg and he fell to the mat in a heap. When the black belt said that he couldn't get up, the master smiled broadly. The tests were over. Nothing to do now but wait for the results.

Ronin

Literally, "wave man."
A masterless samurai; a rogue.

We spent our last day packing suitcases and marking time until the results of our tests were announced. I knew I'd done well but I tried not to show it. The virtues of skill and strength have their limits. Where they end the virtues of honor begin, and perhaps the first responsibilities of honor are the practice of courtesy and restraint. Thaiwell, who was always much more of a man in the ring than out of it, restrained himself not a whit. He knew he had aced the tests, but he showed us no courtesy. Instead, he swaggered around the camp as if the results were already in and he had placed first. In fact, he *had* placed first, but with a caveat, for when the results were finally posted two students had tied for the top spot—Thaiwell and I.

I was in the clouds. First place! The fact that I was tied with Thaiwell didn't bother me at all; in fact, I considered it an honor to be ranked in a tie with him. Of course

Thaiwell didn't see it that way, and as soon as the results were announced he fixed me with an angry stare. He wasn't about to share top honors with anyone, least of all a gaijin upstart.

Our group spent most of the rest of that day and night drinking sake. We drank to the past; we drank to the future. We drank to the day when we would all meet again to compete in the freestyle championship. We drank so much that I have no clear recollection of just how it started. Perhaps I said some harsh words, perhaps Thaiwell did, but when Thaiwell threw his drink into my face he crossed a line that had to be answered with something more than mere words, and so, like an idiot, I stood up to fight and promptly got punched in the face. Then I did the unthinkable: I charged him. It's embarrassing, even now, to admit that I could do something that stupid, but I did. Being drunk was no excuse. For the past six months I had drilled and trained for just this sort of encounter, but now that it was actually happening all my training seemed to fly out the window. Not Thaiwell's. In one fluid motion he stop-kicked my leg and shin-kicked my throat. I fell to my knees, gasping for air, and before Thaiwell could do me any worse the other guys rushed in and stopped him.

For me the party was over. I returned to our sleeping quarters to nurse wounds and a grudge that grew stronger with each passing moment. When finally I couldn't take it anymore, I went out looking for Thaiwell. I found him still partying with the others, and boasting that he, and not I, was the best fighter in camp. The way he'd countered my drunken lunge was his proof.

Right then I decided to kill him; it was only a question of how. I slipped into the shadows outside the compound and waited. Then, when Thaiwell came out to piss, I stepped up behind him and whispered so that only he could hear me. "Hey, motherfucker, you want to see who's really best? Meet me in the dojo. Come alone. I'll be waiting."

I went back to the sleeping quarters, unpacked my *gi* and put it on. Then I went to the dojo. Twenty minutes later Thaiwell showed up. I stared at his face. The bastard grinned as he dropped into his stance. My rage had burned through the last of my liquor high long ago, and before Thaiwell even knew what was happening I kicked him in the nuts and head-butted his forehead. As he dropped, I kicked him twice more in the face with my shin. I could tell he was finished, not that I cared; I hadn't even gotten started.

"Stop!" The word came from the entrance to the dojo where several instructors and students now stood. "Stand aside!"

Thaiwell lay defenseless on the floor. His cheekbones were high, his nose broad. An extended knuckle strike to either and he would be dead.

"Don't do it," the instructor shouted again.

I let a moment tick by, then unclenched my fist and stepped away.

Later that night I was called to see the master.

"The sculptor goes to the quarry to search for a stone," the master began. "In his mind he knows the work of art he wants to create. He looks at many stones, but none of them are right. Some have fissures, barely visible, but the sculptor senses them. Some stones are too hard and will never yield to the chisel. Others are too soft and will break before the carving is through. After weeks of searching, the sculptor finds the right stone. He brings it back to his studio, begins to carve, and in time creates a great work of art.

"You, Dominiquie, are the right stone. You can be turned into a great work of martial art if only you would surrender yourself to the chisel."

I nodded, a flush of shame reddening my cheeks.

"Go then and think about what I have told you. And, no matter what you decide, never again drink to the point that you lose control."

I bowed and left the master's room. Out in the courtyard the other students were waiting. As soon as I reached them, they pounded my back, pumped my hand and congratulated me for the beating I'd served Thaiwell. As we drifted into the night, I looked back and saw the master's silhouette framed in the doorway. He had placed the chisel in my hand, but it would take years for me to gather the courage needed to carve art from living rock.

The World

From the Vietnam war, a slang term for home,
or anywhere that wasn't Vietnam.

I slept. I slept for hours, and when I woke up I was home, or at least they told me it was home, though to me it seemed more like some strange waking dream. I pushed through the airport, through a jumble of people, past hundreds of earnest, unimaginative faces with no light shining in their eyes. I caught the usual collection of buses, trains, metros, and jitneys, all the time getting closer to my own little corner of Europe, to my mother and my father and the reassuring sameness of my village.

As soon as I walked through the door, my parents made straight for me. My dad, aloof, vaguely curious, and even more vaguely proud of what he called "my Asian adventure" greeted me with a smile. My mom, tearful and expectant, ran a hand over my newly shaved head and eyed me like she'd just cooked up some fancy new recipe and was waiting to see if I liked it. Both of them were just as I remembered them, just like my friends, and their friends, and all the rest who had come to greet me—unchanged.

I thought it would put me at ease, this constancy, but it didn't. It only pointed out how much I had changed. The training had done more than just toughen me; the six months of Kunto had chipped away all the tailings of civilization, leaving me dark, sharp, and hard as obsidian—a living weapon. But in the stifling closeness of my parent's front room I felt more like a curio than a killer.

"Come on, Dominiquie, show us how high you can kick."

"Hey, can you do that thing like in the movies where they spin around and stop their foot an inch in front of your face?"

"Dominiquie, never mind that, taste this torte. Come on, one bite, what can it hurt?"

It was awful, impossible, and the more they plied me with questions and comforts the more uncomfortable I became. I wanted to strip down to bare feet, shout *"kiai,"* and kick out. I wanted to run, punch, anything to prove to myself and to them that what I'd been through mattered, that I was now a different man, a world apart.

I wondered why no one could see the change. I thought maybe they were all just pretending that I was the same boy who had left. Maybe they thought that, by acting as if I hadn't changed, in time they could win me back to the fold. Then an even worse thought hit me: What if they were right? What if I could be worn down like a rock in a river, all my hard work dissolving under the constant pressure to conform?

After the guests left, my family and I sat down to dinner. The perfectly set table, the rich foods, their soft faces all looked a million miles away. And something in them was saying something to me, and something in me was saying something back. But what? I didn't know and hardly cared. None of it seemed real. It was like watching television with the sound turned off. Inside, my head was a jungle. And I could feel the psychopathic heat, the familiar craving for blood, war, and animal violence, rise through my body like a purifying fire, and then, just as suddenly, it sputtered and was gone. Impossible, I thought as I searched within myself for some new ember of anger that I could fan into a fiery rage. I'd been unmade. A few hours in polite society and I was coming apart. Soon all I had become would be no more. Already there was a change. And still the treatment continued:

"We kept your room just like you left it."

"I'll bet you didn't get to eat food like this over there."

"No matter what, you'll always be our son."

"Pass the noodles, please, son."

But I was beyond passing noodles, beyond table talk, beyond anything they could ever understand. Open your eyes, I wanted to shout. You see these hands? With a single pinkie I could gouge out your eyes. With two fingers I can crack bones, with five stop a heart. You know what that means? You know what it's like to hold power like that in your hands?

"Your father says they've still got an opening for you down at the butcher shop."

"Good place to work out your aggression." My father jabbed at the air with his fists. "Like Rocky, eh?"

Work out my aggression? God, if they only knew how much I needed to fight right now, if only to clear my head.

"So what do you think, son? You going down to the shop tomorrow to see about that job?"

I met my father's eyes and chewed my food without saying a word. I lifted another forkful and slid it between my lips.

My father rose up in his seat. He felt the challenge of my silence as plainly as if I'd set a bomb on the dining room table and lit the fuse. In that moment I wasn't his son anymore but a dangerous stranger set loose upon the family table setting.

"Is that your answer?" he finally sputtered when he saw I wasn't going to speak.

My mother tried to calm things. "Honey, now you said yourself he'd probably need some time off. Let's give him a chance to relax, get his strength back after what he's been through. Just look at his color; you ever seen him so white?"

Poor mother. Like most women she would never understand the demonology of men. If only she had come to see me fight, just once, perhaps then she would have been able to grasp what it meant to be a man—how simple it was, how right.

I stood up and faced my father. Sooner or later I was going to have to hurt him. I might as well do it now. Why pussyfoot and run the risk of going soft? Better to hit him now with everything. Maximum violence instantly.

"I'm not going to be a butcher or any other normal bullshit job. I'm going to be a fighter. You understand? I am a fighter, the best goddamned fighter in the world. That's how I'm going to make my living because that's what I am. If you can't live with that, fine. I'll leave your house right now because you're never going to change my mind. I'm going to fight."

It took a few days before my parents broke down and agreed to let me do things my way. I could live at home and train for the upcoming championship. The fight was a year away. First prize was twenty thousand dollars in cash, but I needed money now. My parents hadn't asked me to contribute to the household, but I didn't want to be a burden—no man does—so I went to see my old trainer Frank Merton. I figured he could line up some paying fights for me. Bare-knuckle stuff. Blood sport. Illegal as hell, but Frank knew the score; he'd been around.

When I told Frank my plan he thought I was crazy. He wanted me to fight in sanctioned bouts. Nobody on the Continent could touch me. He was sure I would be the next European Pro Champion. Then I could make lots of money endorsing clothing and gear. I could get my face plastered in karate magazines, teach seminars, even start my own dojo if I wanted. Why jeopardize a future like that by fighting in bouts where I could get my nose or fingers bitten off, where I could lose an eye or even my life if I wasn't careful?

I asked Frank to pad up—headgear, cup, the works— and challenged him to a fight. Frank had always been a good fighter, a champion himself in his time. He could take punishment and dish it out too. Before I'd been to Okinawa he was better than I was, but now I beat him easily, effortlessly, again and again.

"You see," I told him, "there's no challenge in this for me. For fighting to mean anything to me it has to be real. All or nothing. No holds barred. Fighting with padding and rules just makes me frustrated, like being stuck in traffic in a Ferrari. You want to see how fast I can really go? Show me some open road. You won't fucking believe it."

Frank said he'd see what he could do. There were blood sport fights all the time in Eastern Europe; money could be made. If you had extra cash to bet with, you could make even more. Only one problem. If you wanted to survive the blood sport circuit, you had to be as good at hustling as you were at fighting. If you bet too heavily or beat the local favorites too easily, they were just as likely to rob or kill you as pay you. It was a dangerous business all the way around.

"You're a crazy motherfucker, Dominiquie."

"I know. So when do we start?"

I walked home cocky as a comic-book hero. I didn't know that on the kitchen table a letter from the Belgian government was waiting. When I opened it and read it, I started shouting and didn't stop until my mother came running into the room, shouting herself. "What is it? What's wrong?"

I handed her the letter. She read it, and, for the first time since I returned from Okinawa, her bruised and anxious eyes seemed to soften. "I guess this means you won't be able to fight for a while."

She'd guessed right. The letter was a draft notice. I'd been called to serve in the Belgian army, the last place on earth a single-combat fighter wanted to be. For the next twelve months the army would own me. That meant I would miss the championship fight, I would lose a year of training, and my skills would wither.

I cursed the country that seemed so determined to rob me of myself. If the lottery that had chosen my name was blind, my rage was not. I cursed the politicians who had concocted this criminal scheme, the ministers who preached its justice from their pulpits, and all the rich sons of bitches who sat home nursing their bellies while we had to serve. You never saw any of their sons standing in the ranks. For the rich and the powerful there were always deferments. But for people like me, for the sons of mechanics and bricklayers and farmers, there was no way out. We had to serve. Or did we?

I did some investigating. If I volunteered to be sent to a Belgian army base located in Germany, I would only have to serve eight months instead of the usual twelve. That meant I would still have two months after I was discharged to prepare for the World Championship. I figured it was a better deal than going AWOL and having to leave Belgium forever, so I signed up to be stationed in Germany.

Pisser

Belgian military slang for a new recruit.

Two weeks later I was on a train full of draftees heading to the city of Turnout for three weeks of basic training. Basic was just that—a three-week handshake introducing us to the tedium and stupidity that is military life. When they weren't teaching us how to stand, march, or make our beds, they kept us busy cleaning. We cleaned walls, fields, toilets, floors, and kitchens. I began to think that the military was actually training an army of cleaning men, that all the talk of war and weapons was just a ruse. The real enemy of the Belgian state was dirt. With brooms, buckets, and mops we marched out to do battle.

Our training sergeant tried to act like he was training us for war, but it was a bad acting job straight out of an American B-movie and none of us believed it for a minute. We all knew we were just marking time. Even the officers who had decided to make a career in this pathetic excuse for an army knew that theirs would never be a true path to glory. Not that any of them could have handled glory. Most were drunks and shirkers who couldn't hold a job in the real world and so had joined these ranks to play out their time as soldiers before retiring on fat government pensions. Their days were spent hiding, avoiding work, avoiding us, and maneuvering themselves into bars and brothels where they did what soldiers everywhere do best.

It wasn't much different in Volgelzang, the German base where I was stationed after basic. The base specialized in laying mines and detonating explosives, though I never saw much of either the whole time I was there. Instead, I taught Karate. In a small country like Belgium news travels fast, and when the officers heard that a Belgian Junior Freestyle Karate champion was being stationed at their base they flocked to me for training in hand-to-hand combat techniques. The training was pointless. Most of the officers were in no condition to attack anybody. They'd practice halfheartedly for an hour or so, then pull out their cameras and ask me to pose with them for pictures that proved they had trained with a champ. A lot of good the pictures would do if they ever got in a fight.

Training the officers, though, did have its rewards. Within a month I'd been excused from almost every work detail and even from most of the military training. That left me plenty of time to train on my own. There were still a few techniques I wanted to develop before the championship bout. One of them was the ability to deliver an internal strike. In a normal strike, the power of the blow comes from the muscle power behind it. A normal strike will either knock a target down or push it away. An internal strike, however, doesn't damage or even move the surface of the target. Instead, the force of the blow is transferred inside the target; all the damage is done internally.

To deliver an effective internal strike, you have to be able to direct the force of your *ki* into your blows. To do that, first you have to become aware that you even have *ki;* you have to locate the *ki* in your body and learn to move with it and through it. I'm sure you've all seen Tai Chi practitioners going through their ambulations; well that's what they're doing—they're moving with *ki.* Once you learn to control your *ki* your striking power increases ten-fold. You can fight faster, harder, and longer, and deliver more damage with each impact. Controlling *ki* is some-thing any serious martial artist spends a lifetime perfect-ing. I had eight months, so what did I do? I went out every chance I got, drinking and whoring with the boys.

The town of Cologne was a soldier's wet dream of pros-titutes and bars. I'd lost my virginity with a village girl right after I returned from Okinawa. She didn't mean much to me nor I to her, but I'd gotten in, and now, like all the rest, I followed my dick into town, eager for another crack at it. Getting laid in Cologne was a no-brainer; all you had to do was open your wallet. At first, I hated myself for hav-ing to pay. It was insulting to my dignity and to hers, but after awhile I got over that. When you're seventeen, horny, and in the army you'll get over just about anything for sex.

One night, three of us came whooping into a bar like prospectors after a big strike. In the past two days we'd fucked our way through half the town's whores and just about all of our cash. With our leave almost up and just enough money left for a few drinks and maybe a quick round of blowjobs, we figured this joint was as good as any.

We looked the place over. The bar was littered with weary losers and snakebit drunks. Up on the stools, a cozy of ancient potbellied whores sat tonguing lipstick off their fossilized teeth. It looked pretty grim and I wanted to leave when my buddy Victor spotted a Gypsy girl sitting alone at a back table.

"She'll do," Victor said as he eased his hands into his trouser pockets and ambled over to meet her.

While Rene and I sat at the bar, Victor struck a deal with the Gypsy and they retreated toward the bathroom. The Gypsy didn't look bad; she was soft and sultry, and her ass moved with a bounce that looked like it would give a fine ride.

Since there was no one else in the bar to equal her, Rene and I debated over which one of us would go next. Soon we were swimming in a pink cloud of imagined sex that would never be. Between us we had just enough money for a single blowjob or a few rounds of drinks. It was no contest. While Rene called for the drinks, I unglued myself from the barstool and headed back to the bathroom to piss.

"So, how's the blowjob, buddy?" I called out to Victor, who was seated in one of the closed stalls.

When Victor didn't answer I got worried, so I bent down and looked under the stall. From my vantage point I could see that the Gypsy was on her knees and that Victor's pants were down. What I couldn't see was that the Gypsy was holding a knife to Victor's balls in order to rob him. Still, the dead silence in that stall was enough to convince me to get up and yank open the door. As soon as I did though, the Gypsy was ready. She hit me with a blast of mace that caught me like a fireball. Before she could spray me again, I side-kicked her in the chest, punched her once in the head, and she fell unconscious to the floor.

Just as Victor and I were about to make our getaway, a German burst into the bathroom. I didn't know if he was her pimp, or just a local Good Samaritan, because as soon as he saw the girl out cold on the floor he attacked me. His mistake. A right, a left, and a middle kick to the stomach later and he was sprawled out next to her. After that, Victor and I scuttled out of the bathroom, grabbed Rene, and ran into the night.

The next day we caught a train back to Vogelzang. All of us were hung over and I wasn't in the mood for any kind of trouble when four Turkish teenagers boarded the train. There weren't many empty seats and the Turks, in their hurry to grab some, pushed past an old man who toppled and fell to the floor. I got up and helped the old man to his feet. He was badly shaken and could hardly stand, so I guided him over to my friends and offered him my seat. Then I looked back at the Turks. They were laughing and pointing at me like I was some kind of jerk for the kindness I'd done the old man. It was more than I could take. A testosterone rage swept the sour hangover haze from my head. I walked up to the Turks, who by this time were too busy harassing a pretty girl sitting behind them to even notice my approach.

"Hey!" I shouted, and when they turned I kicked two of them in the face. Crack! Crack! One shot each and they were out. I grabbed the third by the hair, lifted him out of his seat and punched him in the face until I felt him go limp. I let him drop just in time to dodge the fourth Turk, who had pulled out a knife and was charging. With the Turk's knife cutting the air in front of me, I stepped back and whipped off my belt. Before the Turk could close, I swung the belt and caught him in the face with the buckle. When he winced, I grabbed his knife hand, threw him to the floor and started playing soccer on his head until my buddies rushed in to stop me.

"You're going to kill him. It's enough!"

As I stopped kicking the poor Turk's head the other passengers sat frozen in their seats.

"No more trouble. Everything's okay now," I shouted in German to the passengers. Most of them looked away. They were now as afraid of me as they'd been of the Turks. Not the old man though; from him I got a smile and a thankful salute.

At the next stop, my buddies and I rushed off the train. So did nearly everyone else. Nobody wanted to get into it with the German police, who I'm sure soon found the Turks, moaning and bloodied after our little dance together.

Three months later my duty was up. I'd done my time and that was that. Under no circumstances, I thought, would I ever stand in the ranks again. In fact, if you'd told me back then that in less than a year I'd be slogging through some African hellhole with the French Foreign Legion, I would have laughed, then I would have punched you in the mouth.

Primus Inter Pares

Latin for "first among equals."

I came home to another letter, this one from Thaiwell, challenging me to a rematch. He wrote that he wanted an honest fight this time, not like what had happened in Okinawa. The hypocrite. Our fights had been honest. In a fight without rules there can be no dishonesty. Total honesty of the most extreme and violent sort is the very soul of Kunto. I couldn't believe Thaiwell didn't know that. I figured his loss to me had eaten the heart out of him. Good. When the time came to face him again, I wouldn't have to do much to beat him; he was already defeated.

I started training like a madman. I battered speed bags and heavy bags until they were as familiar to me as my own body. I practiced kata and drills until my fighting responses were entirely ganglionic. To fight, I didn't have to think anymore; I simply sat back and let my hands and feet paint the air like a performance in automatic writing. I did calisthenics, strength-building exercises, breathing exercises, and routines to develop flexibility, coordination, balance, and endurance. I trained until I felt like the last man on Earth. I was intoxicated by my own pure warrior spirit. The blind tenacity, the unremitting ordeal, was so wonderfully healing, so completely sensible, that I never wanted it to end.

Only one thing intruded on my otherwise hermetic universe—sex. The sweet sighs of sex. The smell of sex. The dewy, giddy, wriggling rush of sex. I tried to put it out of my mind, but against the pirouette of flesh on flesh I was defenseless. I swore that, as soon as the championship fight was through, I'd do nothing but fuck and fuck and fuck and fuck.

I'd already pumped my body hard as a full-on erection; I was a perfectly muscled creature. Now, if I could just maintain it, the championship fight would be my ultimate fuck. At night, I dreamed of myself in the ring, my oiled body shining like the flanks of a stallion, ready to fuck or be fucked, not for passion, or comfort, or money or love, but simply for release. I let go with a spinning back kick and woke sweating and pulling at the covers, a sticky wet spot spreading through my pajama bottoms.

In my delirium I told my father that if I could I would cut off my own balls to get over the insane longing that was distracting me from my training. My dad thought I was crazy, and in a way I guess I was.

I threw myself at my training even harder. Frank helped out a lot. He brought in wrestlers, boxers, Karate men, kickboxers, weightlifters, street fighters—all sorts of brawlers. I wanted to experience every fighting strategy I could, because in freestyle competitions you never knew who or what you were going to be facing. It's not like boxing where there are set rules and forms and you can see tapes of your opponents before you fight. In freestyle you step onto the mat without knowing anything about your opponent or how he is going to try to fight you. All I knew,

all any of us knew, was that the competition being sponsored by the NTK Federation was called the World Open in
Bare Knuckle Karate and that it would take place somewhere in Budapest. In the competition, which would last
for three days, each of us would be fighting between three
and five bouts a day. Each bout would go three rounds or
more, with each round lasting four minutes. You won either by knocking your opponent out or by getting him into
a hold, in which case he would usually tap the mat to signal that he gave up before you snapped one of his bones, or
choked him unconscious or dead.

When the day came to leave for Budapest I was more
than ready. I'd already gone beyond the limits of lesser
men and I pitied the hopeless human bastards who were
going to have to face me.

Frank was more practical. When we met on the morning of our drive into Budapest he introduced me to Martin,
a cut man, who'd be coming along just in case. I looked at
the cut man and shook my head. He was short and fat with
a spotty bald head and a face that looked like a crushed
fender. When I got close enough to shake his hand I could
almost see the alcohol fumes rising off him in waves.

Martin farted wetly and excused himself. "They're rip-
pers but I swear they don't stink, as long as I don't shit myself," he laughed.

Then he farted again. "Hey, mind if I sit in front? I got a
boil on my ass that's killing me."

I opened the car door and shot a look over at Frank.

"He's the best there is. I'll tell you that right now."

"He fucking better be," I growled as I slid into the back
seat.

Once in Budapest, we checked into a cheap hotel and
Frank made some calls to let the fight committee know that
we'd arrived. Because the fight was unsanctioned and only
quasi-legal, we still didn't know where it was going to be

held. They wouldn't tell us either, not until the morning of the fight, which was still two days away. I guess the fight sponsors were afraid the authorities would find out, or the press, or the gamblers, all of whom they were trying to keep at arm's length. It was Master Takimuro's wish that full-contact freestyle fighting be kept pure. The last thing he wanted was to see it debased by betting men, or spectators, or press people hunting for a bloody tale to spin.

I passed most of the two days before the fight alone. Frank said I was acting like a woman with PMS. Sure, I told him, if PMS stands for Pissed-off Murderous Sociopath, that's me. Then I pushed him out the door and went back to replaying in my head every fight I'd ever had.

The morning of the fight we were told to go to an old school gymnasium not far from where we were staying. We drove over. From outside, the place looked abandoned. From inside it looked worse. A dim gray light percolated through greasy windows set high above a tier of exhausted bleachers. About forty or fifty fighters and their assistants sat in the bleachers or milled around a tatami mat that had been placed in the middle of the floor. Almost no one spoke. The whole place stank and was cold as a crypt. It felt like a meat locker, and you could sense the fatality, the immense frozen solitude of the fighters hanging in the air.

While Frank went to check us in, I went over to say hello to some of the guys I recognized from Okinawa. Of the ten who'd been invited, only four, including myself, had come. I shook hands with two of them. They barely acknowledged me. I wasn't surprised; we'd all pulled the trigger on our kinder emotions weeks ago. After all, this was war, and every man was a potential enemy.

I looked around for Thaiwell. I planned to walk over and sniff at him like shit, but he hadn't shown yet. Oh well, it was early; there'd be time.

I went to the changing room that I shared with five

other guys, stripped down to bare chest and black pants, and waited for Frank to come in and help tape up my hands. Some of the other fighters were starting to warm up. I watched and tried to guess what fighting schools they came from. Of course, I knew that even if I placed their moves, I could never be sure of how they would actually fight. These men were experts in the art of inflicting pain, and that meant they were experts in the art of deception as well. Whatever moves they were using to warm up were probably a fake-out. None of them had gotten this far by telegraphing their intentions.

As I rubbed liniment into my legs, I could hear the muffled whip-crack of karate strikes coming from the gym. The competition had started. When Frank came in and told me that it would be at least an hour before I got to fight, I went out to watch.

On the floor, a little guy was beating the tar out of a fighter who was two, maybe three times the little guy's size. The little guy moved like a tornado. He was every-where, his arms and feet flying in swirling patterns. When the big man stumbled, the little guy launched a flurry of vicious kicks and punches at the big man's face. Picture a ventriloquist being mauled by his own evil dummy and you'll get an idea of what it looked like.

The big guy tapped at the mat. For him, the contest was over; he'd be going home. Though I didn't know if anyone there would recognize him; his face looked like the inside of a shattered watermelon.

I watched three more fights, then it was my turn. I stepped onto the tatami. My opponent, a local Hungarian Kyokushinkai Karate stylist, stepped out as well. We stood toe to toe and raised our hands above our heads. I looked into his eyes. They were black and atrocious as the space between stars. We touched palms and the fight was on. The Hungarian charged me. I sidestepped his attack and turned to face him again. Again he charged and again I side-stepped. The third time he came at me with his hands down so I let him close. As soon as he stepped into range, I elbowed him in the chin and followed up with a spinning back fist that caught him straight in the throat. He fell unconscious to the mat. I raised my fists. My first victory had taken less than thirty seconds.

As I stepped off the tatami, I spotted Thaiwell watching me from the bleachers. I raised a finger and pointed at him like a baseball player signaling the direction of his next hit. Thaiwell stood up and crossed his arms across his chest. He looked good, really good, not at all like the ruined man I was expecting. In a way I was pleased. When the time came to beat him I wanted to leave him without remonstration. This time, I wanted him to know for sure that I was his better.

An hour later I fought my next fight. An hour after that I fought my third. Both my opponents came from Tae Kwon Do, a martial arts form that's beautiful to watch, but not very effective against freestyle fighters. The first one I took out with a series of low leg kicks that put my opponent on the mat before the first round was out. The second one I closed on and knocked out with a left hook to the jaw.

I spent the rest of the day watching the other fighters. Some of them were stronger than me, and some of them were faster, but none of them had my ferocity, my stamina, or my sheer will to win. Thaiwell came close. I could tell his internal motors were all souped up, because he didn't waste any time toying with his opponents; he just blew through them and moved on. Though we never spoke a word, we both knew we were on a collision course.

I started the second day facing an Australian Judo champion and tough-man contest winner who weighed 360 pounds. Get him mad, which he was, and he looked like he could lift buses. As soon as the fight started he roared straight for me. But what his bulk gave him in power it took away in speed. I figured as long as I kept moving I would have the advantage. So, after tagging him with a couple of low shin kicks, I moved in and pelted him with body shots, then backed up and caught him with kicks again. I went at him back and forth like this until I caught him with a shot that bent him over, then I stepped in and kneed him in the face. He went down like a stone, and they had to bring in the smelling salts to get him up and off the mat so that the next fight could go on.

My second opponent was a traditional Karate fighter whom I dropped fairly quickly after catching him with a roundhouse kick to the throat. My third opponent that day was a former European boxing champion turned Karate expert. When I saw that his hands were faster than mine I did what I could to avoid them while hammering his legs with low kicks. He had no real defense against the kicks, and at the end of the first round he hobbled into his corner and forfeited the fight entirely when he was unable to stand and meet me in the second round.

I figured my second day of fighting was over when suddenly Frank was telling me I had one more fight to go. Before I even had time to warm up, I was led to the tatami. I recognized my opponent immediately. Hoerst was a reputable German freestyle and street fighter who made his living as a close combat paramilitary instructor.

Just before the signal to fight was given, Hoerst extended his hand to shake mine. As soon as I took it, I realized my mistake, because instead of shaking hands Hoerst spit in my eye and kicked me in the face. Then he kicked me a couple more times in the ribs. Ignoring the pain, I countered with a series of lefts and rights. Hoerst was good, and we fought to a standstill through the first round and the second. By the third round, though, Hoerst was exhausted while I was still going strong. Now it was my turn. I moved in and caught him with a six-punch combination. He was out on his feet, and any second would drop, but first I wanted payback for the dirty way he'd opened the fight, so I put all my power into one final right hook. It caught him under the jaw, lifting him clean off his feet before he slammed into the mat and lay still.

While the paramedics carried Hoerst off, Frank and Martin sat me down. My right eye was swollen and my nose had been dislocated. With a quick wrench, Martin snapped my nose back in place. Though I didn't feel anything except a dull tug, I knew it would hurt like hell the next day. Frank was more worried about the eye. If the swelling didn't go down my vision would be impaired. I was facing the possibility of maybe five fights the next day. If I wanted to make it through, I would have to protect the eye. No easy task. Everybody in the gym had seen what happened. They would all be gunning for my eye. I looked over and saw Thaiwell do something I'd never seen him do before—he was smiling.

That night, I knelt by the side of my bed and prayed to God for help. Now I know, to a lot of you, the idea of asking God for help in beating other men half to death must seem comical and maybe even a little crazy, but that night I would've prayed to Buddha, Moses, or even Zoroaster if I'd only known how. As it was, I stuck with the prayers I knew, which worked out fine, because the next morning the swelling around my eye was completely gone.

When Frank and Martin saw the eye they put it off to the ice bags and tinctures they'd prescribed. Maybe so, but I like to think there's still room in the world for a small miracle now and then.

My first fight of the day was against a champion rocklifter and lumberjack from Russia. He wasn't a trained martial artist, so he had nothing to prove in that department.

When I learned that he competed in illegal boxing fights strictly for the money, I thought he must be nuts. A man who was willing to take this kind of punishment for money alone had to be. Nuts or not, if he'd made it this far in the competition, it meant he was dangerous. I'd have to take him out fast.

As soon as the fight started he rushed me, throwing front kicks and punches. I backed up, firing back fists until both of us fell to the floor outside of the tatami. Time was called and we both moved back into the center of the ring where the fight began again. Just as before, he opened by rushing me, only this time I was ready for him and as he got close I connected with a spinning back kick to the spleen that sent him to the mat, screaming in pain.

Usually, that would be enough to finish a man, but, just as I feared, this guy was crazy—instead of surrendering like he should have, he sucked up the pain, got up, and came at me again. Since I couldn't get inside his defenses, I backed away. I figured I'd work him with low kicks for a while. I was a master of low kicks; I'd practiced them almost every day of my life, often for hours on end, but this time something went wrong, and instead of connecting with the kick, I missed.

It was just the break the Russian needed. He closed on me and we grappled. We were fighting his fight now—a stand-up free-for-all. I threw punches and kicks, all of which he deflected while raining his own blows down on me. Finally, just when I thought I wouldn't be able to take much more, I snaked out a fist that all but disintegrated his nose. As the Russian opened his mouth to breathe, I snapped an elbow into his throat and that was the end of him. There'd be no prize money for the Russian today. All he'd won was a free trip to the hospital courtesy of the local ambulance squad.

My next opponent was a Kung Fu Wushu stylist. I

squashed him like a louse. It took me all of about ten seconds to kick him out—which was good because I was in desperate need of rest. The competition was taking its toll. I was stiff and tired and had long since descended from the elegance of my best style.

I went back to the changing room and slathered myself with liniment. Only two more fights to go, but I was so damned worn out I had to wonder, could I make it? My skin had been tattooed with welts and bruises. Every inch of me hurt. All across my chest, back, and legs, the skin that wasn't black was blue, and what wasn't blue was brown or red or a sickening purple-green. But when Frank came in to tell me that my next opponent would be Josei Thaiwell I forgot all about the colors of my skin. The pain evaporated. The exhaustion disappeared as the old rage rose within me on a pulsing column of blood.

A half-hour later, the ref barked out the single word I'd been waiting a year for: "Fight!" Like a dog released from its tether, I rushed at Thaiwell only to slip and stumble to one knee. Though he could have attacked, Thaiwell just stood there, shaking his head in disgust. I attacked again, this time in an even blinder rage. It was exactly what Thaiwell wanted. He caught me with two stinging side kicks to the ribs. I backed up fast, but again Thaiwell refused to press his advantage. What the hell was his strategy? And, for that matter, what was mine?

Maybe it was the pain radiating from the spot where Thaiwell had kicked me, but all at once I smartened up. I realized that my tactics weren't working. I was fighting like a street brawler. All I wanted was to get my hands on the bastard and kill him. Thaiwell could see that and he was using it to his advantage. But what else did I know about Thaiwell's game plan? Not enough. I decided to study him for a while before committing myself to another rash attack.

For the next two rounds I collected intelligence while Thaiwell and I played cat and mouse. Whenever I attacked, Thaiwell withdrew or parried. Whenever he attacked, I blocked or picked off his strikes. Since neither one of us was willing to commit to an all-out attack, the fight quickly sank into a stalemate.

When the second round ended I had all the information I needed. Thaiwell's strategy was clear. He was fighting a defensive fight. He figured that as long as he controlled the range and the terms of engagement, he could drag the fight on forever. But we didn't have forever. If Thaiwell could hold me at bay through the next round, the winner of the fight would be decided by a board-breaking contest. I couldn't let that happen. Thaiwell was one of the best board-breakers I'd ever seen. He could easily break ten or more hardwood boards with a single strike while I had to struggle to break more than four. That meant I had to press the fight, bring it to him, and soon, or I would lose by decision.

Bringing the fight to Thaiwell had actually been my plan from the beginning. My fundamental strategy had been to close on Thaiwell and bring him down with leg kicks. But getting through Thaiwell's formidable stand-up defenses wasn't easy. I'd already tried to rush him and gotten my ribs kicked to shit in the attempt. I'd tried coming in using feints and timed combinations but that didn't work either. Thaiwell was too smart; he could read me, and each time I tried to close, he was able to avoid or evade.

When the next round started I came at Thaiwell full out. Soon he was backing up, but that wasn't good enough. If I was going to take him out, I had to get through his gauntlet of fists and feet. I knew that would be like trying to go through a meat grinder, but I had no choice, so I tucked in my chin, steeled my defenses, and charged. As soon as I did, Thaiwell blasted my injured ribs with another hard side kick. I sucked in the pain and kept coming. He hit me again with a glancing blow, then we collided, and I caught him in a cinch hold. While he struggled to break free I peppered him with knee strikes. When one of them connected with his balls I heard Thaiwell gasp. As he fought and dipped and tried to back away, I kneed him again, this time in the face. I put so much power in the shot that it drove Thaiwell backwards, and me with him. We fell to the mat with Thaiwell on his back and me on top of him, but even as we were falling I was punching. And before the ref could step in and stop the fight I had already landed between fifteen and twenty hard shots to Thaiwell's face.

It was more than enough to finish him. As I stood up, sweaty with victory, and looked around the gym, the other fighters sat stiff in their seats, staring at Thaiwell. He wasn't moving. Not a muscle. Not a twitch. Not even when the medics held the salts under his nose.

A wave of terror swept over me. I'd expected ultimate things of this fight, but not death. While the medics worked on Thaiwell, an acid bath of self-recrimination ate at my insides: "I shouldn't have kept hitting him. His blood is on my hands. Please, God, don't let him die."

I waited—we all did—and finally, when Thaiwell began to stir and we saw that he would live, the whole gym heaved a sigh of relief. I said a silent prayer of thanks and then went back to hating him the same as before. The bastard—even in defeat he'd managed to rob me of the fullness of my victory. Well, at least this time I'd get no argument about which of us was the best. I was. The point made, I marched back into the changing room to await my final fight.

Every fighter deals with waiting in his own way. Some sit, some pace, some talk or shout or even try sleep, but I can tell you none of it helps. Waiting is hell. No matter how you try to face it, waiting is like a stake through a fighter's heart, and as I sat under the ticking clock on the changing room wall, listening to the slow creep of time, I could feel myself growing weaker. Tick tock. Damned waiting. Damned clock. I closed my eyes and tried to concentrate my energy. I imagined myself as a vein of uranium buried deep under a mountain. Above me, men dug with picks and shovels, their Geiger counters jumping wildly. Soon I would be unearthed, and, when I was, there would be an explosion the likes of which no one had yet imagined.

An hour later, I took my place on the tatami for the championship bout. This was it, the final contest. My opponent was a Kunto stylist who had already won several freestyle tournaments. That made him the favorite, but I didn't care. I was so full of my own white-hot fire that his presence seemed almost mothlike. I would burn him down.

I moved towards him and we touched palms. Normally, after you touched palms, you broke off, then fought. But this time, instead of breaking off, I slid my hands down, grabbed his wrists in a hold and yanked him towards me. Then I head butted him and kicked him in the stomach. He fell to the mat and started to rise, but I never gave him the chance. I punched him hard in the jaw and he dropped backwards, out cold. Not ten seconds had elapsed since I'd stepped on the mat and it was over. I'd won! The World Open in Bare Knuckle Karate championship was mine! I was eighteen years old, the youngest person ever to win the title. I felt like a god. Like the conquering heroes of ancient Greece, I was filled with the power of myth.

But any illusions I might have harbored about being crowned with a wreath or lifted on shoulders and carried around the gymnasium in a victory parade were just that—

illusions. Aside from the cut man, and Frank, who handed me an envelope fat with American money, not a man in the gym stepped forward to congratulate me. Instead, they all hurriedly packed their gear into bags, pushed through the creaking doors to the street, and were gone.

I watched them go. In the end these roughest and toughest of men turned out be human after all—only human, all too human. For, even though they would never admit it, I knew they were running. They were running from defeat. They were running from me. It was the sweetest victory parade I could have asked for.

La Petite Mort

French slang for an orgasm. Translated literally
it means "little death."

I spent most of the ride back to Belgium spitting out
ideas like a popcorn machine. "We could go around the
world fighting freestyle bouts. Asia, South America—
what do you think? Hey, what if we tried making videos?
Full-contact videos would be vicious."

"Before we do anything, we need to let a doctor see
your ribs."

Oh yeah, the ribs. We were all pretty sure they were
broken, a memento of Thaiwell's kicks. The wheezing rasp
that sounded when I exhaled, the pain that rode my chest
when I inhaled pretty much spelled it out, but I wasn't
going to let a little thing like a couple of busted ribs get in
my way.

"Hey, the ribs'll heal. I got twenty thousand bucks to
use as a salve. Believe me, they'll heal."

And they did. They healed as I sucked up sun on the
beaches of southern France. They healed as I laid down

money for top-dollar hotel rooms and luxury meals. They healed as I fucked my way through a conga line of women. Oh boy, did they heal. They healed the way only money and sex can heal. They knitted up so well that even my laugh improved. I called for more champagne. It went well with the caviar I'd lumped on my bedmate's nipples. She giggled uncontrollably as I licked the briny treats.

Riding high on greenbacks, I rolled through southern France like a porno loop bucking its way through a super 8 projector. Every night a new face, a different background, but always the action the same. It began with a zoom-in as the bra came off. A bit of backside teasing and then a pan down to the panties where the camera held to reveal that stunning shock of hair, sometimes red as a candied apple, others in shades of caramel, buttered toffee, or licorice whips. All the colors of a candy store were there between their legs, and after lingering over the sweets it was on to the money shot and the big bang-up finale.

Yes, I was fucking, but in my mind I was already in Hollywood, the next stop on my wallet-draining tour. And why not? Where else in the world could you live like this and get paid for it? Throw the crowd a little simulated violence and they rewarded you with real sex and real money, as much as you wanted. Christ, it sounded like a miracle. Not that I thought it would ever happen to me. I just wanted to get a taste of the dream close up but still second-hand. Like tourists everywhere I was after vicarious thrills: The dojo where Bruce Lee once worked out. The famous gyms where Stallone and Schwarzenegger trained. The Hollywood Walk of Fame. Venice Beach.

I quickened my pace against the girl. She began to moan and buck. The champagne spilled. Caviar matted the sheets. It was too good to last, and after a few more quick thrusts I came in a sweat-soaked surge.

"You're pissing your money away. Twenty thousand,

forty thousand, what difference does it make if you just piss it away?"

Right organ, wrong activity, I thought, but I wasn't going to say that to my dad, especially with my mom and grandma sitting in the room.

I'd just gotten back from the south of France. I hadn't even been home two hours and this was how they greeted me.

"You know how you're going to end up, don't you? All those punches and kicks to the head. They're going to turn your brains to mush. You're going to end up with oatmeal for brains and nobody to take care of you."

Oatmeal for brains? I must've had oatmeal for brains when I decided to travel home for a few days instead of flying straight out to Los Angeles. But it was Christmas and I thought it would be nice to spend the holiday with family.

"And another thing. You think you can just waltz in and out of here whenever you want? A little money and all of a sudden you're Mr. Jet Setter?"

"Marcel, please. It's the holidays."

"No, it's time he heard this. You know it's true."

My mother's eyes caught mine for a moment and then fell away as my grandmother leaned into her handkerchief.

"Nicky, now you listen to me," my grandmother said after giving her nose a good blow, "This fighting all the time, it's no good. In the war it's one thing, I understand. But now, for what? For money? For excitement? Is that why you do it?"

I nodded and she went on.

"Look, *mijn jongste,* I know you're strong, you're full of energy, but I'm telling you, as someone who knows, these things don't last."

"You hear your grandmother? You hear what she's telling you?" my father cut in. "I've been telling him the same thing for months, but he doesn't listen to me. The boy thinks he'll fight forever."

"Ten years. I said I was going to fight another ten years."

"You see," my father tapped his head, " Up here I think it's already oatmeal."

"Don't you want a wife and children?" my grandmother went on.

"I'll have a wife and children."

"Then you need to settle down now, not ten years from now."

"That's right."

"Take a regular job. Find a nice girl from the village."

"Why're you making that face?" my father asked as if he didn't know.

"Don't think I don't know what you're thinking, Dominiquie," my grandmother said, wagging a finger, "But you're wrong; a village girl is just what you need. You marry one of those, those—what did you call them, Marcel?"

"High-maintenance women, Ma."

"Yeah, you marry one of those women and maybe you'll have fun for a while, but, mark my words, in the end you'll have nothing but heartache. Now you marry a good village girl, a girl who'll have dinner waiting on the table, a girl who'll give you children and take care of them. You marry a woman like that and ten, twenty years from now you'll be a happy man. And, God willing, I'm still here, you'll thank me."

"Grandma, you don't have to wait that long, I'll thank you right now." I swooped down and smothered her in a hug. I think it surprised her; it surprised them all, because for a second they shut up. I seized the moment. "Look, I know you all only want what's best for me, but it's Christmas—let's just enjoy it, okay? I'll be gone in a couple of days anyway."

"You'll be gone? To where?" they all seemed to ask at once.

"To California."

"California? Why? What for? When are you coming back?"

I answered as many of their questions as I could, and when it started to get ugly again I went to my room and knocked off a couple hundred push-ups.

"Eh," I heard my father muttering as I left, "he's going to blow all his money. It's hopeless."

At night from the air, Los Angeles looked like an immense open jewel box shining just out of reach, and I could hardly wait to dip my hands into its riches. But, once on the ground, I quickly discovered that the jewels were all made of paste and that even these faux treasures were unreachable. The beautiful California girls, the celebrities, the laid-back party lifestyle, even the city itself seemed always just beyond my grasp. In a rented car I cruised the famous streets and boulevards thinking, It's all here somewhere; it has to be—but I never found any of it the whole time I was there. Instead, I found pollution, and a city that had become a growth without landmarks, a solid mass made terrifying by its sameness.

I checked into a Hollywood hotel and went out to walk the famous Boulevard. It was just after Christmas and the town was in its glory. Everything was wrapped in lies. The streetlights were hung with them. The palm trees were stripped with them. I even saw a car caked with phony snow. Plastic icicles fluttered from the windows. The driver had a sign mounted on the roof. He was advertising himself for acting jobs.

While he idled by the curb, he offered pictures of himself to strangers in the passing crowds. Most people laughed in his face. And what a face. The eyes looked dull and plundered. The lips were aloof, hanging open around a perpetual smile that seemed more like a scream. The whole face looked as if it'd been gang-raped then plastered over with rouge and bronzing tonic to give the appearance of health. I took one of his glossies and looked at it. The face in the photo shone with an anonymous optimism and at the same time a vast and cretinous emptiness. I looked back and forth between the photo and the man.

"Who's your photographer? He's really good, " I heard a girl ask the man after glancing at his picture. I dropped the photo into the gutter where it fell next to a hundred others, and rejoined the throngs of tourists who were moving down the street.

In front of Mann's Chinese Theatre I stopped to look at the cement prints of hands and feet that had somehow become even more famous than the real hands and feet that had made them. Later, I drove through Beverly Hills and saw the façades of houses where the famous hands and feet had once lived. I took a studio tour in which the star-making machinery that had stamped out those hands and feet was exposed for all to see. I found the whole tour about as interesting as staring at the guts of a broken film projector. I didn't care how it worked—I just wanted the show—so I plunked down my money and went to see a movie.

Up on the movie screen men were dying. Cars and buildings were exploding without anyone on screen even casting a backward glance. The actors were all too busy chasing money. They had to find the money—a hundred million dollars hidden somewhere on an old abandoned ship. They were fighting and dying over the money right up until the end of the last reel.

I came out of the movie thinking that maybe my father was right. I was pissing away my money. With the money

Seventeen years old in Los Angeles.

I'd blown in a week in California I could have lived for six months in my village. For that matter, I could have taken the whole twenty grand and moved out of the village, found a little place in Antwerp and tried to make it on my own. Why hadn't I? Was it love or fear that held me to my parents and their simple village life?

In another few days I'd be home and my dad and I would start our tired call and response all over again: "Work in the butcher shop." "No." "Marry a village girl." "Never." "Save your money." "No." "Give up fighting." "Never."

What a mess. Things were always so much simpler in the ring. There the answer was always yes: "Are you ready?" "Yes." "Can you take him?" "Yes." "Are you better than anybody, the best in the world?" "You bet."

I figured I needed a little head-clearing violence, but I'd already visited the gyms and dojos of Los Angeles and knew I wouldn't find any there. Most of the city's dojos had been infected by the New Age sickness. Instead of fighting centers, these dojos were more like self-confidence emporiums whose sole reason for being was to dispense nostrums to lonely Angelenos who wanted their twelve-step programs with a little more kick. Other dojos had re-sisted this trend only to fall prey to another equally pernicious disease. Beltism, I called this one. In these dojos people trained not to improve themselves or their skill, but to win belts of ever higher grades. They were ob-sessed with their belt colors, with color in general, and it wasn't uncommon to see people in these dojos wearing not just a new belt in yellow, red, green, or brown, but a whole *gi* in a color either matching or complementing their belt. When a group of them worked out on the floor, it looked more like a Chinese New Year parade than any martial arts practice I'd ever seen.

I went back to my hotel and worked out in the gym for

five or six hours. Then I got cleaned up. It was New Year's Eve. Might as well try to make the best of it. I'd met a couple of girls the night before and they'd given me the address of a party in East Hollywood. I decided to go.

The party was just getting thick when I walked in. The crowd, I learned later, was fairly typical for an East Hollywood party: art-house types, punks, bikers, rockers, retro-beatniks, a smattering of slumming Westsiders, and the ever-present leavening of actors and actresses rounded out the scene. The music was loud. You had to shout to be heard, which didn't bother me because there wasn't a whole lot I could say in my fractured English anyway.

Since I'd come to California I'd given up trying to get laid. Without language it was impossible. In the south of France I'd been able to seduce German, Finnish, Dutch, Swedish, English, and Italian girls using only broken English, but here the girls wanted banter from their men. They needed to be seduced with big talk before they'd even think of lying down.

With nothing to say and no one to say it to, I passed most of the night with a bottle. By the time midnight rolled around I was blind stinking drunk.

"Happy New Year!" a woman offered, then she planted her lips on my mouth and we were soul kissing. The next thing I knew it was morning and I was lying beside her in bed. She was still asleep and since I couldn't see her face— it was buried in the well of her pillow—I lifted the covers to get a look at the body I'd just spent the night with.

"Never drink again!" Master Takimuro's words echoed in my head when I saw what was hidden under those sheets. No, it wasn't a penis. She wasn't a man, just another overweight desk jockey, maybe forty-five years old, with a career woman's pallor and an old girl's hunger for young cock.

I climbed out of bed, collected my clothes and padded

toward the bathroom. I wondered where the hell I was—her place, I supposed—and just how the hell I was going get out of there without waking her. Waking her was the last thing in the world I wanted. She might ask for another go-round in the sack and I didn't want that. No, a quick piss and I'd be gone. Let a taxi take me home; that is, if I could find a taxi in this transport-forsaken city.

I was standing at the toilet, scraping the crust of her sex off my dick when she walked into the bathroom. She was naked and for the first time I saw what forty-five years of gravity could do to a girl.

"I thought you'd snuck out on me, lover."

"I, uh, no, but I need to get back."

"Well, I'll take you back, that is, if you're sure you want to leave."

She moved in and snaked her arms around my waist.

"No, it's okay, really. I'll take a taxi," I said squirming out of her hold under the pretense of needing to use her towel to dry my hands.

"No, I insist. I'll take you home. After all you did for me last night, it's the least I can do." She moved to the shower and turned on the tap. "You are quite the artist, you know, martial and otherwise."

So she knew I was a fighter. I wondered what else I'd told her.

"You know, I meant what I said last night; I really can get you in the movies."

I threw her a puzzled look.

"I'm a casting director, remember? It's my job to recognize talent, and, honey, that's one thing you've got plenty of." She ran her hand down my chest, then stepped into the steaming water. "All you'd have to do is hang around for a while," she called out from the shower; "I know I can make it happen for you."

"No. Thank you, but no."

"Why? What do you want to go back to Belgium for? So you can work in a butcher shop? So you can ruin those beautiful features of yours in a fight? I don't think so."

I didn't believe it. This goddamned woman knew everything. I'd told her everything.

"You know, you could always stay here with me. I've got plenty of room. You wouldn't have to worry about money. I'm telling you, you'd be a hot property in this town, Dominiquie. You're the real thing, not just another wannabe. People respond to that." She poked her head out of the shower. "I know I did." Then it was back under the spray. "Of course we'd probably have to change your name, get you a green card, but that's no problem; it's done all the time."

I'd be lying to you if I said I wasn't tempted, because I was. I spent the rest of that day and most of the next with her while she carted me around to meet her friends and pitch them on the idea of turning me into an action star. In the end, though, I told her no. I wasn't cut out to be a gigolo, no matter what it might mean down the road.

And so I said goodbye to Los Angeles. As the jet lifted off and circled east, I looked out on the city. Somewhere down there the Van Dammes, the Norrises, the Segals, and all the rest were scowling into cameras pretending to be hardcore, bad-ass tough guys, but I'd made my choice and wished them well. From now on I would lead the life they only played at.

Submission Hold

A grappling technique that uses pressure
applied against joints to force an opponent
to submit or suffer injury.

"Hey, Dominiquie, hurry up with those steaks. I got customers waiting."

"Coming right up, boss."

I redoubled my effort at boning out the side. As I sliced through the raw meat, I felt as if I were opening wounds in my own body. I edged the fat and brought out the steaks on a tray.

"Where's the flanken, Dominiquie? You know Mrs. Martens always gets flanken with her order."

I muttered under my breath and went back to cut the flanken.

Three days a week I worked in the village butcher shop; that was the deal I'd made with my dad. I'd made another deal with my trainer, Frank. For the next six months I would do tune-up fights, and then we would go to Thailand to compete in some big-money freestyle fights. I wanted to go to Thailand sooner, but Frank wouldn't have it any other way.

"Those Thai guys are crazy," he told me over and over again. "They're vicious little fuckers, and they're all on the juice."

"What kind of juice?"

"Shit, everything. Uppers, downers, steroids, jungle potions, crap we've never even heard of. I'm telling you, they're all drugged off their nut. You can beat 'em half to death and they still won't go down. I've heard stories, man, scary stories."

Frank was serious, but his stories didn't scare me. In Thailand you only had to fight one guy to win. It wasn't like the freestyle competitions in Eastern Europe that went on for days. In Thailand, you just had to beat one guy and you could take home a purse of forty to sixty thousand dollars. Just one guy. I didn't care how hopped up he was; I knew I could take just one guy.

"I want you to prove yourself here first. We'll start with a couple of wrestling bouts, then we'll do maybe two, three world-class freestyle fights, then we'll go to Thailand, okay?"

"Well, all right, but I don't know what I've got to prove; I'm telling you I'm ready now."

"Man, you don't know. These Thai guys, they fight in competition maybe once, twice a month—to them it's like eating breakfast."

"All right, fine. Let's get on with it, then."

My first tune-up fight was a freestyle wrestling bout in Livorno, Italy. The competition in my weight class took a day but I blew through the thing so easily that we decided to stay an extra day so that I could compete in the open weight division. I fought three heavyweights and beat them all to become the overall champion of the meet.

We returned home to a surprise celebration. The whole

village turned out, even the mayor, who used the occasion to make a windy speech before presenting me with a village sash and trophy. I donned the sash, held up the trophy and thanked them all even though the hypocrisy of the award made me sick. Weren't these the same villagers who'd rather see me cutting meat than fighting, who thought I was nuts for going to Okinawa, who looked at me like I was dirt when I was a kid? I get one little victory written up in the local paper and suddenly I'm treated like a hero. It didn't wash.

But I didn't have time to dwell on it. An old friend had called. He'd broken his hand in a training bout and wanted to know if I would stand in for him in a full-contact Karate fight. Eight rounds against a single opponent in Antwerp in three days. The purse was six thousand dollars. Would I do it, and if I won, would I give him a thousand; he was getting married and needed the money. Even though I'd been training for wrestling and not Karate, I agreed to do the fight, and three days later I was standing on a mat in an Antwerp gym.

My opponent was a tall, skinny guy with lots of speed but no power. The ref went over the rules: "No elbows, no knees, no kicks below the belt." Stupid rules, I thought, but I'd live with them for now. We went at each other. I let him fight the first two rounds his way. I knew Frank wanted me to get all the experience I could, but this was ridiculous. The guy couldn't hurt me even if I let him. By the third round he'd exhausted himself, and rather than play it out any longer I cracked him in the jaw and ended the fight. I gave the thousand to my friend, and then I gave him another thousand and wished him good luck in his upcoming marriage.

Two weeks later I fought another wrestling competition. This one was held in Germany and was a Greco-Roman-style event. Again I won easily. I was getting bored sleepwalking through bouts and I started pressing Frank to push up the timetable on Thailand.

"What are you trying to do here, build my self-confidence with easy matches? Because that's the last thing I need, you know."

"Hey, I can't help it if you're good. I told you you could be the next European champion."

"Is that what this is about, becoming a wrestling champ? I thought we were going to Thailand."

"We are, but would it be so terrible if first you got a sponsorship from the Belgian Wrestling Federation, and maybe some endorsement money from a couple of sports-wear manufacturers?"

"I don't care about endorsements or sponsorships. I told you, I think it's all bullshit."

"What about an Olympic gold medal, Dominiquie? You think that's bullshit too, because you could win one if you just stayed on track here."

"Hey Frank, you know what? I don't care. As far as I'm concerned they can take their rules and their medals and shove 'em up their asses. I told you, to me that's not fighting. It's not anything. It's just bullshit."

"What is it with you? What do you got against a couple of rules? You still win, don't you? Isn't that what counts?"

"No, you know what counts? What counts is that I'm true to this." I squeezed off a fist and pounded it against my heart. "This is what matters to me. Right here." I pounded my chest again. "I don't care if I live, die, make money, or starve as long as I do it from here. And in here there are no rules. In here, it says Thailand."

"What're you so obsessed about Thailand for?

"They're the best, aren't they?"

"Yeah, at what they do they are."

"Well, now there's one better 'cause I'm going to rip their fucking heads off. Understand? I'm going to burn every goddamned one of those motherfuckers to the ground. Now are you with me or aren't you?"

Frank stared at me like a civilized man facing an unfathomable barbarism.

"All right, okay, we'll go to Thailand."

"When?"

"Soon."

But it wasn't soon enough, because a few nights later I stepped out of a bar and got hit by a speeding car.

I came to in the hospital. My leg was shattered. My hip was a mess. I was in traction. A pair of metal pins jutted through the skin of my thigh. My hamstring muscles were so badly injured that doctors had to install a plastic shunt to feed them blood and keep them alive. They told me that I would be in traction for at least two months, that I wouldn't be able to walk normally for six months to a year, and that I shouldn't even think about competing in martial arts for another two to three years. But really, they said, if I knew what was good for me, I'd give up fighting; I'd never fight again.

Two weeks later, a nurse caught me doing push-up on the floor next to my bed. The nurse called a doctor who made me swear that I wouldn't slip my leg out of traction again. But I did. At night, when the nurses weren't looking, I did push-ups and sit-ups and whatever else I could manage. I couldn't just lie there like a lump, which, when you got right down to it, is what I was. I couldn't stand. I couldn't walk. I had to piss in a bottle. I couldn't even sit in a wheel chair. I was a lump. I was worse than a lump; I was a lump with no prospects, unless you consider limping to and from a butcher shop each day a rosy vision of your future.

I began planning my escape. Should I use pills, or would a quick cut up my wrists be better? Maybe I could drag myself across the floor and throw myself out the window. A plastic bag over the head? I'd heard that large amounts of aspirin and whiskey taken together would do it. After playing out every option I decided on seppuku—ritual disembowelment—a slow, agonizingly painful death. That's how a samurai would do it, with a short sword drawn across the stomach.

I'd met a girl from a town near my village shortly after I got back from California. She was a fashion model, tall and thin, with long brown hair and light green eyes. Of course my parents didn't like her. "She's high-maintenance"—my father trotted out the damning phrase. "Bad breeding stock," my mother added. "Her hips are too narrow." But to me her hips were perfect. I'd spent many a long night nestled in those hips. Making love with her had been like performing an act of grace. Our sex filled the sky and always left us both feeling immortal for hours afterward. But, now, when I looked at her sitting across from me in the visitor's chair all I saw was death.

"Bring me a katana sword."

"What are you talking about? "

"You heard me—bring me a katana sword."

"What for?"

"Don't ask me, just bring it. Go buy one if you have to and bring it here."

"Dominiquie, stop it. You're scaring me."

"Are you going to bring me the sword or not?"

"No."

"Then get out. Go on! Get out of here! Don't ever let me see you again. You whore! Bitch! Get the fuck out!"

She left. They all did, all my so-called friends. Not that I blamed them. I would have left too if I could have. Just turned my back and walked away. But I couldn't. I was too much the lump. And like lumps everywhere I lacked even the conviction to die. Oh, I kept exercising, secretly pumping off push-up and sit-ups, but that was just rote. Inside I was empty. There was nothing but despair.

I was sent home with orders to take it easy. But ease has never been my way. For me there's only struggle, either victory or defeat, and since I couldn't kill myself I was left with no option but to fight.

As soon as I got home, I hobbled out to the garden where my punching bag hung limply from its chain. I stared at the bag that I'd spent hours training on to become the champion that I was but wasn't anymore. Maybe the doctors were wrong; it wouldn't be the first time. Maybe I could fight again. I threw a weak punch, then another, this one stronger at the bag. Punch long and hard enough, I thought, and the spark would come back. Soon I was whaling against the bag, transforming despair into white frenzy. Instinctively, my leg shot up to throw a kick and I collapsed. What an idiot I was. What a stupid, doomed idiot. I started crying.

The next day I worked the bag again. Again I fell. But this time I didn't cry. I just got up and went back at it. Soon, I was training like a demon, snapping out thousands of punches, pull-ups, whatever I could muster to get back in fighting trim. I was healing faster than the doctors thought possible. After two weeks, I abandoned my crutches and started running, dragging my gimpy leg behind me as I went. When I built up my run to six miles, I found a backpack, filled it with sand, and ran with it on my back.

But despite my best efforts I knew that I would never be the same. There was a kink in my hip that wouldn't go away. It felt as if my right leg and hip didn't belong to me any more. There was a dislocation between them and me, a sense of stopped time. That little extra second it took messages to pass from injured leg to brain and back would be death in the ring. Any world-class fighter would destroy me.

Frank took pity on me. He found me a part-time job as

an assistant martial arts instructor for cops and soldiers who wanted to improve their hand-to-hand skills. It was a kind gesture on his part, but for me it was torture. I was training people who didn't have any of my talent or desire, but they could kick without impediment. They could snap their legs high in the air all day long without pain. Envy was a new emotion for me and I didn't like it. It signaled a turning—this time, I feared, a permanent one—away from victory and toward a life of defeat.

Among my martial arts students, one stood out from the rest. He had a hard edge about him, a sense of purpose and pride that reminded me, more than a little, of the qualities Kunto instilled in a man. We got to talking. I learned that Mark was a paratrooper in the Belgian army, an officer, but, as he was quick to explain, it wasn't the Belgian army that had molded him into the man he was, but the five years he'd served before that in the French Foreign Legion.

I'd heard about the Legion, but I'd never actually met a legionnaire before. I pumped Mark for facts.

"A legionnaire is an adventurer," Mark told me. "A legionnaire is a professional. A legionnaire is a fanatic; he has to be to survive."

I started reading about the French Foreign Legion. Mark was right. The legionnaires were anything but regular soldiers. In the Legion, poets and priests had fought side by side with perverts and pimps. Scholars, doctors, princes, and painters had all served at one time or another as brothers in the Legion. One of their famous marching songs made it clear that this was a unique army with a special view of itself:

> We are sharp, we are warriors.
> Not ordinary fellows;
> We are often bored stiff.
> We are legionnaires.

What sort of men were these, I wondered, who fought for none of the usual reasons, not for country, or spoils, or in defense of a political ideal? I asked Mark.

"A legionnaire fights for the image he has of himself in his heart," Mark explained. "A legionnaire fights for the dream of who he is and the honor of the Legion. But, most of all, a legionnaire fights in order to be able to die, because it's better to die well than live badly."

Right then I knew that the French Foreign Legion was for me. I started training even harder than before, only now, instead of worrying over my next fight, I imagined myself in the Legion. Running through the Flemish countryside with a sand-filled pack on my back, I was a lonely legionnaire toting ammunition through enemy territory. My injured leg was a war wound. My heavy heart was for my fellows who'd died in an engagement a few miles back. Those weren't cows ahead of me, but a band of mounted Tuareg raiders. I loaded a clip into my imaginary rife and began shooting. Blam! Blam! Blam! I went down firing. A beautiful death.

Yes, the Legion took me out of my dead-ended world and gave me something better; it gave me dreams of glory and of being born anew. Where else but in the Legion can a man's past be forgiven and forgotten so completely? Where else but in the Legion can a man come together with men of every country all of whom are willing to give their lives for their brothers? *Legio Patria Nostra* is the motto of the Legion. It means "the legion is our country." It became the slogan of my heart.

I asked my dad about the Legion.

"Eh, bunch of misfits and lunatics. I knew a guy once who joined; he'd had a bad romance he wanted to forget so he joined up. He deserted after about six months. I remember when he first came back; he'd been unhappy when he left, but when he got back he was so happy to be home he kissed the ground and cried for three whole days. For three whole days he did nothing but cry and complain about how awful the Legion was. If you ask me, they should do away with the whole damn thing. It's nothing but a breeding ground for criminals anyway."

I never mentioned the Legion to my dad again.

I'd just stripped off my bloody apron after serving another enervating shift at the butcher shop when one of the countermen burst into the back.

"Hey Dominiquie, sorry, but the baroness is up front."

"So?"

"So, she wants eight *blinde vinken* made up."

"Sorry, not me, buddy."

"Come on, you gotta do it—you're the only one back here. The boss'll have a fit."

"No way. I'm outta here."

"You'll be out of here permanently if she doesn't get her *blinde vinken*."

"Ah, shit."

I put the apron back on and began grinding up the pork and beef like the poor bugger I was, working my balls off for so much a week. I mixed the ground meat in a bowl with raw eggs, breadcrumbs, and seasoning. My despair had reached the point that I didn't even notice it anymore. I laid some skirt steaks on the table and pounded them into thin strips. Even my dreams of redemption through the Legion were just a fantasy. I knew that. The Legion didn't want a gimp. And I was a gimp. I didn't walk through the relics and the ruins of my life—I limped. Better to forget the Legion and join the common misery completely. Learn to work when I didn't want to work. Smile when I didn't feel like smiling. Live when I didn't know why and everything in me was dead. What good are dreams anyway to someone who is already dead, except as a cruel reminder that they had once been alive? I spooned the pork mixture onto the pounded skirt steaks and began rolling them tight. No room for dreams here, or pity. I tied off the rolls, tucked in the edges, and set the *blinde vinken* on a tray.

In Flemish, *blinde vinken* means "blind finches." I'd made eight little blind birds for the baroness. I picked one up and stared at it. Poor little blind bird, I thought as I squeezed it in my fist and watched the filling ooze out between my fingers. I threw the rest one by one across the room. Fly, little blind birds. Fly! Fly!

"Hey, Dominiquie, what's going on back there? Let's go!"

I took off my apron and tossed it to the ground. I was going all right, but first I picked up the *blinde vinken* and brought them out front on a tray. After what they'd been through the *blinde vinken* looked more like eight struggling turds than anything you'd want to eat. I set them on the counter. "Here's your *blinde vinken,* Baroness," I said and stormed out the front door.

That night I packed my bags. After my parents had gone to bed, I snuck out of the house and walked the distance to the train station and bought a ticket to Brussels. From Brussels I went to Paris. From Paris I took the train to Marseilles. It was morning when I arrived. Back in Belgium my parents would be wondering where I was, but I didn't care. I was in Marseilles. Hidden somewhere in its twisting streets and warrens was a recruiting station for the French Foreign Legion. Soon I would find it, and when I did I would join. Somehow, I would convince them to take me, gimp and all.

Pissant le Fort

"Storming the fort."

I arrived in Marseilles and with my dwindling cash reserves bought as many books about the French Foreign Legion as I could afford. I checked into a hotel and lay down to read. I figured I had enough money to last me a week, no need to rush things. Besides, I was scared. What if the Legion wouldn't take me—or, even more frightening, what if they did? Then there'd be no turning back. The standard Legion hitch was five years, not an easy mistake to get out of unless one deserted, which for me was out of the question. My word is my bond. Once I took the oath I would be in for the duration no matter what, so I figured I'd better be sure. I opened one of the books and started reading.

I read about Camerone, where on the 30th of April, 1863, a depleted force of sixty-four legionnaires was besieged by an army of two thousand Mexican soldiers. The leader of the Legion force, Captain Danjou, after suffering the loss of sixteen men in the field, retreated to a farmhouse where, hopelessly outgunned and without hope of reinforcement, he demanded that each of his men take an oath to fight till the end. They did. The end came in the evening after a day of nonstop fighting. By 6 P.M., the original company had been reduced to one officer and eleven men. Captain Danjou was dead, shot in the head. Ammunition was low, and when the Mexicans attacked in an all-out assault the remaining Legion officer ordered a bayonet charge. At the head of his four remaining men, Lieutenant Maudet rushed into the courtyard where he was cut down by a murderous crossfire. Mexican casualties were nearly three hundred, but the Third Company of the Second Legion Battalion had been wiped out.

Camerone produced some of the greatest heroes in Legion history, among them Captain Jean Danjou, whose wooden hand, recovered after the battle, now lies in state in a museum crypt located on the Legion's main base at Aubagne. Once each year, legionnaires march with the Captain's hand at the head of a parade dedicated to his memory and the "glorious defeat" he and his men suffered at Camerone.

Reading about Camerone was exactly the tonic I needed. It assured me that I wasn't alone, that there were other men in the world like myself, and that if I was going to find them anywhere it would likely be in the Legion.

That night I went out hunting for legionnaires. I was especially interested in meeting men from the *Deuxième Régiment Etranger de Parachutistes,* the 2REP for short, because that's what I planned to become. The 2REP were an élite group based near the city of Calvi on the island of Corsica. Like the U.S. Army Green Berets, or Britain's SAS, the Legion's 2REP were a force to be reckoned with, and only the best made it into their ranks. Though I wandered from one waterfront dive to another searching for men wearing the distinctive red lanyard of the 2REP, I didn't find a single legionnaire.

The next morning I went to the local gendarmerie and asked the policeman on duty where I might find legionnaires on leave in Marseilles.

"What do you want to know that for?"

"Because I want to become a 2REP legionnaire."

The gendarme called to his buddies, and soon a whole group of them circled me.

"The kid wants to be a legionnaire."

"Just what France needs, eh? Another mercenary. Why don't you go back and fight for your own country?"

"You must have done something pretty bad to want to join the Legion. You a criminal, boy? Are you wanted?"

"How old are you, anyway?"

"Eighteen."

"Well go home and think about what you're doing before you waste your life."

But I stuck to my guns, and finally one of them told me the names of a few bars where legionnaires were known to hang out.

"Make sure you're out of these places by ten. It gets pretty rough after the legionnaires have had a few drinks."

I thanked him and left the station.

"You're making a big mistake, boy. Go home while you still can," one of them shouted out after me.

"It's too late for that," I called back. And it was. As far as I was concerned I'd burned all my bridges. Not telling my parents where or why I had left had been the ultimate disrespect, but for me it was the only way. If I'd told my parents of my plans, they would've raised such a stink that I probably would have joined the Legion just to spite them. But I wanted the decision to be mine, and mine alone. If I was going to do something this drastic, I wanted it to be a leap of pure faith and not some last desperate act of escape.

That night I went to all the bars the gendarmes named but didn't see a single legionnaire. Dejected, I started back toward my hotel. I guess I wasn't paying attention, because soon I was hopelessly lost in what I'd already been warned was one of Marseilles' worst neighborhoods. When I paused to try to get my bearings, some movement in a dark alley caught my eye. A man was coming toward me. I steeled myself for conflict, but as soon as the man stepped into the street I recognized him for what he was—the white kepi cap, the green uniform—he was a legionnaire! I rushed up to introduce myself.

"Excuse me, sir—" But before I could utter another word he was shouting, "Don't call me 'sir,' civilian. I'm a legionnaire." Then he turned and walked off. I thought about chasing after him, but in the few seconds we'd faced each other I'd looked into his eyes. They had that look that all the books on the Legion mentioned but I'd never seen in the flesh. It was a look of pure murder, a look that stunned and chilled, like staring down the barrel of a loaded gun. I'd seen mad eyes on fighters before, but none of them held a candle to this. I stood and watched the legionnaire disappear around a corner, then I turned the other way and ran blindly into the night.

When I finally got back to my room, I lay down and tried to sleep, but I couldn't get that look out of my mind. I wondered, would I get that look if I joined the Legion? Would my face become a mask, my eyes two gelid pools of solitude and fury? I fell asleep with the chill image of his eyes fixed inside my head.

The next morning I thought about packing up my things and going home. I had a million reasons not to join. It would hurt my parents terribly. My grandmother was ninety-five; I'd probably never see her again. Who wanted to live under the strangling discipline of an army anyway? Taking orders was not for me. Since when was there room in my heart for rules? I was a single-combat warrior, not a soldier. But what other options did I have? The butcher shop? I'd pretty much closed that door. School? Not for me. Learn another trade? I'd go crazy. Martial arts instructor? I hated it.

I went out and wandered the streets of Marseilles, but the sights, sounds, and smells of the city disgusted me. Everything about the practical world, its buildings and sewers, streetlights, staircases, automobiles, newspapers, even the people, especially the people, filled me with contempt. Their lives seemed so ugly and senseless, so absolutely absurd that I wanted to kill each and every one of them, if only as an act of mercy. But I knew that would never be, that more than likely they would kill me with their demand that I get a steady job and become a useful member of society.

Some men can live quite happily in the soft city world they have made; they can work, raise a family, and grow old and die, and for them it is enough, but not for me. For me, and for men of my temperament there is only one life—the life of a warrior. To train with indifference to physical hardship, to practice courage and honor, to run risk, face death, and survive, these are the things that make life sweet.

I sat on a bench and listened to two old men harangue about the rising price of everything.

"I'm telling you, things are out of control. Soon we won't be able to afford even bread, and, then, revolution."

"No, no, it's all a question of how much you're willing to pay for things."

"How much you're willing to pay for things." I wondered how much I was willing to pay to live the life of a warrior. Was I willing to become a soldier? Would I pay that price? I got up and walked down the street. Yes. The word rose up from deep within me and spilled out into the world. Yes, the water said as it splashed from a fountain. Yes, my boot heels clicked on the cobbles. Yes! Yes from the crowds. Yes from the streets and the buildings—they all joined in a chorus shouting, Yes!

They say that when your heart is pure serendipity rules, and I agree, because after deciding to join the Legion I hadn't walked two blocks when I suddenly spotted a legionnaire, and not just any legionnaire, I saw as I drew closer, but a soldier wearing the red lanyard of the 2REP. As I watched him through the window of the restaurant where he'd just sat down to lunch I thought I was dreaming. But, no, he was real. More than real, he was ideal. From his spit-shined boots to his snow-white kepi, his uniform was immaculate, his bearing completely dignified. I watched him address the waitress like a gentleman to the manner born. As he sat, ramrod straight, and waited for his food, I went in and took a table near his. Though I wasn't at all hungry, I ordered a meal and sat fidgeting like guys sometimes do when they've spotted a beautiful girl but don't know how to break the ice.

"May I help you?" the legionnaire asked after he caught me staring at him for about the umpteenth time.

"I want to join the Legion. Can I talk to you about it?"

"If you want to join the Legion, son, don't talk about it, don't think about it, just do it," he said and went back to his food.

But when I asked if he would be willing to show me to the nearest recruiting station he perked up.

"Come, sit with me." He lifted his kepi off the chair and motioned me over.

I sat down and soon he was telling me about his experiences in the Legion and what it took to be a legionnaire.

"If you like discipline, adventure, and hard physical training you should do it. You have to do it when you're young, because once you're twenty-five or thirty you just won't take the abuse anymore, and believe me it can get pretty hard."

I told him about all the books I'd read on the Legion.

"Just remember, the Legion is a mystery. No matter how much you read about it, no matter how much I tell you, you can't know what it is till you're in. And even when you're in, you still won't know because it's bigger than any one man."

Then he talked about principles and honor, and about how a legionnaire always sticks to them no matter what.

When I told him about the legionnaire I'd met the night before he took it in stride.

"There're some pretty hard cases in the Legion. There's no denying that, but they're still legionnaires, and in a pinch they'll be there for you."

I was impressed. I liked the way this man spoke about honor and the importance of being true to your word. I liked the way he treated me. He didn't pull any punches, and he didn't condescend, and when I asked him again if he would show me to the recruiting station he agreed.

An hour later we were standing in front of a pair of massive gates that marked the entrance to Bas-Fort Saint-Nicolas.

"There it is."

"Well, I guess this is it."

I put out my hand and he took it.

"Good luck."

We shook, and after he left I turned and pounded at the gate. It opened with a groan and a tall, bearded legionnaire stepped out and stared down at me.

"What do you want, son?" he said in a voice deeper than any I'd ever heard.

"I want to become a legionnaire."

The gatekeeper stared at me for what seemed like an

eternity. Finally, he knitted his eyebrows together and spoke.

"Are you sure you want to do that?"

"Yes, sir," I answered without hesitation.

"You have anything besides what you brought?"

I told him I still had some things back at the hotel.

"Well, go get them, and before you come back I want you to think twice about whether or not this is really what you want to do."

Then he closed the big gate.

I went back to the hotel and packed my things. I don't know why I bothered. I could have walked right through the Legion gate with what I had on. It wouldn't have mattered. I'd already been told that once I was sent to the base at Aubagne, the Legion would take everything I carried with me and donate it to the Red Cross.

I brought my bag downstairs and sat down to have my last cup of coffee as a free man. There was only one task left to me now and I didn't relish it. I had to tell my parents. After I finished my coffee, I went to the phone and dropped a fistful of change into the slot.

"Hello, Dad?"

"Dominiquie, where are you?

"I—"

"Son, you have to get home right away. Mom's had a relapse. The leukemia's back. She's in the hospital."

No, I thought, not now.

"How bad is she?"

"She's not good, son. She wants to see you."

"Dad, I can't."

"What do you mean, you can't?"

"I'm in France, Dad. I joined the Foreign Legion."

"What?"

"I joined the French Foreign Legion. I can't come home."

"Oh, my God."

"Tell mom I love her; tell her I'm pulling for her, okay?"

"Dominiquie, where are you, exactly?"

"I have to go now, Dad."

"No, Dominiquie, wait. Tell me where you are. Which base? I'll get you out on a medical emergency—"

"No, Dad, I'm sorry. Look, I've really got to go, okay? Goodbye."

I hung up the phone while my dad was still talking. "God forgive me," I muttered into empty air, then I picked up my bag and walked out.

A short time later I was back at the fort and banging at the gate.

"So, you decided to do it, huh?" the bearded giant said.

I nodded and stepped inside. He pushed the gate closed and threw the latch. I wondered if I'd ever see my mother again.

Le Réveil

"Wake-up call."

as-Fort Saint-Nicholas, a thick-walled stone keep set high on an escarpment overlooking Marseilles, was a relic of another time and an older way of doing battle, and so were many of the soldiers who manned her. The bearded gatekeeper, for instance, was well into his sixties. I'd read about such men; *le Pionniers,* the Legion called them out of respect for the lifetime of service that they'd given.

The Pioneer handed me off to another who led me deeper into the fort. We entered a storage room where my bags and clothes were taken and I was told to change into an old tracksuit. After that, I was brought into a small windowless room where two new recruits were already ensconced.

"Inside," the Pioneer barked.

I stepped into the room and he slammed the door behind me. As his footsteps echoed down the hall I turned to face the other recruits. They were stretched out in their bunks like dead men. One of them was gaunt, almost skeletal. The other, a Greek from the looks of him, was pockmarked and greasy and he smoked incessantly. They both looked on the edge of complete dissipation and I wondered what calamities had cast them up here.

"So, how long you guys been here?" I greeted them in French, but it was hopeless; they didn't even glance over. Instead, the Greek lit one cigarette off the stub of another, flipped the old butt to the floor, and went back to the hard business of staring at the ceiling.

Five hours later a Legion guard led us to dinner. We ate as we roomed, without speaking, separated from the other legionnaires. After dinner we were escorted back to our room, where another volunteer was waiting. He was fat and German and had two black eyes—a recent addition to his features from the looks of them.

"Anybody got a cigarette? *Zigarette*? *Tsigaro*?" The German pantomimed the act of smoking and the Greek tossed him a smoke.

"I bet you're wondering how I got these, huh?" The German pointed to his twin shiners, and when the Greek shrugged and fell back in his bunk the German went on anyway. "Well, I got myself into a fight with some gendarmes. Pretty stupid, huh? But, hey, I was drunk and the bastards were hassling me, and they got the worst of it. I ain't in jail, right? Right? Hey, goddammit, I'm talking to you, asshole."

"Forget it. They don't understand," I said, diverting the German's attention to me.

"Hey, you speak German?"

"A little."

"Thank fucking God. If I was stuck with those two all night, Jesus, I'd go mad."

"So why are you joining the Legion?" I asked him.

"Why not? It's a paycheck, ain't it?"

I nodded and the German went on. "What a fucked way to spend a Friday night. When the hell you think we're going to get out of this rat hole and into some real Legion action?"

I didn't know, but I hoped it would be soon. The Legion fort at Aubagne was only an hour away. That's where the selection process would begin. For three weeks we would be poked, prodded, questioned, and drilled. I'd already been told that about half of the men wouldn't make it. I figured the German to drop. He didn't have the discipline. As for the other two, they looked desperate enough, but the one was so thin and the other such a heavy smoker that I doubted either would ever make the grade. After listening to the German ramble on for a while, I rolled over and spent a night of dreamless sleep.

The next morning I came awake to the sound of a legionnaire shouting out my name.

"Vandenberg!"

"Yes, sir?" I mumbled, half asleep.

"It's corporal to you, shithead. Now get the fuck out of bed—the warrant officer wants to see you."

He stood there while I rose and dressed, cursing at me the whole time.

"You better be glad you're not signed up yet, Vandenberg, because if you were I'd show you what Legion discipline is, with this." He waved his fist in my face. "I'd teach you respect, you dog's-ass piece of worthless monkey shit."

I wondered what I'd done wrong. Had my father called the Legion? Was this about my mother? Were they going to ship me home? I didn't know at the time that this was standard operating procedure. In the Legion, the NCOs ruled over men. Discipline was harsh. Insults were the least of it. Step out of line and you could expect a fist or a foot in your face. Worse still were the unexpected fists and feet, the ones that came at you out of nowhere, for no reason except that you, for some mad reason of your own, had decided to become a legionnaire.

The corporal led me to an office where an old Arab warrant officer sat behind a desk. On either side of him, two young, barrel-chested legionnaires stood at ease but wary.

"How old are you, Vandenberg?" the Arab asked.

"Eighteen."

"Why do you want to join the Foreign Legion?"

"For the adventure. To become a soldier in the best army in the world today."

"Okay, good. Now give me your passport and papers and you can go."

I did as he asked. One of the younger legionnaires saw me back to the room and the next volunteer was called out.

Two days later we were bused to Aubagne, where our bags and clothes were taken away and we were given old

Elèves légionnaires in our moth-eaten tracksuits.

green running suits and cheap sneakers to wear. I put them on and was marched to a barracks room where about twenty other recruits were bunked. On either side of our billet were others, making us altogether a selection of about sixty-five men.

For the next three weeks we sixty-five would be put through the mill. It started with five straight days of medical tests. Eyes, ears, nose, asses—the doctors probed everything. They took x-rays and scans and monitored our vital signs. They made us read eye charts, took blood, and inquired as to the state of our bowels, and then under the misapprehension that we'd either cheated or somehow changed our physiology overnight, they did it all again.

When they discovered that I had a double fracture in my left leg, they pulled me out of the selection and sent me to the military hospital at Laveran. I thought for sure that I was finished, and but for another act of serendipity I would have been.

At the hospital they ran another series of tests on my leg.

"I know you," the doctor in charge of the tests said after looking over my paperwork, "You're Dominiquie Vandenberg, the fighter, right?"

When I nodded, the doctor opened one of his desk drawers and pulled out a stack of karate magazines. He opened one to an article that had been written about me.

"Son, does the Legion know that you're a karate champion?"

"No, sir, I haven't told them."

"Why not?"

"I didn't join the Legion to fight in the martial arts, sir."

"But aren't you proud of what you are? There's nothing wrong with being a champion."

"I'm very proud, sir, I guess I was just worried they

might try to send me to Fontainebleau, to the sports school."

"Not with this leg," he said, pointing to a picture of my x-ray.

"Look," I practically begged him, "the leg's not a problem, really. I can run all day on it. I can march. I'm in better shape than just about any recruit out there."

"I can see that."

"Then will you take me in the Legion?"

"Why did you join?"

"I want to go 2REP."

"I don't know, son—the 2REP? I don't think you should be jumping out of planes on that leg."

"Sir, please, I only broke it four months ago. It hasn't even healed up all the way yet. Just give me the chance."

"The doctor thought for a moment. "Are you sure that's what you want?"

"Yes, sir, more than anything."

"You know that only the top five graduates from Castelnaudary are allowed to pick their posting."

"I know."

"Well, I suppose if you're good enough to make it into the top five in your section, you'll be good enough to jump."

"Yes, sir."

"Okay, I'll tell you what I'll do: an autograph for an autograph, how's that sound?" He handed me a karate magazine and had me sign it to his son, whom he said was a big fan of mine. Then he signed the medical waivers that would release me to serve in the Legion and sign on with the 2REP if I made it.

The next day I returned to my company just in time to receive our first issue of military uniforms. Following Legion tradition, no measurements were taken and everything was handed out piecemeal, so that once I was fully dressed I looked even more pathetic than I did in my old moth-eaten tracksuit. My shirt and vest hung from my body like clothes on a scarecrow. My pants ballooned around me, and my beret was so big it made me look more like a character in a Rembrandt painting than a soldier. But I didn't care. It was a uniform and I was in it. I was on my way.

The next week the mental testing started. They hit us with tests of our IQ, perception, spatial relations, you name it. Worst of all were the question-and-answer sessions with the men we called "the Gestapo." It was the Gestapo's job to find out everything they could about you—and I mean everything. They would sit you down and grill you about things you couldn't possibly remember but that they already knew because they had full access to every school, police, government, and business record that had ever been kept on you.

The questioning would go on for hours. What was your first-grade teacher's name? A distant relative's phone number? Then they would type up your responses, and three days later you would be back again, answering the same damned questions until you wanted to scream. Of course, that's exactly what the Gestapo wanted. They wanted to catch you in lies, trip you up, see if you could stand up to their verbal assaults without snapping: "We heard that your mother is a whore. Is that true? Is your mother a whore? Your father an alcoholic? Do you have sex with animals?"

And some men did snap. A Canadian ex-paratrooper and helicopter pilot I'd befriended broke a chair over the head of one of the interviewers. I heard that the two legionnaires who were always standing guard during these sessions beat the pilot pretty badly, but I didn't hear it from him, because as soon as they were done beating him they threw him into the street, and I never saw him again.

"Elèves légionnaires, appel!" the NCO shouted.

We lined up next to our bunks.

"Corvée!"

The hated *corvée*—cleaning duty. It was as much a part of Legion life as breathing. Every day, members of the company were assigned various tasks. Some cleaned the yard; others scrubbed floors or toilets. Each day a different recruit was put in charge of the company's *corvée* duty. It was his job to make sure that everyone else's job got done. If some men slacked off, if duties weren't performed to Legion specifications, the recruit in charge would be punished for everyone.

When my turn came to take command of *corvée,* I was determined to succeed. I'd already seen the many ways a man could fail. Some failed because they bullied, and men would sabotage their cleaning work just to see the *corvée* leader made to "smoke the cigar," as the Legion called punishment—which at this point in our training usually meant standing all night at attention in front of the barracks. Other men failed because they were weak, and many a man put in charge of *corvée* ended up being punished twice, once by the other, stronger recruits who beat him rather than work, and then again by the Legion, who had him smoke the cigar for failing to get the job done.

I decided I would be fair but firm, direct and precise in my oversight of the men. I checked the yard. The detail was coming along nicely. I looked in on the kitchen and barracks, giving instruction when I thought necessary. Then I came to the bathroom. A tall black African had been assigned to the toilets. He was loitering aimlessly when I walked in.

"What are you doing, recruit? Get to work."

"Fuck you. Do it yourself," he spat in broken French and turned his back.

I slammed him face first into the wall and spun him around.

"Clean the fucking toilets, now!"

We locked eyes, neither of us willing to give an inch. I knew I could beat him senseless if I had to, but I didn't want it to come to that. None of the men knew that I was a trained martial artist and I wanted to keep it that way; otherwise, I figured I'd be fighting nonstop against every clown in the company who wanted to make his reputation as a tough guy. If the African figured he could take me, fine; there were other ways than fists to put fear into a man.

"You may think you can take me," I told him, "and maybe you can, but if you don't fucking clean those toilets right now, I'll get you. I'll wait until you fall asleep, and when you do I'll slit your throat, crawl back into my bunk, and nobody will ever know. You understand what I'm saying? You got to sleep sometime, and when you do . . ." I drew a finger across my throat. "You die."

The African's eyes went wide and I left him to his work, which, when I returned to check on it, exceeded even my expectations.

In the final week they started us on a régime of hard physical training. For me the exercise was a relief. Two weeks of doing nothing but waiting, cleaning, and testing had taken their toll; I was frazzled. We all were, and a lot of the men had taken to fighting just to let off steam.

Now there was no time to fight. When we weren't working out we were given instruction in close-order drill. Even more important, we were taught the intricacies of saluting Legion style. As soon as we got to Castelnaudary, we were told, we would be required to salute everyone from a legionnaire first class right up to a general. The unofficial punishment for failing in this duty was a swift punch in the face.

A few days before final leave we were awarded the red patch of advanced *engagés volontaires.* Then our heads were shaved in the regulation crop called a *boule à zéro,* and the Gestapo interviewed us one last time. Finally, we were marched into a classroom and invited, Legion style, to sign our first military contract.

"Once you sign this contract," an NCO bellowed as he paraded back and forth in front of us, "you will be expected to complete basic training. That usually takes anywhere from four to six months depending on you and the state of your training company. After that, you will be free either to leave the Legion, or sign up for a full five-year hitch. What you do at that point is up to you, but once you sign this contract you cannot leave the Legion until your basic training program has been completed. Does everyone understand that?"

When we shouted that we did, the NCO unsheathed his pistol and continued. "Once you sign this contract," the NCO said as he stepped up to a man at random, "you may not under any circumstances leave the Legion." The NCO leveled the barrel of his pistol against the man's temple. "Because if there's one thing the Legion hates, it's deserters," he said, cocking back the hammer on his pistol. "This is what we do to deserters in the Legion." He pulled the trigger, letting the hammer fell on an empty chamber. "Once you sign this contract, there will be no deserting. Understood? Now I want you to line up and sign these contracts right now!"

One by one we stepped up to sign the contract. No one read it. No one had to. With a squeeze of his trigger finger the NCO had spelled out everything we needed to know.

The next day, three corporals and a master sergeant from Castelnaudary arrived to take charge of us.

"I want you men to put your kit bags and rucksacks in

the trucks. The trucks will take you to the train station in Castelnaudary, where vehicles will be waiting."

While the corporal gave instructions, a volunteer standing behind me in the ranks started whispering to another fellow. It was a stupid thing to do, because as soon as the master sergeant saw it, he walked over and sucker-punched the volunteer in the face. The volunteer collapsed to the ground. The master sergeant let him lie there as an example.

"From now on, *élèves légionnaires,* you talk, shit, piss, and whisper only when I tell you. You don't whack off, you don't even think unless I tell you to. You're in the army now. The most disciplined army in the world. Remember, we didn't come to get you. You all came to us. All with your own reasons, but I don't care about reasons. All I care is that you're here. And now that you are I'm going to make you into legionnaires."

"Is that understood?" one of the corporals shouted.

"Yes, sir," those of us who spoke French shouted back.

"It's 'Yes, Corporal,' you idiots! Now drop down all of you and give me sixty push-ups."

What the fuck had I done to myself? I thought as I dropped to the ground and started knocking out push-ups. I'd signed my life over to a cabal of madman. I wasn't able to kill myself; now I was going to be trained to kill others. Is this what I'd come out of the womb for? To end up an old and bearded *Pionnier,* opening gates to younger men whose lives had already run out. God, the world is cruel and destiny a liar. God, what a malicious cripple I'd become. God, how I longed for the sweet dance of the ring. Just one more turn with fists and feet, a pas de deux to the death. But I was only boxing at shadows.

"Come on, *élèves légionnaires,* you call those push-ups? Let's go! I wanna see some effort."

I surrendered myself to the rhythm of the push-ups. I wished I could do them forever.

Marche ou Crève

"March or die."

When we arrived at the train station in Castelnaudary the trucks were waiting, just as the corporal had promised, but they weren't waiting for us. Instead, we were instructed to load our kit bags and rucksacks into the trucks and then ordered to run to the camp. The run took over an hour; we were dressed in parade shoes, and by the time we arrived most of the men's feet were bloody messes.

"Appel! Appel!" The corporals shouted for us to form up for roll call. I'd read that *engagés volontaires* who wanted to desert would often do so during the trip between Aubagne and Castelnaudary. Now I knew why. The look in the eyes of the civilians who saw us as we marched on and off the train was enough to make any man want to run. Their stares of shock and pity, the undercurrent of fear, spooked even me. I felt like an animal, like all those cows must have felt before they ended up on my butcher-block back in Belgium.

Prodded by kicks and punches delivered by our corporals, we lined up in front of our barracks to await further orders. The master sergeant walked our ragged line:

"I'm not here to welcome you. I don't want to shake hands or even say hello, because as far as I'm concerned you're all shit. You're not men—you're just punks, rock-and-roll wannabes, party boys. Well, from now on that's all going to change. You can forget all about your lives before the Legion; that's over with. Your family, your friends, that's all behind you now. Even your girlfriends—they're not going to wait; they're already out fucking somebody else, so forget 'em.

"Beginning tomorrow morning at 5 A.M. we're going to start making soldiers of you. It's going to be tough, and I hope a lot of you wimps try to go AWOL because if you don't it means I'm not doing my job right. It means the training's too easy, and we don't do anything easy in the Legion."

The next day we woke up at five, washed, shaved, performed our *corvée* duty, and did a five-mile run. In the weeks to follow, we fell into a routine of forced marches, calisthenics, military instruction, more marches, drills, and field instruction. It went on and on, with no pick and no choice possible. If you got tired you were shit out of luck. You marched or got trampled underfoot.

After only a month, eight men petitioned the Colonel to break their contracts. The requests were routinely denied. If you wanted out of the Legion you had to earn it by dying, deserting, or collapsing so completely that the Legion judged you unfit for further service and discharged you. Men in our section did all three. After three months, of the fifty or so who started less than twenty-five remained, and a new section had to be called up from Aubagne and joined with ours to bring us back up to full complement.

The training continued, and with it came the punishments for which the Legion was famous. If a man was caught wearing dirty underwear, he was forced to march back and forth across the yard with the offending underwear stuffed in his mouth like a shit-smeared gag. If a man showed up at roll call with a bad shave, one of the corporals would hold a cigarette lighter to the man's face until the whiskers and often a good patch of his skin were burned away. If a man's uniform wasn't in order top to bottom, the whole section was disciplined with extra hours of running, or guard or *corvée* duty. The corporals left it to the section to punish the man, which we always did without fail.

I remember one poor slob who couldn't seem to do anything right. After he showed up late for inspection, with his shoes half-polished and without his belt, the corporals exploded. They made us all strip and march naked into a freezing lake where they had us stand at *garde à vous* (attention) for an hour, the whole time shouting "thank you" to the slob. When lunch came, we were given five minutes to eat. Again we were forced to thank the slob. Then hours of exercise punctuated by thank-yous. Then more drills and more thank-yous. And finally, when night came, instead of crawling into our bunks, a six-hour march in full pack. "Thank you." When we returned to the barracks, it didn't take long for four or five of the men to surround the slob and thank him again, this time with fists.

A few hours later, when we lined up for *appel,* the slob stood in the ranks, his uniform spotless except for the blood that ran from his nose and his mouth and stained the front of his tunic. The corporal stepped up to him. The slob's face was covered with bruises, one eye was swollen shut, and two of his front teeth were missing.

"Look's like the mosquitoes were biting pretty bad last

night, eh?" the corporal asked, and we laughed long and hard until even the slob had to join us.

But worse than the punishment meted out to the slob were the torments saved for the whiners and weaklings. Some got the "blanket treatment" until they deserted. Night after night the corporals would slip into the barracks, throw a blanket over the head of the sleeping man they wanted out and beat him until he deserted. Others were lifted from their beds and carted off, never to be seen again. Rumor had it that they were sent to mental institutions, but we never knew for sure.

Sometimes the corporals eschewed stealth altogether and would openly practice their cruelties. Once, as we stood at attention in front of our bunks, a black man was stripped and stuffed into his metal locker. A propane burner was lit and placed underneath the locker. For ten minutes we stood and listened to the man scream for his life while the corporals cooked him alive.

I thought I'd go mad listening to those screams. I wanted to fight, to rush in and help, especially since, as best I could figure, the only reason the man was in there was because he was black. But instead of helping I stood and did nothing. *"C'est la Légion,"* I said to myself as the corporals extinguished the burner and had four legionnaires drag the locker to the steps. *"C'est la Légion,"* I repeated as they tipped the locker over and I watched it tumble end over end down three flights of stairs. *"C'est la Légion,"* I said to smother my shame as they carried the locker back up to the second floor and then threw it out the window with the man still inside. By then he'd stopped screaming, but I hadn't; inside my head was a slaughterhouse screaming for blood and vengeance.

It was exactly the mindset the corporals were after. They wanted my mad killing rage. How else could they get me to march into death, storm a hill, or hold a fort against impossible odds? How else but with rage?

As several legionnaires lifted the black man from the locker I suddenly realized how else, because as soon as I saw his burned, bloodied body, my rage gave way to an excruciating fear: what if I was the corporal's next victim? What if that was me down there instead of him? Right then, I swore to myself that I'd try harder, do better, whatever it took not to end up like him.

This was the other half of the Legion equation—fear. It was fear that made us rise before dawn and clean toilets till they shined. It was fear that propelled my arms and legs when they both felt like rubber and I thought I couldn't go on. Pure raw fear. The rage might make us fighters, but it was the fear that turned us finally into soldiers. How the corporals were able, eventually, to transform our rage and fear into feelings of pride and esprit de corps I never knew, but they did. Between the twin stones of rage and fear they ground us into legionnaires.

A few weeks later I came down with the flu but that didn't stop me. I slogged on, marching through rain and cold, singing Legion songs until my voice disappeared. I developed blisters on my feet that burst and became infected. When, finally, I couldn't stand unassisted without falling, they sent me to the hospital where I lay next to other men whose minds and bodies had been ruined by the Legion.

Of the six men in my wardroom, three were completely insane. During low points between doses of medication, two of them would start to weep and whimper, the one setting off the other until they would chorus together like wolves. A third was there because he'd tried to kill himself. Though he never spoke a word, the evidence was clear; the red oozing bandages that covered his wrists said it all.

He wasn't the first suicide attempt I'd seen. About a week before, I'd walked into the bathroom during the night and found a man from our section hanging dead. That he'd killed himself was no surprise to me. His father and older brother were both officers in the Legion and they'd wanted him to become an officer too, but it was clear he didn't have the stuff, so he hung himself.

I'd like to tell you that I felt some compassion for these lost and dead men, but I didn't. We were all lost, all dead. All of us losers, killers, sinners—a brotherhood of the broken, locking arms with the mad. We had no need for kindness; we let the notion drop. We'd long since marched past the frontiers of sympathy, across the boundaries of mercy, into territory that for most of us was entirely uncharted.

The corporals led us forward; they'd all been this way before. If we wanted to survive there was nothing for us to do now but follow.

"A legionnaire doesn't need compliments, " I recall a corporal once saying. "When you're out on a campaign, all a legionnaire needs to do is his job; all a legionnaire needs to know is that the men around him will do theirs without thinking, without flinching, no matter what."

I was released from the hospital and returned to my section where I proceeded to do my job. Marching, running, cleaning, drilling. I surrendered myself to the corporals' every order and carried on without a word. I only spoke when spoken to. I ate and slept when I was told. To the corporals' cruelties, I turned a blind eye. My own agonies and hardships, I ignored. Wrapped in a cloak of silent discipline, I pursued the mechanical perfection that the Legion demanded, fully aware that even the slightest mistake could mean not just failure, but death.

"Hey, Vandenberg, how come you don't talk to any of us anymore? You think you're too good for us?" A towering

Serbian confronted me as I walked to the toilet after a day of hard training.

"No, man, I just want to do my own thing my own way."

"Well, I think you're a pussy."

"Well good for you," I said and started past him. I don't know why the Serb suddenly turned on me. Maybe word had gotten out that I was a martial artist; perhaps one of the officers had talked and now the Serb, who was a black belt in Karate, figured he could build his rep by besting me.

"Hey, where you going, pussy? Don't you turn your back on me; only pussies turn their back."

The Serb stepped in front of me and barred the bathroom door with his arm. I didn't want to fight him, but if he didn't let up it looked like I'd have to.

With the whole section watching, I stooped under his arm to get to the bathroom.

"Fucking pussy!" the Serb shouted. Then he grabbed me by the throat and cocked back his other hand to strike.

I reacted instinctively with a back kick to his ribs, a back fist to his face, and three low kicks to his leg. He dropped to his hands and knees, and before he could get up I kicked him in the face and dragged him by the ears into the bathroom, where I pushed his head into a toilet and started flushing.

"Next time, I'll shit on your head before I flush."

I let him go. The Serb fell to the floor and lay there gasping while I pissed, washed, and walked back out to the barracks.

The next day, the military police showed up. It turned out that my first kick had broken three of the Serb's ribs. He was in the hospital. I was sent to prison.

The small concrete cell held eight prisoners. At night there was just enough room for the eight of us to lie side by side on the floor. We slept without bedding of any kind. It was the middle of winter and most nights we froze. They woke us at four. If we were lucky they fed us slop. Often, we got nothing to eat at all. During the day they worked us out doing push-ups, sit-ups, running till we dropped. We performed hours of *corvée.* Sometimes they made us clean the same spot over and over just to break our balls. Other times they had us carry heavy stones back and forth across the yard.

For just under three weeks I was forced to endure the guards' every whim. Rumor had it that one of them had once beat a prisoner to death. I wasn't surprised. Almost all the men in prison were there because they'd been caught trying to desert. As far as the Legion was concerned we deserved to die.

"Get up!" a guard ordered a prisoner who'd fallen to his knees.

"I can't. I just can't anymore; please, send me home. I just want to go home," the prisoner begged.

"Get the fuck up now, prisoner!"

But the man would not obey. Even though he knew what would happen if he stayed on the ground, he would not get up; he just couldn't.

The guard called another. Together they stood over the man and told him again to get up. But the man only sobbed. The guard's first kick caught the man in the face. The blows that followed caught him everywhere. After they were through, the guards had us carry the man to the hospital where, a week later, rather than return to prison to serve out his term, the man killed himself.

I came out of prison and was sent back to my section. I was weak and thin. A man in our section who had been a doctor in civilian life looked me over. He was an interesting case, the doctor. While driving drunk with his wife and three children in the car he'd gotten into an accident that had killed them all. He'd joined the Legion to atone, and I guess it was working because the harder things got in our training the more serene he seemed to become.

"You get any more relaxed, you're going to turn into a Buddha," one of the men in our section joked. But there was truth in the remark. The doctor wouldn't be the first man the Legion had redeemed, or the last. As long as there was suffering in the world, men would find their way here to be lost or saved on the Legion's altar of pain.

"You need food and rest," the doctor told me.

No kidding. I'd been dreaming about candy bars and Coca-Colas for weeks. Since we didn't have either, I stuffed my face with the usual Legion fare. It did the trick. My strength returned, and just in time, because the training had entered its final stage. The thirty of us that had made it this far now began to take the tests that would qualify us for the white kepi cap. Among other things, we had to complete a night run of fifteen miles in less than three hours while wearing a thirty-pound pack. We had to stand guard duty for 192 hours, rotating two hours on and four hours off. We had to pass written and oral exams proving that we remembered, in French, what we'd been taught about weapons and war.

I came out first in all the physical tests, except for the long-distance runs. My leg and hip were still off. As soon as I slipped a heavy pack on my back my left leg would start to quiver. After five or ten miles, the pain was incredible, but I never complained, I never quit, and the corporals, always quick to rebuke even our smallest failings, said nothing. Even when they saw me hobbling through the last few miles of our runs, grimacing in pain, they said nothing. I suppose they were impressed by my tenacity. Either that or they or they were too busy enjoying my agony to admonish me.

Before us lay one final test, "the march for the white

kepi." Pass it and we would become full-fledged legionnaires.

The march would last a week. For seven days we would march, outfitted with full packs and FAMAS rifles, through the French countryside. We would march all day and most nights. Two to three hours of sleep was all we would be allowed during any twenty-four-hour cycle, and sometimes we wouldn't get that. Our food allotment consisted of one can of sardines and a chocolate bar per day. Water would be distributed along the route. If we quit at any point for any reason, we would not be allowed to graduate with our section. Instead, we would have to go through six more weeks of basic training, wait for the next march, and try again.

We climbed out of the trucks that had delivered us deep into the woods and broke into groups of ten. A corporal led each group. It was raining when we started and for the next seven days it would rain almost continuously. The first day came and went. Then the second and the third. By the fourth day we were starting to fray.

On the fifth day we set up camp in a downpour. Most of our gear was already wet but this clinched it. In the driving rain everything from sleeping bags to chocolate bars got soaked. The next morning my pack weighed a ton and my last pair of socks ripped clean through when I tried to pull them on. For the rest of the march I would have to walk without socks in wet boots too big for my bare feet.

The rain slowed us down, and to make up for lost time the corporal began calling fewer and fewer breaks. Men, forbidden to stop and relieve themselves, now pissed and shit in their pants as we marched. By the next to last day we were one ugly, stinking group of soldiers. One thought drove us on—the white kepi—it hung in the air like a Grail, but with each step I took toward it a sizzle of pain shot up and down my left leg. Worse still were my feet.

Without socks to protect them, my feet had become a sickening pulp of puss and blood. Thinking that urine would eat out my blisters and help fight the spreading infection, I decided to piss in my boots. When I slid my feet into the piss-filled boots it burned like hell but it did the trick. I put my mind on empty and kept marching.

In the Legion, every man is paired with a partner, a *bon ami,* we called him. It was your job to watch your *bon ami*'s back. If your *bon ami* went down and you left him behind, you would never again be trusted by anyone. So far, my *bon ami* had kept up. He'd hung tight while many around us dropped out. But now, with less than one day left to go, my *bon ami* was falling apart.

"Leave me here. I can't make it any more," my *bon ami* slurred and stumbled forward like a drunk.

"You're going to make it. You have to. Come on, we're almost there."

And we were. Another six hours at most and we'd be at the town where the general was waiting with kepis for all who marched in. But my *bon ami* was beyond caring. Even when I took his pack and carried it on top of my own he continued to fall behind. I'd already tried pushing, shouting, cursing, promising, but still I was losing him. Finally, in desperation, I took his belt, tied one end to my back and cinched the other end to the front of his pants. For the next six hours I pulled him along like a dog that didn't want to walk. But he did, and together we marched into the village where the general was waiting.

A short time later, after we had changed into clean uniforms and polished our boots, and were standing at attention, the general began his speech.

"Congratulations, you are now part of the best army in the world. Be proud. Be brave. And keep your heads up always, for you belong to a gallant tradition."

It was a grand moment, and would have been grander

still if we had just been allowed to rest and eat beforehand. But we hadn't, and, as the general went on, men already pushed to their limit and beyond began to drop where they stood. Some fell in a heap. Others pitched straight forward, smashing their faces on the ground. While the corporals rushed to drag the fallen men away, the general continued his speech, oblivious to the mayhem going on in the ranks.

"Coiffez le képi blanc!" The general finally gave the command that would make us legionnaires. We donned our white kepis and went wild.

After returning to Castelnaudary, I was sent to see the colonel of instruction. He told me that the Legion had assigned me to military karate training. I was to be posted at the sports school at Fontainebleau.

I told the colonel I was sorry but I'd already made my choice; I was going for paracommando training on the island of Corsica, home of the 2REP.

The colonel tried to talk me out of it, but he never stood a chance. Since I'd graduated among the top five of my class I was free to pick whatever posting I wanted.

In my brand-new kepi and eager for action.

"There's no doubt in my mind, Colonel. I want to be a paratrooper. I'm going to the 2REP."

After six months of taking orders, it felt great to give one for a change. Perhaps, if I'd known where that order would take me, I wouldn't have been quite so smug.

Le Bleu Bite

"The beginner."

Six months of basic training had supposedly made me a soldier, but as soon as I stepped into camp with the Second Foreign Parachute Regiment, I could see right off how far I still had to go. The 2REP was an élite airborne rapid deployment force, and, like crack units everywhere, the men of this regiment were proud. You could see it in the way they held themselves, in the rakish tip of their kepis and berets. Don't even think about fucking with us, their every move seemed to say. No idle boast either. From their scorched, scarred faced to their tattooed, butcher arms they were tough. *Bailaise,* we called them in the patois of Legion. It meant a man who knew his way around and was able to take care of himself, the exact opposite of a *bleu bite,* or beginner—which, when it came to the 2REP, is what I was.

The instruction started with three weeks of jump training. There were night jumps and day jumps and jumps round the clock. From a packed Transall aircraft screaming over drop zones at heights as low as five hundred feet we would run and leap as if it were the most natural thing in the world. And after a while it was. We even found ourselves getting addicted to the kick of the slipstream and the gut-rush of falling through space. We wanted it to go on forever and regretted the jerk of the canopy when it deployed.

Drifting under a fluttering chute I felt like my old hero Spider-Man again. Then I hit the ground and it was back to the shit storm of Legion training: The push-ups, the pull-ups, the time-tested runs. The endless calisthenics, drilling, training, and marching, always to another in the Legion's endless litany of songs. The songs were about death, loneliness, hardship, and loss.

In this one, a legionnaire has just boarded a boat for Algeria:

> Goodbye old Europe, may the Devil take you.
> Goodbye old country, for the burning sun of Algeria.
> We are the wounded from every war, the world's
>   damned ones.

Here, a legionnaire sings of his misery:

> Not a single bird sings in the dry, hollow trees.
> O land of sadness, where we must suffer endlessly.
> Sounds of chains and sounds of arms,
> A sentry guards us day and night.
> Oh unhappy land, land of tears,
> Death awaits he who flees.
> But one day in our lifetime,
> Spring will flower again.

Ah, the French. Can you imagine any other nation trying to forge its men into warriors by making them sing these doleful songs? But forge us they did, and after three weeks we marched before the regimental colonel, who awarded us the silver parachute wings and red lanyards that signified we were now full fledged soldiers of the *Deuxième Régiment Etranger de Parachutistes.*

That same day I received my assignment to the Second Section of the Regiment's First Company. The First Company was known as the craziest company in the 2REP. They specialized in night fighting and urban combat, though there was little in the way of war and killing that they wouldn't or couldn't do if ordered. To bad for me the Second Section had just returned from a tour of Central Africa where a mission had gone out of control.

The mission specs were clear enough: the Second Section had been assigned to track and capture poachers who'd been decimating the African elephant population. But, when one of the captured poachers tried to escape during the night, a legionnaire shot the poacher in the leg. Now a bullet from a FAMAS rifle has a lot of stopping force. When the 5.56 mm round hits bone it can do a lot of traveling in the body, and the poacher was pretty badly torn up. There was no way the section could hump the poacher out alive, and after a day of listening to him scream and suffer they asked for volunteers who'd be willing to finish him off. They buried him in the Savannah, and that would have been the end of it, except that when the section returned to town somebody talked, the story leaked out, and the whole section got sent back to Calvi in disgrace, their mission aborted, their extra pay gone.

Now, all the anger of these men was about to come down on us *bleus bites.* Our first day with the section, three new guys got the shit beat out of them for no reason at all. Another showed up at the barracks without the required case of beer. I guess he didn't know that whenever you get a new billet in the Legion you're supposed to show up with a case of cold ones. He knows now though,

With the 2REP.

because as soon as he knocked at the barracks door, a mad-as-hell legionnaire answered:

"What do you want?"

"I've been assigned here."

"Where's the case of beer?"

"Case of beer?"

Bam! The legionnaire broke the *bleu bite*'s nose.

"Don't come back without a case of beer, asshole."

When the *bleu bite* turned up at the Post Exchange with his busted nose and his face full of blood and plunked down some money for beer, nobody even looked twice. I guess he wasn't the first sorry broken-nosed asshole they'd had in that day.

Even the corporal got in on the act. While we stood at attention in front of our bunks, the corporal paced our line swinging an ax handle and spouting racist jokes. Then, when one of the men in the ranks dared to laugh at a punch line, the corporal clubbed him to the floor with the ax handle.

"You think my joke was funny, legionnaire?" the corporal shouted at the half-conscious man. "Well, think again because you're not here to laugh. Remember that!"

I remembered. Not that I felt much like laughing. Not when I realized that this was going to be my life for the next five fucking years. I thought things would get a bit more relaxed after basic, but I was wrong—not in the 2REP.

A 2REP legionnaires' life, I was quickly discovering, was one long, ugly butt-fuck without privacy or freedom. You lived under the constant threat of punishment. You were deprived of sleep, forced into a daily routine of spit and polish, and could go for months without ever seeing a woman. You trained and you trained. And for what? For the glory of the Legion? For the honor of being called a soldier of the 2REP? Sure, I liked playing with all the deadly toys—the rifles, the rockets, the helicopters and tanks. After nearly five months with the First Company I knew how to blow up a bridge, storm a house, and take a town by force. I could recognize the tanks and planes of a dozen nations, and parachute lower, faster, and in a more tightly grouped formation than a soldier in any other army in the world. I liked pushing myself beyond the limits of the average Joe. But it wasn't enough. Something was missing.

That something was action. I was itching for battle. We all were. To a man we were restless and sick at heart. When we weren't training, our soldiering consisted of the most mundane and menial tasks imaginable. We stood for roll call twice a day and if our lockers and bedding weren't perfect everything got tossed in the air. The shirts we wore for guard duty and on parade had to be ironed with fifteen different creases, each one spaced exactly three and a half or five centimeters apart. Our kepis had to be kept spotlessly white and our boots shined even on the soles. A scuffed heel or a little fleck of fly shit on your hat could earn you a punch in the stomach or the face.

To deal with the tedium, most of the men drank. After a long day of training and pointless routine, they'd rush en masse to the foyer, where they'd belly up according to their nationalities or native tongues—English-speakers with English-speakers, Germans with Germans—to drink themselves deaf and dumb.

Though I never once joined in these bouts I understood the need. We all wanted to forget, and not just our past but our present as well. After a few months in the 2REP I began to realize that the Legion's mournful songs were right after all. For the lone legionnaire there is only hardship and loss. Love, home, happiness—these are impossible for the Legion's lower ranks. The best we could hope for was liberation through death:

> Our forbears knew how to die
> For the glory of the Legion;

We too shall learn how to perish,
Following tradition.
In the course of our far-off campaigns,
In the face of fever and fire,
We forget, along with our sorrows,
The death that so seldom forgets
Us, the Legion.

But the Legion couldn't give us that death. Its far-off campaigns were but a memory: Dien Bien Phu, Algiers, Kolwezi. We were all "soldiers in order to die," but not in a goddamned training accident, and so the men drank.

To pass the time others filled by drinking, I practiced the martial arts. Every night after training, I would make my way out to the yard where I would kick, punch, and do katas. My left leg was still weak and to compensate I tried reversing my stance. It worked wonders. By leading with my left and using my right leg for power I was able to mount a ferocious, if limited, frontal attack.

Soon other martial arts–minded legionnaires started joining me in my workouts, and before long a small team of us were going at it every night. While it felt good to be sparring again, ultimately the practice depressed me because it brought me face to face with the inescapable fact that I wasn't meant to be a soldier, even in a crack unit like the 2REP. I was a single-combat warrior. That's what I'd been born to, and with luck it was how I would die. If I was going to fight somebody, I didn't want to shoot him down, blow him up, or bomb him. I wanted to look him in the eye and struggle man to man. I wanted it to end in blood, not some distant puff of smoke.

Another day of training over, I rushed as fast as my injured leg would carry me to the yard where I practiced my art.

L'Armée d'Afrique

The Army of Africa.

"*Levez-vous!*" the corporal shouted above the roar of the engines. We stood and hooked our static lines to cables that ran the length of the plane. Each of us pushed as close as possible to the man in front so that when we jumped we would exit the aircraft in a tight formation. The jump doors were thrown open and a wind like a million howling mourners beat its way into the plane. I bowed my head and waited while a thousand feet below the African desert spread its desiccated arms.

A week before I'd been standing at our base in Calvi, listening to the colonel regale us through a loudspeaker. "You are my war machines," the colonel's voice echoed through the camp, "the best fighters in the world. My sons. My legionnaires. My animals of war, created to succeed where all else fails."

Yes, I thought, all else had failed, that's exactly why we were here. It wasn't courage or patriotism that had pushed most of us to the soldier's life. It was failure, and rage, and, if you must know, self-pity. To a man we'd been beaten, broken, and cast out by the world. To a man we hated the world that started just outside our gates. That's what held us to this field where we stood and listened to the colonel vomit forth. Just give us the order, *mon colonel,* and we would march against that world. Like unchained beasts we would hack and rend until the entire world was as dead and cold as your gaze.

Inside the plane, the smell of aviation fuel mixed with the stink of fear and sweat. What were my comrades afraid of, I wondered. The leap into nothingness? The possibility of death? Didn't they know when they joined the Legion that this was an army of last stands and impossible assaults—that we were all expendable? Besides, this was only a training mission; it wasn't like we were going down to face fire. The leap into the Djibouti desert was just another leap that would lead nowhere and to nothing. Just another dry hump.

While the men around me prayed to their private gods, I ruminated on pussy. It had been a year since I'd gotten

Living with the nomads of North Africa.

laid. For the past month of that year I'd been based at a North African training compound in the hills above the shantytown of Arta. Arta was a shit smear of a town where life meant nothing and death less. The black Africans who lived there scratched out their living by servicing the soldiers of our base and a French Marine base located a few miles to the south. As a consequence, alcohol and sickness polluted the locals.

For a few hundred Djibouti francs you could get blind stinking drunk on the awful North African whiskey. For the price of a tin of sardines or a few cigarettes you could buy a man's wife, or his daughter, or both at once if you wanted. And boy did I want it, though I guess not bad enough to bring myself to fuck any of the women of Arta. For one thing, they stank. They smelled so bad that at night, on guard duty, you could smell them coming from fifty yards off. For another, their clitorises had been hacked off during childhood to satisfy some sick local custom. Worse still was the illness that many of them carried. Later, we would learn its name was AIDS, but at the time none of us knew or even suspected that the men and women we saw in the streets, covered with sores and gaunt as skeletons, were its victims.

Since I was going to be based in Africa for at least another three months, it looked like I'd be stuck with my own right hand for a while longer. Standing over a stinking latrine, eyes clenched, a perfect woman splayed out in my mind, I let my fist thrash away at my dick. "Ugh," I grunted, and opened my eyes as Africa wheeled back into view in all its unwelcome clarity.

Suddenly, the green jump light flashed red, the klaxon wailed, and the dispatcher shouted, *"Allez! Allez! Allez!"* I rushed toward the door, dived into the slipstream, and fell with a cruel swiftness. It was wonderful and terrifying, and for an instant I felt on the verge of some great

Preparing to jump.

breakthrough, as if something new and strange was about to reveal itself to me. Then my canopy deployed and the feeling was gone. I was drifting in silence, swaying underneath the open parachute like a stick figure in a child's game of hangman. I pulled the retaining pin on my rucksack and let it drop on its length of nylon rope. A second later the rucksack hit the ground and I took my dropping position: feet and knees together, chin tucked into chest. I landed, packed up my parachute, and regrouped with the rest of my unit. After everyone had rallied, we consulted our maps and started out.

Four days later we marched into camp, dropped off our equipment, changed our uniforms, and were assigned to a twenty-four-hour guard duty that ended up lasting sixty-eight hours because there was no one available to replace us. For the past year the regiment had been hemorrhaging men. So many had deserted that even the addition of our section to the African camp couldn't cover the loss or plug all the gaps in our ranks.

Desertion wasn't an option for me. I'd given my word that I would stay, and no matter how miserable the Legion made my life I would never abandon my word. Besides, if I left, where would I go? What would I do? There was no place for me in the world anymore. The world was a place for individuals with individual wants and individual desires. But my unique self had been subsumed. I no longer was an individual; I was a legionnaire, and like legionnaires everywhere I had worked long and hard to kill off every gentle trait in me that could be humanly killed. With one swift blow I murdered kindness. With another I crushed charity. In basic we'd been forbidden to use words like "please" or "thank you." Such words made you weak. I clubbed them down. Strength and skill were all that mattered; that and a willingness to endure mindless tedium, discipline, and injustice were what made you a legionnaire.

I had no illusions about the Legion or myself. As far as I could tell I was no longer human; I had dropped below the animal, beneath the vegetable to the mineral. I had become a man of stone. For a year the Legion had quarried me and still it wasn't through. I wondered where the next hammer blow would strike and if I'd be able to take it.

When the time finally came for me to have my first night off I presented myself to an officer. If one line in my uniform was badly ironed, if my shirt had a wrinkle or even a sweat stain, I could forget about leaving the base.

After a group of us passed the inspection we caught a ride to the city of Djibouti, some two hours away by truck from our mountain camp. As soon as the truck arrived in Djibouti, most of the legionnaires scurried out after prostitutes. Not me. I sauntered off to a bar with my English friend Pat. Pat liked his liquor. He liked it so much that within fifteen minutes of sitting down at the bar he'd downed half a bottle and was stoned, stupid drunk.

We weren't the only military force in the bar that night. Sitting across from us were eight French Commando Marines getting just as drunk and stupid as my friend. But it was Pat who started things when he leaned over and used his cigarette lighter to set one of the marine's pants on fire.

"Française de merde!" Pat shouted and threw a punch, decking the marine. Then all hell broke loose as seven screaming mad marines charged us at close quarters. While Pat picked up a chair and broke it over some heads, I was busy chopping a marine in the throat, kicking a second in the chest, and head-butting a third. It felt pretty good to get back to the old give and take. After I flipped a marine onto a table and back-kicked another through the bar's front

window, I figured we'd given them enough. I wanted to end this Wild West show before the cops showed up, so I grabbed Pat and together we ran out of the bar.

We'd just rounded the corner and were about to get away when two Djibouti policemen appeared and shouted for us to halt. We kept on running, but when one of the cops drew his gun and shouted, "Halt or I'll shoot!" we froze in our tracks.

Before the cops could reach us, I tore the red lanyards off our uniforms and stuffed them in my pocket. Without the lanyards, I figured the cops would mistake us for regular legionnaires of the 13DBLE Brigade that was headquartered here in the city. But in removing the lanyards I'd made a decision that I couldn't go back on. Now there was no way I could let the cops take us in. For what we'd done in the bar we'd go to Legion jail for sure, but that would be nothing next to the punishment we'd receive for dishonoring the regiment by removing our lanyards.

"Papiers!" the cop holding the gun barked. I rooted in my pocket like I was searching for my papers, stepped toward him, and head butted him hard in the nose. At the same time I jabbed the other cop in the eye. Then I cracked the cop with the gun again and watched him drop. Pat was so drunk he didn't even know what had happened until I was pulling him and telling him to run.

The next morning Pat and I lined up for *appel,* expecting the worst, but when not a word was said about the bar fight or the cops we knew we were home free.

The following day our section was sent north to the vast dried salt plain known as Lac Assal. Lac Assal is one of the hottest places on Earth, with daytime temperatures of 130 degrees Fahrenheit. We started out at dawn on a march across the dry lake, our boots crunching on salt and sand so hot that if you stopped walking even for a minute it would blister the soles of your feet. Far off to our left and right, skerries of volcanic rock rose and fell in petrified black waves. Before us stretched the lake, featureless and white. Nothing grew. Even the withered grass and shattered trees of Djibouti's other deserts could find no purchase here. It was a naked, haunted, dying place. Supreme and primitive. A perfect place to march a Legion cohort.

By midday I'd gone through all my water and white-hot needles of pain were stabbing at my head. My skin had gone pulpy from sweat and every step became a burning agony as my clothes cut into tender flesh. What a way, I thought, to spend my nineteenth birthday. Suddenly, a canteen was thrust into my hands. I took a swig and passed it back to the parched soldier who'd handed it to me. His face was seared, his lips cracked and branded by a sun that wouldn't stop. That a man tortured by thirst would share his last water, would do so without asking, as if it were the most natural thing in the world, is what the Legion at its best is all about. And in that moment I knew that there was no place else on Earth that I would rather be than here, together with my Legion brothers, sharing all we had while marching lockstep through hell.

We returned from the march and picked up another long guard duty. A week later I was granted an overnight leave. This time, I was ordered to spend it in Arta.

I walked into the village and made straight for the bar. I drank quickly, without pleasure, to steel myself for what I planned to do. I was going to buy a whore. I didn't care anymore if she was clitless or diseased; I just wanted to feel something soft against my skin. A little honeymoon of flesh. A night of sweet forgetting before I lost even the desire to remember what it had been like to hold a woman in my arms.

I found a whore and took a room where we engaged in a low-morale and sullen fuck. Afterward, I sank into a postcoital undertow that no amount of drinking could relieve. When I heard the sounds of a fight going on outside my door, I threw on my pants and rushed into the street, grateful for anything that might distract me from my misery. There, five Africans were beating the tar out a soldier of the regular French army. I rushed in and took three of the Africans down. When the other two ran off I helped the soldier to his feet. He'd been badly mauled and could barely stand, so when I saw two French MPs rushing toward us I thought for sure they'd come to help, and it was a real surprise to me when, as soon as they got close, they began clubbing me in the face with their batons. I dropped the soldier and fought back. In no time both MPs were on the ground, unconscious. I let them lie there, lifted the French soldier, and helped him the mile or so back to his base.

The next day I returned to the Legion camp to find both private and military police waiting for me. I was taken into custody, and, after consulting with the captains and colonels of the various forces I'd offended, the Legion decided on my punishment—thirty days in the Legion jail called *le Plot.*

More than a place or a punishment, the Plot was a plan to break you. Beatings, isolation, and lockdowns in an iron-walled cell that radiated heat like an oven were alternated with sessions the Legion euphemistically called "exercise." For three hours every day I was forced to run in place while holding a large truck tire filled with sand around my neck. Then I would be handed a hammer and told to shatter rocks, which I would then carry from one place in the yard to another and back again.

After two weeks in the Plot I looked and felt like shit, but I refused to let it break me even though I knew that my punishment was undeserved. Sure, I shouldn't have hit those MPs—the idiots, they thought I was the one who'd beat the soldier, and that's why they'd tried to club me. But I knew that I'd saved that soldier's life, and would do it again if I had to, no matter what.

I came out of the Plot gaunt and haggard, but what I lost in fat and muscle I'd picked up in respect. It seemed every man in camp now nodded when I passed. They all knew what I'd been through and agreed it wasn't fair, but even more important to them was that I'd done my time without complaint. I didn't whimper. I didn't whine. I just took it and moved on. That meant I was someone to be taken seriously. I'd proved myself a soldier deserving of respect. As far as I was concerned it was about time. A man can only press his face against the glass for so long before something's got to shatter, and I was starting to worry that something might be me.

The day after I got out of the Plot the Legion held a riflery contest. I came out first in my section and was sent together with about forty other top shots from various Legion outfits to participate in the CTE 1 Sharpshooters Course.

The course was held close to the border with Ethiopia near a desert village called al-Sabieh. The border area was dangerous and we were warned not to wander too far outside of camp. The year before, two legionnaires had deserted across the border into Ethiopia, where rebel fighters had quickly caught them and thrown them into jail. It was months before the Legion was able to buy them back for its standard bounty of thirty-five thousand Djibouti francs for each captured deserter. But when the swap was finally made, and Legion officers tried to march the men off to prison, they quickly learned that the deserters were way beyond any punishments that the Legion might inflict. The first was completely insane, and the other, after being fucked up the ass day and night by the rebels, had come down with AIDS and was dying.

I did the best I could at the sharpshooter course, but it wasn't good enough. Through the whole first two weeks of training I just couldn't find my groove. I kept jerking at the trigger and missing all my shots. The gun jammed. The wind changed. I went half-blind from the sun. I tried to make corrections but it only made things worse. I was one of the worst shots in the course.

The final shooting tests were coming up. If I failed, I'd be sent back to the Plot. Legion policy was strict—anyone who failed a training program was carted straightaway to jail, and there was no way I was going back there. I wasn't about to see all the respect I'd won from the other men lost down the crapper because I couldn't hit the mark. I wouldn't surrender myself to those sadistic bastards again for something as stupid as this, especially since I really was a good shot. Now all I had to do was prove it.

"Easy," I whispered under my breath. "Steady now." The final tests were underway. So far, I'd done great. After three rounds, I was tied for first place with a legionnaire named Zanardo. My leap from last to first had shocked everyone but me. But, then, I had discovered a secret. I'd stopped caring about what happened to me and that's why I was in first place. By caring less and letting go of worry, I had freed myself to perform to my limits and beyond. How stupid I'd been not to use this technique earlier in the course, but my fear of being sent back to jail and losing the respect of the men had blinded me to the simple truth that in this life less is always more and nothing everything.

The tests went on and on. We shot long range at moving and stationary targets. We competed in rapid-fire exercises and were tested at night, firing with and without a scope. We shot across the open desert and from escarpments in the mountains. While lying prone, standing, and squatting we blasted away at all kinds of targets under all kinds of conditions.

For the final test we were handed five bullets and told to hit five targets that rose and fell on pulleys from a distant trench. After hitting my first four targets, the wind changed. I reset my scope, stayed centered on my breathing, eased down on the trigger, and Bang! I caught the last target dead on. After taking out my magazine I looked over at Zanardo. He'd just nailed his fourth target and was waiting for his fifth. It popped up and he fired, but the shot went wide. He missed, and I ended up coming out first overall in the course.

Only three other men from the regiment passed. The rest were sent to the Plot. At least they didn't have to suffer for long. About two weeks later we were all shipped back to Calvi. As our transport lifted into the sky I waved farewell to Africa and thanked God for getting me this far. What's next, I wondered, and could it get any worse? If it did, at least I knew I wouldn't be the first man who had fallen into an adventure that had crushed him.

Faites Comme Moi

"Do as I do."

From the desert in summer to the mountains in winter, you could always count on the Legion to send you where it hurt. This time it was to Mont Louis in the Pyrenees, where the Legion ran a winter commando course for its combat paratroopers.

Each day started with a circuit run over an obstacle course of walls, cables, pipes, tires, and ropes. Worst were the cables, a hundred-meter run of braided steel slung between two high towers. In the summer, crossing the cables hand over hand might have been fun because the run was high and the view spectacular. But in the winter, if you hesitated even for an instant, your hands would freeze onto the steel and you'd have to tear them loose with a sickening rip that you could hear even above the raw howl of the wind.

Like all Legion training courses, this one required more than just physical prowess. You needed heart, discipline, and esprit de corps to make it through. It took heart to run for hours through the mountain snow while dragging heavy wooden boxes filled with sand. It took discipline to jog from the mountains to the sea and back while gripping a tin cup filled with water in your teeth. Over and over we made the trip until we filled an empty jar set on top of the mountain with the water we'd carried in our cups.

Sometimes they would make us dress and undress from full combat gear to underwear and back again, faster and faster until we beat a measured time. Then they would march us straight down to the sea where we would stand chest deep in the freezing water for half an hour, singing. We hated every minute of it, but it built esprit de corps as men, united by shared suffering and triumphs, were forged into a unit hard as stone.

At night we were never permitted more than an hour or two of sleep. As often as not they would rouse us early and march us out to the yard, where we would practice bare-hand fighting. Imagine fifty tired, cold, and angry men throwing vicious kicks at one another's balls and you'll know what we were up against. It was pain plain and simple, unadorned by any kind of comfort, and with no one watching out for us but God.

But it wasn't all mindless exercise and fighting. Over the next several weeks we learned how to read the enemy's intentions by observing his deployment. We were taught techniques of infiltration and attack. We overran houses, practiced night insertions by land, air, and sea, and learned how to deal with booby traps and mines.

Short of war itself, if anything could sate the appetite of men who dined on battle it was this. For the first time since I joined the Legion I was beginning to feel like a real soldier. I guess others were too, only they didn't take to it like I did, because many used their time here to desert. It was a near perfect spot from which to do so. All you had to do was wait until you went out on a small group maneuver, slip away, change into the civilian clothes you'd secretly hidden in your pack, find a road, stick out your thumb, and pray that the first car that came by didn't belong to the Legion. If it did you went to jail. If not, you caught a ride across the mountains into Spain.

To our group leader, a hard bastard named Daniels, the increasing numbers of deserters were just part of the proof that he was doing his job. He drove us all well past our limits, and there wasn't a man under his command that didn't curse him for it night and day. But he was fair, a great soldier, and those who stayed he turned into rock-hard motherfuckers, and for that I respected him. By the time we'd finished our training, our group had broken every timed record for the course. We were fast, sharp, and tough as nails, and we owed it all to Daniels and his head-on, full-force, take-no-prisoners approach to leading men.

As the course moved into its final days we started conserving all our energy for the tests. By now we'd all learned how to sleep while standing up. We could run the obstacle course with our eyes closed, assault a beach, scale a cliff, or take out a tank on instinct alone.

The tests started with a fifteen-mile run in full combat gear. Then we had to defend ourselves against a line of men each of whom would attack us with knives, with guns, or barehanded. After that, we had to lie on our backs and play chicken with a speeding tank. Just as the treads were almost on us we would roll out of the way. Then we would do the same thing from a crouch, but this time we had to touch the tank with our hand before we bolted. Then we did it again, this time by ducking into a trench just as the tank rolled overhead.

That night we had a shooting test in a labyrinth that passed in and out of buildings and wound down a dark and twisting trail. It was a target-rich environment, but woe unto you if you missed or, worse, accidentally hit one of the "hostage" or "civilian" markers that dotted the course.

Next, they sent us into the tunnels. We started by sliding down a small tunnel that dropped us into a pitch-black room. I fell into the room with a thud, and before I could get up four men surrounded me and started kicking and punching. Even though I was exhausted, I defended myself well and the men were unable to handcuff me. That meant I could continue. I slid feet-first through another tunnel that trailed down sharply and ended with a long straight drop to the ground. Luckily I was able to stop my slide and grab onto the rope that hung near the mouth of the tunnel before I fell. The man behind me wasn't so lucky. He flew out of the tunnel like a bat and landed far below, breaking an arm.

Those of us who made it through the tunnels regrouped, threw on our packs, and started out on a four-day raid march through freezing rain and snow. By the second day my gear was soaking wet and I was too cold to sleep even the two hours they allowed.

After the raid march we endured another ten-mile run in the snow. Then we changed clothes and were driven to an old air force base where a Transall plane was waiting. We climbed aboard and took off for a low-altitude, low-opening jump that went off without a hitch. And that was it. The tests were over. We had passed. The next day we shipped back to Corsica, where we received our commando insignias and berets.

After what we'd been through the men of our section were given rights to a few days' leave. Most were eager to take it. Not me. I wasn't ready for the outside world. I didn't want to be reminded of what I'd lost. I didn't want to have to see my mother or father. I knew exactly what they'd say: "Are you insane, Nicky? Is this how you want to spend your life? We want you to come back with us

Burned out from Legion training.

right now; put this madness behind you once and for all
before its too late."

I didn't want to hear it. What I wanted was to fight
again in freestyle competition, and every spare moment I
could find I spent practicing my art. At least I didn't have
to worry about sparring partners. The Legion had plenty.
There was Havio, a ex–heavyweight boxing champion and
former Brazilian MP; before he joined the Legion he'd
worked for one of the death squads that roamed the streets
of Rio killing drug dealers, stray children, and thieves.
There was Mikal, a Russian Spetnaz Special Forces fighter
who'd defected in Afghanistan and found his way straight
to the Legion. There was Wilson, who'd made his pre-
Legion living collecting bad debts for the mob. Throw in a
few ex–SAS British Special Forces members, SBS Raiders,
a Jujitsu street fighter, and a generous leavening of black
belts and bone-crushers trained in dozens of fighting

styles, and you had the makings of a fine freestyle training camp.

Still, it wasn't enough. To be a winning freestyle fighter you had to be brought to your absolute peak, and a few stolen hours of rough-and-tumble with the boys wasn't going to do that. For that kind of edge I'd need Kunto-style training, but since the Legion didn't offer anything even close I settled for the hardest thing they had—their advanced training courses—and as soon as I got out of the commando course I volunteered for a sniper course that started the next day.

Like the commando course, the sniper course demanded lots of running and marching with little food or sleep. It was tough, and more than a few men cracked under the strain and begged to be sent back to base, to jail, or anywhere as long as it got them out of the course. I didn't blame them; if I hadn't been harboring a secret ambition to fight again I'm not sure if I would have made it through either.

After I graduated from the sniper course I enrolled in a parachute course, and after that in an urban combat and explosives course taught by Warrant Officer Harris, a hard-ass Irish bully out of the Fourth Company.

At least Harris was a solid soldier with lots of experience and balls. As I was quickly finding out, in the Legion that wasn't always the case. Many Legion officers came directly from the French Military Academy. We called them *girons,* slang for "babies," because they looked like little children and knew even less. For the most part they were know-it-all prigs who thought they deserved respect just because they were born to the French upper class. But what they really deserved was a swift kick. A good officer is supposed to lead by example. It's up to him to set the standard and then live by it. If an officer wants to instill bravery he has to be brave. If he wants his men to go hell for leather in everything they do he'd better be willing to do the same himself.

Sadly, most Legion officers fell far short of my expectations. They weren't brave or tough; they weren't even good soldiers. Most of them were just working to get by, to get up in grade, or to protect the turf they already had. It made me sick. I'd joined expecting heroes, but these men had no honor, at least none that I could see. I'd given myself 100 percent to the Legion because I believed all the things I'd read about Camerone and men dying for their brothers. Maybe I had a romantic view—most new legionnaires did—because it took a romantic view to endure the bullshit and brutality that the Legion threw at you every day.

They say that no man feels more betrayed than a man whose ideals have failed him, and once I began to see the Legion officers for what they were I turned against them with a vengeance. At night I dreamed of murder. By day I fantasized about all the baroque tortures I would inflict on them if I ever got the chance. After I learned what happened to my friend Havio, my rage grew even worse.

Havio had been sitting in a bar in Calvi minding his own business when he noticed that a Legion sergeant was having trouble with seven members of the Corsican Mafia. The Mafia guys were angry because the sergeant owed them money, but that didn't matter to Havio. All he saw was a fellow legionnaire in trouble, so he did what any self-respecting legionnaire would do—he jumped in to defend the sergeant's back. He didn't know at the time that the Sergeant's back was streaked with yellow. He never dreamed that as soon as the fighting started, the sergeant would run, leaving Havio alone to face all seven. Havio got the shit beat out of him that day, but it didn't end there. A few days later Havio caught the sergeant going about his business on the base and challenged him to an honor fight. When the sergeant refused, Havio beat him up anyway. In fact, he beat up three sergeants after two more rushed in to defend the worthless officer. For what he'd done, Havio was transferred out of the regiment. I stayed on, nursing a hatred that grew stronger every day.

A few months later I decided to put that hate to work in the ring. With a fifteen-day leave coming up, I called two old friends from the Netherlands. Roberts, a former Judo champion, and Smits, a Kyokushinkai Karate fighter, had been encouraging me by letter to get back into the single-combat game. Now I would take them up on their offer. Since I couldn't fight in Europe, (you had to show medical papers to fight in any sanctioned European bout and mine would disqualify me) I asked Roberts and Smits what they thought I should do.

"We could set you up in Thailand. They don't give a fuck about medical records over there."

Thailand! As soon as I heard him say it I knew it was right.

"Set it up. Whatever you can put together I'll take."

A week later I boarded a flight from Paris to Bangkok. If the Legion knew where I was going they would have carted me straight off to jail. During his first three years of service a legionnaire is not permitted to leave French soil. While on leave he's not even allowed to wear civilian clothes. Good thing I still had a Belgian passport stashed away. With it and a suit of store-bought clothes I boarded the flight like any other tourist.

"You on vacation?" the words came from the face of the fat old snake sitting next to me on the flight.

"Mm-hm."

"Ever been to Thailand before?"

"Uh-uh."

"Well, you're in for a treat. They got girls over there'll do anything, and I mean anything. Beautiful girls too— wait'll you see 'em. They got that almond skin and those eyes. I'm telling you, I go every year. So what about you? You in the military or something?"

I threw him a look like a pail of cold water. A Legion look. It was a real conversation stopper and it kept him away from me for the rest of the flight.

"Hey, sorry if I offended you. I never meant any harm," the snake said by way of goodbye after we'd landed in Bangkok.

But I did. I meant harm and would do harm just as soon as I got to climb into the ring.

Hoo-uh Laa Hoo-uh Jy

Thai for "head and heart."

The airport was hot and stuffy with people. I chested my way through the terminal, edgy as hell, but excited to be there.

"Legionnaire, hold it!" a voice shouted out from the crowd.

As soon as I heard it all my instincts said run. After all, if the Legion ever caught me here they'd screw me till I hollered.

"Legionnaire!" the voice shouted again, only this time I recognized it as belonging to Smits. I turned to see him and Roberts pushing toward me through the crowd.

"Hey, man." Roberts high-fived me. "Welcome to Thailand."

"You finally made it, you bastard," Smits bellowed. "Hey," he said eyeing the top of my head, "looks like a baby's ass up there. What do they do, razor you?"

"Just about."

"Fuck, I don't know how you take all that Legion shit, man."

"Me either."

"Well you don't have to anymore, buddy. You're a free man now."

"For two weeks, anyway."

Smits and Roberts threw each other a look.

"What is it?" I asked.

"Nothing. Come on, let's get the fuck out of here. You're gonna love this place, man. It's one big party country."

They led me out to the street, where Smits, who spoke Thai, commandeered a taxi. During the ride into Bangkok we caught up on old times. Smits, it turned out, had given up professional fighting and taken to drinking and worse. From the looks of him he'd gotten in pretty deep. Deep into drugs. Deep into violence. Deep into all kinds of Thai shit that I knew better than to ask about. Roberts was another story. He loved the hard life too, but unlike Smits it wasn't Robert's only life. For six months out of the year Roberts lived in Europe, where he ran a big-time gymnasium and martial arts training center.

"Where we going?" I asked.

"Where you want to go?"

"Surprise me."

"Fair enough. Now, come on, tell us about the Legion? What's it like?"

So I told them about the life and some of the bad-ass bad boys I served with. They seemed to like my stories, especially the one about Carlos, the crazy Spanish legionnaire who'd gotten himself sent to a mental institution after a sergeant caught him having sex with a dog.

"What kind of dog?" Smits asked.

"I dunno. Some kind of shepherd, I think."

"Yeah, I've seen 'em do that kind of shit here too," Smits said. "Up on stage, live."

"I thought they just ate dogs here."

"Oh, they do that too. Dogs, monkeys, snakes—they eat fuckin' anything here. Hope you're hungry."

"Very funny."

But he wasn't kidding, and a half-hour later we were sitting beside a sidewalk food cart eating God knows what on a stick. I hardly noticed though. After serving more than two years in the Legion, the freedom to just sit on a street corner without officers or orders was almost overwhelming, and like a man fresh out of prison I found it hard to shake the instincts I'd picked up while under guard.

While Roberts and Smits talked about Thailand I opened my senses to the street—to the busy rush of city folk, to the singsong syllables of sidewalk vendors shouting out their wares, to the potpourri of fish guts, soy sauce, garbage, and exhaust fumes that made up the smells of the city. To me, none of it seemed real, and all I knew for certain was that out there somewhere was a man I'd pledged to fight. In a few days we'd face off. A few minutes after that I would defeat him, and for the first time in years the triumphant power of a warrior would be mine to feel again.

"Dominiquie, you're probably gonna hate me for this." Smits's words snapped me out of my reverie.

"I got some bad news for ya, buddy."

"What's that?"

"Turns out your fight got pushed back."

"Pushed back? Till when?"

"Till four days after you were supposed to leave."

"Four days?"

"Yeah, sorry, man. Nothing we could do. We just found out about it today."

The dominoes started falling in my mind. Four days would put me late into Calvi. I would be AWOL. That would mean Legion jail.

"So, what'd you say, Dominiquie? You still wanna do it?"

I stared into the shadowed craters of Smits's face, thinking maybe he was just razzing me, but he wasn't.

"Four days . . . that really fucks me."

Smits acknowledged the remark with two upraised palms.

"Hey, if you can't do it you can't do it. We can always call the thing off." Roberts offered.

"No, I'm here. I got to do it. I'm gonna fight."

"Good man! All right!" they said and jumped up to pound my back and shoulders. Then they both started talking at once about how we should get drunk and laid to celebrate, but I'd lost the capacity to hear them, and their flood of words was lost.

"Take me to the training camp," was all I said.

"Hey that can wait. Tonight we're gonna—"

"Take me to the camp," I said again, this time with enough force to let them know that I meant business.

They took me to the training camp where for the next two weeks I practiced Thai and Burmese boxing. If I told you that I wasn't scared I'd be lying, because the truth is I was terrified. This was my first fight since the injury. My only fight in over two years, and the whole time I'd been marching in the Legion my opponent had been fighting. After more than two hundred professional fights he was sharp. He was ready, and we'd be fighting by his rules: no wrestling or eye gouging, just straight-out kicks and punches with timed rounds and referees.

The morning of the contest, Smits and Roberts returned to the camp. It was the first time I'd seen them since the day I'd arrived.

"You ready?"

I nodded and they gestured me toward the waiting cab. They both knew better than to make chitchat before a fight,

Getting ready for my comeback.

and we drove to the fight grounds in silence. The fights were being held at the Thai equivalent of a county fair. We entered the fairgrounds and walked down a midway of booths stocked with the same sorts of crafts and farm animals that you'd find at any rural festival. On the far side of the midway a large open hangar had been draped and tented. I followed Smits and Roberts inside the tent where a ring had been set up and some bleachers raised. An amateur bout was in progress. While Smits went off to sign us in with the officials, Roberts and I stood and watched the kids fight.

"Kind of brings you back, doesn't it?" Roberts said, as much to himself as to me.

But it didn't bring me back—if anything it knocked me forward. Soon I'd be up there doing the only thing that ever really mattered to me. If I succeeded, I'd be well on my way to regaining a life that I'd lost to the Legion. If I failed, I'd lose the one thing that even the Legion hadn't been able to take from me—my dream of being the best single-combat fighter in the world.

"See the guy over there?" Roberts pointed to a Burmese fighter on the other side of the ring. "That's your man."

I looked him over. He stood maybe five feet five inches tall. I guessed his weight at about 140 pounds, which gave me an easy thirty pounds on him.

"Bitch looks soft as a fuckin' pillow," Roberts spat.

It was true. The Thai fighter did look soft. There wasn't a cut or a rippling striation anywhere on his body.

Of course I knew that meant nothing. Cut muscle and bulk are a weightlifter's friend, not a fighter's. The most important muscles a fighter can develop are the ones between his ears and the one that pumps his blood. Head and heart are what wins fights, not biceps. When opponents of equal skill and stamina face off it's always head and heart that decide the outcome. Even between fighters of unmatched talents and abilities, it's usually the intangibles of head and heart that turn the fight. Ask anybody who's been around and he'll tell you the same. I've seen street fighters without a lick of technique take apart trained martial artists because the street fighter was the one with the head for it. I've seen otherwise weak men, who, when pushed to a wall, come out swinging stronger and harder than any professional because in that moment their heart was in the right place.

When Smits returned and told me that I wouldn't be up until nightfall I stared at him dryly and shrugged. In the fight game waiting is part of the deal—the worst part, for sure, but that's the beauty of it, because generally the longer you waited, the happier you were when you finally got to face your opponent. Me, I'd been waiting so goddamned long I figured I'd probably kill the poor bastard with joy.

That night, I stepped into the ring ready to hammer out my future on the Burmese boxer's face. As soon as the bell rang I rushed him like he was there for the taking. But he wasn't. Not by a long shot. For two endless rounds I tried to brand his legs with low kicks and cut his head with elbow smashes and all I got for my trouble was tired. I didn't understand it. In training I'd run for hours on end; I'd spar full out for fifteen rounds, do isometrics, endurance and interval training, practice grappling, and clinching, and still feel good to go. Now, after only two rounds my legs were shaky and my chest was heaving like a caught fish. I was exhausted. I'd never punched and kicked so hard before to so little effect.

The next round I tried backing up. I'd always been good at weaving and bobbing, but all my ducking earned me this time was more punishment. In no time, the Thai fighter drove me to the ropes, where he caught me with a spinning back elbow to the right eye that dropped me on my ass. I took a partial count, got up and clinched for the rest of the round.

At the bell, I walked to my corner wondering what else could go wrong. I was already pretty near blind in the injured eye. I knew that in next round he'd be coming at me from my blind side, and that every time I tried to wheel or side step it would open a gap in my defenses. I stared over at the boxer and saw him grinning through a set of randomly angled teeth. He looked like a rat after a piece of bloody cheese. The bastard. He thought he had me, but I wasn't going to be anybody's sure thing. I had too much heart for that.

I opened the fourth round with so much fury that I think it must have surprised him. He stepped back wrong-footed and I moved in and kicked him just above the knee. He winced and I kicked him again, and then again. Now that I'd found the spot it was just a matter of maintaining the attack. Over the course of the next round I pushed everything I had into the breach. I threw it all into that one small spot above his knee. Halfway through the round his leg couldn't take it anymore and he collapsed. When he stood up, I went at him even harder. By now my radar had him locked in. I landed a front kick, then a left and a right, and a left and another right, then I stop-kicked his thigh and *Bang!* I landed a shot right above his knee. He crumpled to the mat. Only this time he couldn't get up; no matter how hard he tried, his leg refused. It was useless. The fight was over. I was the winner by TKO. I'd beat the Burmese boxer on his own rules in his home ground in front of his own people.

For days afterward my vision was blurry and I ached in places I didn't even know I had, but I didn't care. I was on top of the world. In one fell swoop I'd been sprung from my old life. Dominiquie Vandenberg—the fighting machine—was up and running again.

That night I took a lesson in anatomy from two girls at once, and boy did they know their stuff, those mad, jazzed Thai whores. Between their double-hipped torque and thrust they fussed over my erection like hummingbirds buzzing a flower. It was tiptop, no doubt about it, and I came again and again. I figured I could get used to this kind of life. Smits and Roberts sure had. But I didn't want to end up like them, nesting in a bed of flesh and pleasure, only rising when the need for money called, or the lightening crash of violence drove them to the street. No, I still had my honor. I had a contract to fulfill, and no matter what it cost or how much I wanted to do otherwise, I would hold up my end of the deal.

The next day I hopped a flight back to Paris. From there I planned to go straight on to Calvi, but my flight had been delayed and I got in too late to make the connection. That meant I'd be another day late to the Legion. Another day late meant more time in jail when I got there. Oh well; I was in Paris—might as well make the best of it.

With what was left of the money I'd won in the fight I treated myself to an opulent meal at Maxim's. The meal would leave me just about broke, but I figured it'd be worth it, and I was right, because the whole time I spent starving in Legion jail I was able to eat that great meal over and over again in my mind.

After dinner I stopped in for drinks at what turned out to be a firemen's bar. I was dressed in my Legion uniform and before I even ordered my first drink, a knot of firemen were all over me with questions. That happened a lot when you went out in uniform. People everywhere were naturally curious about *la Légion étrangère,* and, if you looked at all approachable, someone usually did. I didn't mind the attention, especially when it came from pretty girls, but the firemen were a good enough bunch, and we ended up swapping stories until they said that they had to go. It turned out they were on their way to work a fire security detail at the *Bercy Palais des Sports,* where a martial arts exhibition was being held.

"Man, are there any tickets left? I'd love to go."

"Nah, I hear it's sold out," one of them said.

Then one of the younger firemen came up with an idea. If I wanted to stand in for him in the fire security detail, he and I could swap uniforms. That way I'd get to see the show and he'd get to spend the night shagging his girlfriend.

We changed clothes right there; his friends thought he was nuts, but what could they do, and while he rushed off to his girl I went with the other guys to Bercy. The show was great fun. There were exhibitions with weapons, staged fights, and lots of so-called "masters" up there strutting their stuff.

After the live demonstrations, they showed excerpts from a Van Damme movie called *Lionheart*. In it, Van Damme plays a foreign legionnaire who goes AWOL and gets hunted down by the Legion. Talk about a weird scene. There I was, AWOL from the Legion, watching Van Damme play someone who was AWOL, while right off stage the real Van Damme stood waiting for the film to end so he could come out and take questions from the audience.

After his question-and-answer was over I caught up with Van Damme backstage. It was easy to get at him. Dressed in my firemen's outfit, I slipped past his bodyguards with ease. We talked for about five minutes, and when I told him who I really was I think he must have believed me, because he gave me his phone number at the King George V Hotel and told me to call him in the morning.

The next morning, the first thing I did was go to the firehouse to get back my uniform. The fireman thanked me. My uniform, he told me, had really turned his girlfriend on, and they'd spent a great night playing soldier under the sheets. By that afternoon I was back at the airport, ready to return to Calvi, but first I decided to call Van Damme. I dialed the number he'd given me and he answered, his voice still heavy with sleep. Ah, the movie star's life. Up all

In a fireman's uniform at the *Bercy Palais des Sports.*

night, sleep all day. I spoke with him briefly and hung up. As Van Damme drifted back to sleep I boarded my flight back to hell.

At the airport at Calvi, two MPs spotted me right off.

"Legionnaire Vandenberg," one of them addressed me, "today is your lucky day, because today you don't have to pay the twenty francs for a taxicab back to camp, because today, we are your taxi. Now let's go. Move it, asshole!"

I followed them out to the Jeep, fully expecting to get punched, kicked or ambushed, but the MPs laid off. They just drove me onto the base and delivered me into a piss-soaked Legion cell where I sat for two days before the colonel would see me. When my turn finally came to pass report I was ready. I marched into the colonel's office, stopped three steps away from his desk, exactly as the rules required, and said:

> *Légionnaire de première classe Vandenberg;*
> *trois ans de service;*
> *Première Compagnie, Deuxième Section;*
> *Fonction Grenadier Foltiguer;*
> *à vos ordres, mon colonel.*

"Repos, légionnaire Vandenberg," he answered. "Now, let's hear your story."

Even though I knew the captain had already given him a full report, I told him my story in every detail. Afterward there was a silence that seemed to go on forever. Finally, he spoke:

"You did well, Legionnaire Vandenberg. You fought like a Legion paratrooper is supposed to fight. You're a champion. But you also broke our rules, and rules and discipline must be followed. For leaving France and returning late I usually give a legionnaire sixty days in prison. Since you're an exemplary legionnaire and your captain speaks well of you, I'm only going to give you twenty. Next time you decide to do something like this I want you to let us know in advance so we can give you more leave. Understood?"

"Oui, mon colonel."

I came to attention, saluted, and was promptly marched off to jail.

Le Continent Noir

"The Dark Continent."

Central African Republic was no place for a soldier wearing the uniform of a European military power. The locals despised us. In Bangui they threw stones. In Bouar, where I was stationed, they robbed and beat us whenever they could, and it wasn't uncommon to see legionnaires stumbling back into camp naked and bloody after too hard a night on the town. Even the local black army cadres, the *Forces armées centrafricaines* or FACAs, whom we trained and outfitted, hated us. They resented our money, our skill and command. In a classic case of postcolonial turnabout, they yearned to rise up and become the oppressors themselves.

Everyone, it seemed, was looking to dominate. You could feel it like an itch that half the damn continent was trying to scratch. The Hutu. The Tutsi. The rebels. The dictators. Even the reformers. All had slipped fingers to the triggers of their guns and it didn't take a genius to see that death was coming. Soon men would fall like leaves to rot untended on the ground, and women would howl and writhe with grief before they too died upon the sword. For the survivors there would be no appeasement and hundreds of thousands would be exterminated before the warring parties finally exhausted themselves and settled into an uneasy truce that wasn't so much peace as prelude to yet another round of killing madness.

In the calm before the storm we went about our business the same as usual. The hundred or so of us who were in Bouar had no idea of what was coming, and most, if they'd known, would have cheered. To your average gung-ho legionnaire the problem wasn't war, but peace—too much peace. During my time in the Legion I met men who'd spent their entire lives jumping from one army to another in search of an honest war. Later, when heavy fighting broke out in Bosnia, I heard there were men who deserted from the Legion just to go. "Surfing the war zones" it was called, and if, before you died, you'd been able to catch just one good wave you were considered lucky.

Shopping for food in Central Africa.

So far, I'd been almost three months in Africa with nothing much to do but train and drink. After I got out of jail, the Legion sent me to Bouar with the Fourth Section of the Fourth Company. We were a sniper/destructor unit, but with little to snipe and nothing to destruct the Fourth lent me to the Béret Rouge, a regular unit of the French army also stationed in Bouar.

The Béret Rouge put me to work driving a garbage truck. It wasn't such a bad gig, really. I had two French army privates working under me, the trash run was easy, and there was always plenty of cold African beer waiting when the day's haul was through. All in all, it was a lot better than jail, and at least it kept me busy, so that I didn't have to spend all day brooding over the fact that I was in the Legion instead of fighting in the ring where I belonged.

I thought a lot about my victory in Thailand; it hadn't been an easy one, but I knew that given time I'd get better. Another year of constant practice and I'd be back in perfect form. Only one thing blocked my progress: my damned contract with the Legion—there were still two years to go.

I aimed the trash truck straight ahead and slammed the pedal to the floor. The truck roared and surged, garbage flew, and seat springs chattered as we bounded down the rutted road.

"Sir?" One of the French privates shouted over the engine noise.

"What?"

"I don't think they're going to move," he said, pointing at the three African men who sat cross-legged in the road around a giant blaring boom box.

"They'll move," I said blasting the horn and bearing down.

I wasn't going to stop. I knew what they were up to. The locals often sat in the middle of roads, forcing convoys to a halt. It was one of their favorite scams. When you stopped they either tried to rob you, or you had to bribe them to get them to move aside. I had my first leave coming up the next day. If I stopped and got into any kind of hassle I'd lose my leave for sure. No thanks. I'd rather run the bastards down. Not that I thought it would come to that. In a game of chicken against my truck, I was pretty sure they'd be the ones to blink. And I was right. At the last possible second they jumped out of the way—not fast enough, though, to save their boom box, which went to pieces under the wheels of the truck. As I spend off I glanced back in the rearview. The Africans were up and hopping mad. Fuck 'em, I thought. Serves 'em right.

"You're a hard man, aren't you?" The black whore snaked a hand around my waist while her other went for my balls. I closed my eyes and for about ten seconds surrendered to the rising feeling, but then I pushed her away. I wasn't there to fuck. My buddies and I had come to the bar to drink and get wild. It wasn't often that we got to let off steam together, and the eight of us who had leave that night were already whistling like teakettles. Inside the mud-floored, thatched-roofed hut that passed for a bar in these parts we drank, danced, laughed, and bellowed. The French Army regulars had left long ago. They knew that when we legionnaires were out to get wild it was best not to get in our way. The twenty or so FACAs in the bar that night, though, had no such reservations. They hated us and wanted to fight, and the anger showed hard in their eyes.

It started like it usually does—over a woman. A FACA tried to steal a whore away from a legionnaire. Feelings got hurt, egos bruised, and the next thing I knew there was a blood-stunning crack as one of the FACAs brought a chair down on a legionnaire's head. The legionnaire crumpled, and a second later the whole bar went to war. I did a two-step on one FACA's head, then took out a second and a third, all the time moving toward the legionnaire who was laid out on the floor. By the time I reached him, the FACAs were on him like flies. In a crunchy half-second one of their boots found his face. In another minute they'd stomp him to death. I grabbed a chair and swung out, clearing a path to the legionnaire. Then, before the FACAs could close, I threw the legionnaire over my shoulder and fought my way out of the bar.

As soon as I backed through the front door, the bouncer, who'd been waiting outside, jumped on my back. Jumping me from behind was one of the worst ideas the bouncer ever had because as soon as I got to my feet I punched him several times in the face and followed up with a hard back fist to his throat. The bouncer flailed and fell onto a barbecue stand that toppled under his weight, spilling hot coals everywhere. When the bouncer landed face first in the coals and didn't move I got worried that I might have killed him, but when, a second later, he rose and ran screaming into the night, his face sizzling like bacon, I heaved a sigh of relief.

As I lifted the unconscious legionnaire back onto my shoulder, the rest of my mates came rushing out of the bar. "Let's go!" they shouted. "Run for it." But just as we turned to make our escape, from out of nowhere a fusillade of stones began to rain down on us. We scrambled for cover and stared into the darkness. Somewhere out there dozens of rock-throwing Africans had set up a barrage. Now we were in real trouble. Inside, the FACAs were roaring for our blood, while outside the villagers waited in over-whelming numbers. Whichever way we went we'd be fucked, so I considered it a real stroke of genius when one of the legionnaires clambered up onto the roof and set fire to the bar. The thatched huts caught quickly and soon a large portion of the village was burning out of control.

While the villagers rushed to save their homes and the FACAs ran to escape the blaze, we slipped off into the night. The next day, the legionnaire who started the fire was given thirty days in the Plot and I was sent back out on garbage detail. Good thing I wore a personal sidearm, because as soon as we backed into the dump I could see there was going to be trouble. The locals were everywhere: hiding in the grass, standing in the road, dotting the trash hills. There must have been close to a hundred, all of them armed with sharpened sticks, bows, arrows, rocks, spears, knives. The French army privates begged for me to slip the truck into gear and get out of there. But I wasn't going to run. I knew how to handle a mob. A mob of men is like a pack of wild dogs—it never attacks against strength. I figured as long as I showed that I wasn't afraid and wouldn't run I'd be okay. I drew my weapon and ordered the privates to stay in the truck. They were so scared they couldn't even find the spit to answer, "Yes, sir."

As I climbed out of the cab, the Africans surrounded me. They stood in shivery readiness, every one of them eager to kill me; it was just a question of which one would have the nerve to strike first. When one of them set arrow to bow and cocked the arrow back I ticked my pistol at him like an accusatory finger. "Uh-uh," I warned. He lowered the bow and I nodded. It meant I'd won the first round, but I still had a long way to go. As I walked to the back of the truck, the Africans watched me like a cobra eyes his charmer, or a tiger his trainer. With their eyes boring into my back I pulled the pins that held the garbage bin in place and dumped my load of trash.

When, finally, I climbed back into the cab of the truck and slammed the door, whatever spell my presence had cast was instantly broken. As I slipped the transmission into gear the mob exploded, and before the truck had even moved a foot, every window had been shattered and angry hands were reaching up to tear us down. Like ants on a carcass they swarmed over the truck, some refusing to let go until we hit the open road and picked up speed.

I reported the incident to the Béret Rouge and for the next few days they suspended the garbage run. A week later I was called back to service with the Legion. Our section was being sent into the field.

The VLRA trucks bounced down the pitted trail. We'd been traveling for weeks, every day going deeper into the jungle. It was all around us now in a riot of unimagined shapes and life forms. When the thin trail on which we traveled gave out, we set up camp, left a few men to guard the trucks, and continued on foot.

We marched for another week, all the time improving our jungle survival skills, but no matter how proficient we became we knew we'd never be as good as whoever was out there shadowing our trail. Sometimes we'd almost see them in a flit of jungle movement or by the light of our night fires. But even our best pickets, night rovers, and patrollers couldn't catch them in the act of watching us, and it wasn't until we accidentally stumbled on their village that we found out why. They turned out to be Pygmies, a tribe of men so silent and surefooted that they could actually sneak to within arms length of a wild animal without being detected.

As we marched into their village their leader came out to meet us. He was old, with a white beard stretching almost to his belly, but what really caught my eye was not his beard but his skin; he was a white man, a European, who'd been living with the Pygmies for almost twenty years. As soon as he saw us he snapped to with a flawless salute. Our section leader answered with a flourish of his own, and in no time he and the old man were chatting like a couple of long-lost friends. I was amazed; our section leader was a hardcore soldier, and until now I'd never once seen him try to bond with anyone; to him everything was always by the book. But, as I would soon learn, when it came to this old man there could be no book. What there was instead was life, gloriously lived, exactly as you knew it ought to be.

According to the old man, we were the first white people he'd seen in six years, the last being another column of legionnaires who like ourselves had come this way by accident. Since the old man knew we were coming, (his Pygmy scouts had warned him), he graciously invited us to stay and join his people in a feast.

That night, the old man shared some of the truths that life in the jungle had taught him: "No matter who you meet, remember, he is you. As you treat him, you treat yourself. As you see him, you see yourself. He is always you, and all that you are or ever hope to become is to be found or lost through him."

As I listened to the old man speak I began to realize what a different jungle he lived in than the rest of us. Where I saw a raw and howling violence, he saw a world of moral sympathy. Where I might raise a gun to kill it, he unfolded his heart to love it. "It's the only way," he said, "to jump clear of the clockwork, and live as we were meant to live by God. Just look at the Pygmies; their life is like a song. They don't defend; they don't explain. They move through every day like an act of pure creation. I know you must look at us and think that we're some kind of throwbacks—that the world has passed us by. That's what I first thought when I came here as a missionary and tried to convert these people to Christ. But, after nearly twenty years here, I've come to believe that it's the rest of the world that's been lost and this right here is grace."

When I asked him what he would do if men ever tried to come and harm him or his tribe, he answered that even though there was no way he could ever bring himself to hurt another human being, he understood that sometimes violence in the service of righteousness was itself a holy act. "There have been many times in history when the path of the holy man and the path of the warrior have crossed. Really, I think the two are both necessary; like a fist and an open hand, each has its place in life."

That night it took all my willpower not to run into the jungle and hide until the legionnaires had gone. I knew that eventually the men I'd warned him of would come. With guns and chainsaws they would bring calamity to the Pygmies and their ways, and when that time came I wanted to be there, ready to fight—an iron fist to the old man's open hand. But it was not to be, and a few days later we left the deep jungle.

Leaving the old man had been hard, and the thought that I still hadn't found my true place in life began to trouble me again, expropriating all other thoughts, until it became my only thought. As we bounced down dusty African roads I took to envying the old man. In the jungle, among his Pygmies, the old man had found his bliss. But what of me? The only place I'd ever known bliss was in the ring. Take me out of the ring and I became a stranger even to myself. Without the spark of single combat, I could sense the magnetic core inside me charging down, and I knew it was only a matter of time before I'd need the jump-start of another major fight to get me going.

That night we made camp next to a small village. We'd stopped near many African villages, but never before had I heard them play such music. It was a wonderful, rich sound that drifted out over our encampment, with subtle halftones like the wings of birds, and pounding rhythms that reminded me of rain and running beasts. It spoke directly to my soul, and after serving my turn at guard I woke three of my friends and together we walked into the village.

As soon as the villagers saw us they greeted us with drinks and chairs, put tam-tams in our hands, and invited us to make music with them. After a long day of tortured thought, it was the perfect tonic, and soon I was deep in musical conversation with people with whom I'd never shared a word. Later, when I looked up and saw a villager sprawled in the dirt a little ways off, I thought he must be drunk, but when I saw him groaning and twitching uncontrollably, I put aside my tam-tam and went over. I shined my flashlight in his face. His eyes caught the light and gave back nothing.

"Got the falling sickness," one of the few villagers that spoke a little French explained. "Die soon."

"Yes, very soon," I said kneeling down to offer what comfort I could. I didn't understand it. One of their own was dying and they didn't seem to care. I tried to imagine how the dying man must feel, left to lie in the middle of the street while all around him people partied as if he weren't even there. How awful it had to be for him to see with his last sight that the only person who cared enough to stop and hold his hand wasn't a member of his family or his tribe, but a stranger, a soldier, whom he'd never seen before. I stayed with him until my friends insisted it was time to go. "Come on," one of them finally said, "forget him. Everybody dies alone."

I got up and walked back to camp, the whole time thinking about my friend's remark. There was no denying its truth. We're born alone. We die alone. That's just the way it is. I guess what makes it so hard to face though, is the loneliness that comes between the two, and the nothingness that comes after, and any man who can stare those two naughts in the eye without flinching is a tougher man than I will ever be.

We arrived back in Bouar, and before we even had time to unpack the entire base was mobilized for an emergency intervention. A rebel army had risen up against the government of Rwanda; there was wholesale slaughter in the streets of Kigali, where many Americans, French, Belgians, and Canadians lived. Our orders, as the closest available fighting force, were to go in, secure the airport, and rescue any and all foreign nationals.

Within hours of getting the call we were on our way by air to Rwanda. Packed into the back of several Transalls, our force of about 120 men was armed to the teeth. Before we took off, FAMAS rifles, light machine guns, rockets, repeating rifles, antitank weapons, and grenades had been passed out like candy, and Jeeps armed with machine cannons had been driven into the bellies of the planes. Almost everyone carried extra bandoleers for the machine cannons, and we all wore backpacks stuffed to bursting with spare munitions and supplies.

As the Transalls began their descent into Rwanda we tensed for debarkation. We all knew it was far too dangerous for the Transalls to come to a stop. Instead, they would disgorge their cargo of men and machines as they taxied. We'd literally be hitting the ground running.

None of us were sure what we'd be facing when we got there. Radio contact with the Rwandan army had been sporadic at best. Last we'd heard they were still in possession of the airport, but that had been hours ago. If the airport was hot the landing could get ugly. Out on the runways we'd be sitting ducks for any fire put on us, and there was a good chance that we'd take heavy casualties. At least we had the night on our side. Coming in under cover of darkness would make it hard for them to pick targets while we, outfitted with night vision scopes and sights, would be able to see and shoot on the move.

Luckily for us, elements of the ragtag Rwandan army were still holding the airport when we touched down, and except for two broken ankles suffered as men jumped from the moving planes we landed without a hitch. After securing the airport we left a small force including the injured men to hold it and headed into the city in trucks commandeered from the Rwandans.

According to information we'd received while in the air, many of the foreign nationals had already gathered at the International French School. Our orders were to secure the school, then use it as a base of operations from which to run rescue sorties into other areas of the city. The distance from the airport to the school was about 5 kilometers and we covered it without incident. Though we all heard the sounds of fighting and explosions in the distance, none of it seemed close enough to pose any direct danger to us. Still, when we got close to the school we proceeded according to plan by debarking from the trucks, infiltrating the grounds and then falling into the buildings in a hostage-rescue-style assault.

For our trouble we gained nothing. The school was completely empty and there was no one anywhere in sight. We immediately went to work setting up our defenses. Perimeter trenches were dug, makeshift bunkers were thrown up, and lines of fire were defined for all the men. Then, after all our mortars and machine guns were set in place, the order of the guard was established. By now all of us were dead tired. While the first guard took his duty, I lay down inside a schoolroom to catch a few hours of sleep. I don't know how long I dozed—it couldn't have been more than an hour—when all of a sudden the windows above my head exploded in a shower of glass.

"*Réveillez-vous! Réveillez-vous, légionnaires!*" the lieutenant shouted as we grabbed our weapons and scrambled to our posts. As I fell into my foxhole a mortar round landed nearby. A moment later, my friend Diaz jumped in beside me.

"See anything?" he whispered as I peered into the darkness through my night scope.

"Nothing." I answered and ducked back down just as a tree behind us exploded in a hail of automatic weapon fire. This was it, the thing we'd all been training for—from the ball-shriveling thump of the mortars, to the ping and thwack of angry bullets, to the light of tracers kindling the sky—this was war!

There was only one thing missing. One thing, but it kept the whole thing from being perfect. We couldn't find the enemy. Not one of us could locate a single target, and we didn't return fire the whole night. It said a lot about our training. Here we were, men under enemy fire for the first time, and not one of us panicked or gave away his position by firing on impulse or out of fear. We all just sat with fingers heavy on our triggers, waiting for the enemy to show. And, when he never came, and the shooting finally sputtered out, it left us feeling disappointed and frustrated, like fucking without coming all night long.

It wasn't until first light, when we went out and surveyed the area around the school, that any of us understood why we hadn't been attacked. It turned out that we hadn't been the real target in the battle; we'd just been caught in a crossfire between the Rwandan army and a sizable rebel force. The proof was in the streets: There were bodies everywhere. The ground was black with them, and the air was already growing heavy with their smell.

Eventually, the sights and smells of death that confronted us that morning would become routine. As we went out, day after day, searching the city for foreign nationals, finding them, shuttling them to the school, and from there to the airport, it got so that we barely noticed anymore that it was a corpse, or a limb, or a mangled bit of torso that we stepped over as we went about our task, and, if not for the looks of shock and horror on the faces of those we rescued as they eyed the grisly carnage, we wouldn't even have noticed the dead at all.

After three days of searching the city and finding hundreds of foreigners, our job seemed pretty much done. A few days later the French Béret Rouge and Belgian paratroopers were brought in and most Legion sections were reassigned to bodyguard duty. It now became our job to protect the rich sons of bitches, politicians, and ambassadors who'd created this mess in the first place. For most of them life went on pretty much as before, only now, instead of their usual retinue of butlers, servants, gardeners, and livery staff, they had us. The whole thing made me sick, and I was glad when I was reassigned again, this time to a Jeep patrol that guarded the road between the airport and the city.

The airport road passed through some pretty rough terrain, and for anyone with half a mind to stage an ambush the three of us in our open Jeep would have made for easy pickings. Not that we were especially worried. The fighting had long since moved to the outskirts of the city and beyond, and it didn't look like we'd be seeing any kind of action for the rest of our posting.

One day, while out on patrol over a patch of mountain road, we heard shouting and ululation's coming from a native village nestled in the valley below. When we stopped to investigate, at first we thought the villagers were engaged in some sort of game or native ritual. The entire population of the village was in the streets. From our perch up on the road we could see them—men, women, even children, slashing at the air with sticks and machetes as they wheeled about the town in groups wide enough to block the streets. Then all at once we realized why.

The villagers had discovered four soldiers trying to pass through their village. The soldiers, one of whom was a women, looked as if they'd been wounded in battle and then abandoned by their troops. They were weaponless and haggard, and made easy prey for the villagers, who by now had trapped the soldiers in the maze of village streets. When the soldiers would run one way, village women watching from the rooftops would shout, and, blocks ahead, others would form ranks to bar the soldiers' path. Back and forth the soldiers ran, down one blind alley after another, the noose around them growing ever tighter as the villagers closed in.

I'd faced all kinds of rage before, and angry mobs as well. I'd felt the hunger for vengeance knot my belly as strong as any man, but what I saw being played out in that village went far beyond all that. This was cruelty in its most naked form, I thought as I watched the villagers pelt the soldiers with small stones, trash, and fresh-laid heaps of their own steaming shit. This was pure evil, I became convinced when I saw a child run up and jab one of the wounded soldiers in the belly with a sharpened stick while his mother watched and cheered. This was hate, and worse than hate, because the villagers were actually enjoying their grim work, and like all things deeply pleasurable they were trying hard to make it last.

As legionnaires we'd been told not to interfere in local conflicts. We'd been given strict orders never to fire our weapons unless our lives were under threat, but this was beyond all such orders.

"Let's waste the bastards! Let's kill them all!" I shouted and jumped up on the Jeep. Mounted on the back was a machine cannon capable of firing 740 rounds a minute in unlimited bursts. At that moment I didn't know which ones down there were the Hutu or the Tutsi, and I didn't care. I just wanted to purge the evil in that village with my own holy fire. Like one of God's avenging angels I was ready to cleanse and punish with a stroke, and, if not for one of my clearer-headed buddies, I would have done just that.

"Wait! Don't do it, man. We got to call this in," he insisted. So I stood and watched and waited for instructions from above while down below the slow torture of the soldiers went on and on and on.

"We're to stand firm and not fire," my buddy said after talking with HQ. I stared at him like one of us was nuts. "Here, you want to talk to them?" he said, offering me the phone. I shook my head no, dropped my hands off the cannon, and walked away.

Down below, the villagers finally closed in on the soldiers and hacked them to death. Afterward, I watched them dance on the dead bodies until many of the revelers were splattered to their waists in human blood.

A week later we shipped back to Bangui in Central Africa. All in all, our unit had done well, and except for one legionnaire who'd lost an arm in a grenade explosion during an attack on the airport we'd come through without any major casualties. Down deep, of course, we'd all been wounded. We'd seen an entire nation goaded into a self-annihilating frenzy by envy and race hatred. We'd seen war brought to a large city and come face to face with men who were willing to wage it. How it's possible fight against such men without becoming like them I don't know, because a war like this remakes everything it in its image—the living, the dead, the righteous, and the wronged. This war spared no one and nothing from its horrors.

Le Cafard

A kind of madness, part violence, part grief, that can possess a legionnaire at any time.

I stood in the hot sandy bucket of the tower and watched ribbons of flame turn to mountains of stone. From the tower, the newly formed mountains shone like tomb- stones in a graveyard after dark. Above me, black clouds rustled hatefully across the sky, stampeding the moon. "Dominiquie." I heard my name drift in on a dirty curl of wind, and watched the desert come alive with the ghost of every carcass that had ever fertilized her soil. They bent to- ward me like wheat, their backs forming a bony carapace, their hands furrowing the sand as they came. I unshoul- dered my FAMAS and started screaming.

Hallucination . . . it was another hallucination. I set down my FAMAS until the trembling passed. I'd been awake for almost forty hours, and, before that, who knows. Certainly not the dead who littered this pathetic country. Chad. I was in Chad, and had been for nearly two months. My God, how much longer could I last?

We'd been sent into Chad not long after Rwanda. A week or so in Bangui, another two in Bouar, and then it was straight on to Chad for another intervention. The country, it seemed, had devolved into chaos, and once again the European big brother was being sent in to hold hands, and, failing that, to kick ass. I didn't know about the hand-holding, but we were all set to deliver the ass-kicking. In addition to the Fourth Section, which I flew in with, the Legion sent in the Second Company and half of the Third as well. They would have sent more, but Saddam Hussein had been rattling cages, and with things in Kuwait getting uglier by the day the Legion couldn't spare another man.

Our mission in Chad had a familiar ring to it: rescue any and all foreign nationals who wanted rescuing, when possible disarm the populace, and at night enforce the curfew. Good thing they packed amphetamines into our ration packs, because without them there was no way the mere two hundred of us that had been sent into Chad could hope to accomplish all that.

As soon as we touched down at the French Air Force base outside N'Djamena we knew we'd stepped deep in the shit. Parts of the city were in flames; there was rioting everywhere. The day before we arrived a white school-teacher had been held down and raped in front of her class and a French diplomat had been killed in the street. The blame for all this, if you listened to official French reports, lay with Idriss Déby. His rebel army was at war with the Chadian government of President Hissène Habré. But did that make Déby our enemy? Well, not exactly. According to the politicians and the international diplomats who specialized in this sort of doublethink, even though the French government favored President Habré, officially we were neutral and would support whoever won this civil war. Theoretically, that meant that while we were in Chad we had no real enemies. In practice, though, it meant that everyone was our foe.

Minutes after landing at the airfield we climbed onto VLRA trucks and drove to the Béret Bleu base in the heart of the city. On a good day it might take all of ten minutes to get from one base to the other, but today was not one of those days. Without police or soldiers to maintain order, the poor people of the city were having a holiday. Nearly every store and home we passed was in the process of being or had just been looted, and the streets were filled with trails of people carrying couches, tables, and whole bedroom sets away. To me they looked like an army of ants after a raid on a picnic lunch, but to the shopkeepers and homeowners whose stores and homes they'd looted they must have looked far worse.

Once safely inside the Béret Bleu base we were given our billet and brought up to speed on the situation confronting us:

"It's a big fucking mess everywhere and there's not a fucking thing you can do about it," one of the Bleus informed us. "So keep your heads down, do as little as possible, and if you do get into any kind of shit don't look to us to save your asses, 'cause we don't give a flying fuck; we just want to get out of here in one piece."

It sounded like a load of shit to me, not the Legion way of doing things, but then again the Bérets Bleus had been here for a while and maybe they knew something we didn't.

We spent the rest of that day checking over our weapons and getting everything squared up for action. We'd been billeted next to the camp infirmary and what we saw there wasn't encouraging. All through the day wounded soldiers of the Chadian army were brought through the gates and dumped on the ground outside the infirmary where they lay, some without arms, others

On patrol in Chad.

without legs or eyes, to bleed and beg and moan for medical attention. Our medics did what they could, but none of them had been prepared for this, and despite their round-the-clock efforts with scalpels and thread, the crush of bodies waiting for attention continued to grow.

That night we took to the streets in our trucks to enforce the curfew. In the morning we went out again, this time on foot, to do house-to-house searches for weapons and munitions. This became our routine. By night we'd drive around, arresting whom we could and chasing off the rest; by day we'd invade houses, rousting whomever we found. We were supposed to be keeping the peace, but after a month of kicking down doors and pushing guns into people's faces I felt more like a thug than a peacekeeper, and a damned tired thug too. During that whole first month I don't think any of us got more than three or four hours sleep a night. At least we didn't have to search too hard for the foreign nationals. Most of them had queued up for outbound flights during the opening days of the trouble, and many of those who hadn't were already settled in temporary quarters at the air force base.

I thought of the foreign nationals all snug and comfy in

their air force cots. What I wouldn't have given to sleep a whole night through. The round-the-clock grind was getting to us, and the men were growing twitchier and sloppier by the day. Not good when there's a war going on, even though all we ever seemed to see of the war were its remains: the blasted trucks and black smoke of tires burning in the street; the bullet-riddled bodies of the injured and the dead; the crying children, hollow buildings, and open, unmarked graves.

Now and then we'd leave the town for the harshness of the desert. On a lead, or an instinct, or an inside tip we'd travel into Chad's lunar hills to search for hidden weapons. What we found there amazed us. Bunkers full of automatic weapons, rockets, and rations, abandoned—the latest in military hardware direct from Russia and the United States piled higher than a man could reach and left to rot. Once, we even uncovered a fully outfitted Russian helicopter hidden in a deserted hangar. Who'd left all this, I wondered? The rebels? The army? It was impossible to tell. Chadian army units were defecting or abandoning their posts all the time, while rebel forces, deprived of booty or easy victories, could collapse overnight. From Chadian generals to soldiers to mercenaries, the war was a complicated game of deceit and cross-purposes with everyone struggling to line up on the winning side before the play was through.

Whoever won, I knew it wasn't going to be us. The Second and Third Legion elements had already taken casualties from sniper fire. Snipers were the last thing we needed. Now, in addition to everything else, we all walked around with that pinched feeling in the back of our necks from jerking our heads at every sound.

We were clearing a village house by house, following the usual routine—except, now that legionnaires had been killed, nothing would be usual again. Even our curfew runs had gotten more intense. While driving down a street a few nights before, we'd spotted a four-by-four and forced it off the road. In perfect syncopation, the result of weeks of constant practice, Master Corporal Gel took the right door and I took the left, while Legionnaire Scaller covered us with his FAMAS. As I yanked open the door and pointed my weapon at the passenger, an AK-47 dropped from behind his seat. "They're armed!" I shouted as I clubbed the passenger with the cross of my FAMAS and pulled him to the ground, while on the other side Master Corporal Gel did the same. Inside the Jeep, in addition to the AK we found a dozen RPGs. But the real score came when we found the diplomatic passport that belonged to a Frenchman who'd been killed. Were these his killers? It looked that way to us, but we left it to the generals to decide, and after delivering our captives to headquarters we went back out on night patrol—three hardcore soldiers dead set on doing our job.

Things didn't always go down so clean and easy. A few days after catching the killers I was sent out on a house-to-house search. With me were two green legionnaires straight out of the Second Company, both novices who'd never seen action before. As I kicked in the door to yet another house they came rushing in behind me. The house was small, only one room. Inside, two black men stood holding Kalashnikov rifles. The instant they saw us they dropped their rifles and threw up their hands, but not fast enough for the trigger-happy legionnaires from Second Company. As soon as the legionnaire on my left stepped through the door he opened fire. His FAMAS was set for full automatic and before I could move a muscle he blasted one of the Africans from ankle to belly. As the African dropped, the legionnaire on my right brought his FAMAS to bear on the other African. "No!" I screamed, pushing his gun barrel up toward the ceiling before he could let loose with a burst. Figuring he was going to die anyway, the remaining African made a move for his rifle. Luckily, I was close enough to him that I didn't have to shoot him. Instead, I stepped in, kicked him in the face and cracked him in the head with my rifle butt. That put him down long enough for us to collect their weapons and secure the house.

While I tended to the injured man, the other two stood gawking like the fuck-ups they were. They didn't seem to realize that they'd just shot a man for nothing, or maybe they did but were too high on the rush of first blood to care.

A few days later I was transferred over to bodyguard duty. Just like in Rwanda, there were plenty of rich assholes in Chad who refused to leave their colonial estates. As soon as I saw the house on which we'd drawn guard I knew why. The place was a palace, with intricate gardens, pools, and opulent high-ceilinged rooms hung with hunting trophies and original oils. No wonder the owners didn't want to leave it and risk having everything plundered.

For the next week I spent my nights sleeping poolside and my days guarding a gate through which no one ever passed. Thanks to the owners, who cooked for us all, I dined on meals of *fois gras* with *cornichons,* roast venison, *cassoulets,* and game hen stewed in wine. It was delicious and I never wanted to leave, except of course when the owners asked us to go into town to scavenge for groceries.

One afternoon, the lieutenant, a driver, and I were coming back from town, our VLRA truck full of market goods waiting to be turned into that night's delectations, when the lieutenant spotted a heavily armed Toyota truck packed with rebel soldiers.

"Cut 'em off. Pull 'em over," the lieutenant ordered the driver, who shook his head in disgust then did as he was ordered.

The Toyota screeched to a halt as we cut it off. I don't think the rebels quite believed what they were seeing as the lieutenant climbed out of the truck and walked up to the leader of their band.

"You'll have to surrender your weapons if you want to travel in this district," the lieutenant shouted at the rebel leader.

While the rebel leader stared at the lieutenant and then at the two of us, I made a quick count of their number; I'd gotten up to twelve when the rebel leader spoke. "Who the fuck do you think you are, you stupid French asshole." He hadn't even finished the sentence when all at once I heard a dozen AK-47s lock and load, and saw the barrel of the heavy machine gun mounted behind the cab swivel until it was pointed straight at me.

The driver and I armed our guns and aimed them at the rebels. I was carrying an M-52; the driver had his FAMAS. Both solid guns, but against that wall of weapons we didn't stand a chance.

"We're not giving up our weapons," the rebel leader said. "You are."

For the next ten seconds no one spoke or moved a muscle. Ten seconds but they seemed like forever. I figured I was dead, and hoped at least I'd get the chance to go down firing.

Finally, the lieutenant spoke. "Tell your men not to shoot." Then he backed up until he was standing next to me. "Disarm," he ordered. I didn't move an inch. "Disarm!" he barked again. The driver glanced over at me then slowly lowered his FAMAS. But I would not shoulder my weapon; I just stood there holding my M-52 rock-steady on the rebels. "Legionnaire First Class Vandenberg, did you hear me? I said disarm!" And still I didn't move.

"Vandenberg, disarm the weapon." This time it was the driver speaking, his voice soft and plaintive. But I would not disarm, not as long as there were a dozen loaded weapons pointed at me.

My adversaries were close—close enough for me to see their eyes, and what I saw there didn't encourage me. These weren't the eyes of men; they were the stony cold optics of insects, the compounded terrors of a heart-stopping dream. Too much war had made them that way, and now too much war would cure them, at least some of them—the ones I killed, that is—before the rest of them blew me away. I wondered how many of those eyes I would see again in hell.

The rebel leader began yammering in dialect at his troops. "Vandenberg, goddammit—" The Lieutenant started in on me again, but before he could shout another word the rebels shouldered their arms, sat down in their truck, and drove away.

That night we sat down to another exquisite meal. Though I chewed the food and swallowed, I didn't taste a thing.

A few days later we were transferred back to the Béret Bleu base. While guarding the estate we'd been out of radio contact with HQ, so it came as a shock when we learned that the Chadian government had fallen and the rebels were now in control of the country.

"When did it happen?" I asked. They gave me a date and I counted back, and that's when I knew that the rebels we'd stopped and faced down in that street weren't rebels at all, but the official army of the newly constituted government of Chad. Though we didn't know it at the time, they could have shot us where we stood and been well within their rights.

Despite the change in government, life went on pretty much as before. The wind still blew, the sun still burned, the desert hid her secrets. At least we'd stopped hunting for illegal weapons and now spent most of our time pulling guard duty or doing work around the base. I thought the change in duties would make our lives easier, but just the opposite was true. The endless hours spent standing alone in isolated guard towers turned out to be maddening. The work we did on base was boring, and at the same time exhausting, because the Legion still pushed us around the clock.

One day, a group of us were standing in a chow line waiting for our turn at lunch. The usual banter was going on: friendly ribbing between us and the Bleus about which of us was tougher, meaner, and harder than the other; like they even stood a chance. Except for the Tahitians in their ranks, who still had a bit of the Polynesian warrior spirit left in them, the Bleus were a sorry lot without any of our flash or soldierly *savoir faire.* Still, we were enjoying the manly give-and-take when suddenly the burst of a machine cannon discharging at close range sent us all into a state of red alert. The machine cannon had only fired for a second, but a second was all it took to blow the head off a Tahitian standing not five feet from me.

Like everyone else I hit the ground and crawled for cover, but not another shot was fired. It wasn't until later, after a full investigation had been made, that we learned the reason for that soldier's death. It turned out that an exhausted Legion master corporal had grabbed hold of the machine cannon as he was boarding a VLRA truck. Apparently, the cannon was armed, the safety off, and the weapon had discharged when he accidentally touched the trigger. Now we legionnaires had another enemy to worry about, because the Tahitians didn't care that it was an accident. All they knew was that one of their own was dead, a legionnaire had done it, and now we were going to pay. It was only a question of when.

That night, many legionnaires and Blue Berets were given leave to go off base. Since *le Rose dans le Vent* was just about the only bar in Chad where a Western soldier could get safely drunk, the bulk of us fell in there. The place was pretty much what you'd expect of a soldier's bar in Africa: take an old blaring juke box, toss it inside a dingy bunker, add some roughed-up wooden tables and a couple of prehistoric chairs, and *voilà*—you've got a bar.

"I'm telling you, even if we gave these sand niggers everything they wanted they'd figure out a way to fuck it up."

"They're not able to run a country; it's genetic. . . ."

I sat, head hunched over my glass and listened to my buddies go on. I didn't need this kind of racist talk. It didn't sit well with the African booze, which was lousy enough by itself. I tuned out what I could and started looking around the bar, where the usual crowd of local whores, pimps, mercenaries, and gun dealers were riding their luck in the undertow.

"What's the smartest thing ever to come out of a bitch's mouth?"

"Einstein's cock."

"Shit, I didn't think you knew that one."

"I know all your jokes, numb-nuts. Gimme a fuckin' break."

Like it always did, my compadres' talk had turned from blacks to bitches. Next would come the urge to fight, and then like clockwork in they walked—a dozen blubbery Tahitians, each one bigger than the last.

"Hey, murderers," they shouted as they passed us on their way to the bar.

Here we go again, I thought. Another jam. Another bar-clearing brawl. It almost made me wish I'd stayed on base. I was getting so tired of this kind of shit that the thought of a nice little house in Belgium with a grinning, wide-beamed wife and maybe a couple of rug rats running around was starting to look good.

The Tahitians stood at the bar and soaked up booze. While the liquor disappeared down their gullets we sat and waited. We knew they were just watering their courage, and that it wouldn't be long before it bloomed into a fight. I wondered as I watched them if they wanted this to be an all-out affair, complete with flying chairs and tables, or if they were after a more dignified row, something perhaps a bit more straight-up and neat.

When one of the Tahitians finally detached himself from his kin and lumbered toward our table I had my answer. This would be a one-on-one fight, a contest of champions between their best man, and—wait, it looked like . . . yes, he was coming toward me. I shot a look of contempt at his subnormal face and watched his ham fists clench. His foreshortened forehead crinkled with effort as he shaped his mouth to speak. "You, stand up. Let's fight," he said to the legionnaire sitting to my left.

So it wouldn't be me after all. Damn! I didn't know whether to feel insulted or relieved, though I did have a fair opinion as to who'd win the upcoming bit of unfriendliness. The Tahitian was a monster, well over six feet, and wide around as a bathtub. The man he'd challenged was the smallest guy at our table. An Englishman by birth, he was maybe all of five foot seven and 140 lbs. As a fighter he didn't look like much, but looks can be deceiving, and what the Tahitian didn't know was that the Englishman had once been a European military boxing champion.

"Come on, you piece of shit, you gonna get up or not?" the Tahitian's voice boomed down from the rafters.

I threw the Englishman a look of concern that was meant as an offer of help.

"No, it's okay," the Englishman said after reading my face. "I can handle it." Then he finished his drink and stood up. "You want to fight me?" he said to the Tahitian.

"Let's take it over there." He gestured toward the dance floor.

The Tahitian nodded and they started toward the dance floor. They hadn't gone three steps when the Englishman spun around and sprang half a dozen good punches straight at the Tahitian's massive jaw. The Tahitian didn't even try to fend them off. He just took them as they came; six straight shots to the face and they didn't even faze him. In fact, the only thing they seemed to do was stoke his anger. Bellowing like an elephant, he stepped back and began unbuttoning his shirt as if the fight hadn't even started yet and the punches were no more than girl slaps.

I had to hand it to the Englishman though, because he didn't lose his cool. He just stood waiting patiently until the Tahitian reached his bottom button, then he stepped in and delivered another lightening flurry to the Tahitian's lug-like face. Again the Tahitian shook it off, but now the Englishman followed up with a move so audacious that up till then I'd only seen it performed on bad TV crime shows. You know, it's the move where the bad guy gains a temporary advantage on the hero by pulling the hero's shirt down around his wrists and then slugging him a few times in the gut. Well, that's what the Englishman did. He reached up and yanked the Tahitian's shirt down, and, while the Tahitian struggled to free his arms from the shirt, the Englishman let lose with everything he had: Fists to the face. Feet to the belly. Head butts to the forehead and chin. It was an impressive display by any account except for the one that mattered because the pummeling didn't even slow the Tahitian down. With his arms still caught in his shirt the Tahitian just dipped his head and charged in a bull rage at the Englishman.

Now, I didn't know about the Englishman, but when I saw that I started to get worried. What the hell would it take to put this guy down? A bazooka? He didn't even

seem human. He was like some kind of comic-book su-
pervillain; you could drop a building on him and he'd just
keep coming.

The Englishman took it in stride; he simply stepped
back and let the Tahitian roar in. Then, when the Tahitian
got good and close he let go with a footballer's punt to the
Tahitian's testicles. The Tahitian collapsed to his knees.
Beautiful! When in doubt, go for the balls. I remembered
Paul Newman in *Butch Cassidy and the Sundance Kid;*
that's what he'd done when faced with a giant. I think it
was the first time in movie history that they'd ever let the
hero fight dirty and I wondered if the Englishman had seen
it. Probably, because now he grabbed a whiskey bottle off a
table and broke it over the Tahitian's head, and when that
didn't work he went back for a chair and broke it.

"Get up! Get up!" the Tahitian's buddies and fellow
Bleus screamed from the sidelines. But the poor fat fuck
did not make it up, because this time the Englishman took
careful aim before booting him square in the face.

The Tahitian went down, this time for good, and before
much else could happen the military police burst in. "All
right, break it up!" came their sharp shouts to the crowd.
As the gawkers drifted off, we told the MPs our story and
the Bleus told them theirs. The MPs' solution was to send
all the Bleus back to camp for the night and to warn us to
keep cool from now on.

They say to the victor belongs the spoils, and we went
at ours with a vengeance. If you had money, which we did,
the bar was a confectionery of delicious dark brown
women with creamy vanilla teeth and supple strawberry
tongues. All you had to do was reach out and pluck one,
and in no time most of us had.

The woman I'd chosen had eyes like a jungle cat
and breasts like two birds in flight. As she sat next to me at
the table, her hot whore's breath on my neck, her hands

rooting at my crotch, I could feel myself drifting in that sweet intermediate zone between arousal and release.

"Let's go to my place, honey," the whore cooed in my ear. "It's not far. I've got a really nice bed."

Maybe it was the way she said it, or maybe it was something else, I don't know, but all at once a premonitory flicker of danger lit the sex-darkened theater of my mind.

"What is it? What's wrong?" the whore asked, thinking maybe it was her, but before I could give her an answer three shots rang out at the bar. The next thing I knew a woman was screaming and a black man fell over dead. For a moment the whole bar went quiet as all eyes flew to the shooter, who quickly turned and walked out the door.

"Gunrunners," my whore told me after the shooter had left. "Happens all the time. Now, you gonna come home with me or what?"

I looked into her cold brown eyes. I had to hand it to her, she was a pro. Through it all her hand hadn't missed a beat at my crotch, and while I wanted very much to slip inside her there was no way I was going to follow her back to the unknown dangers her place held to do it.

"What do you say we go out back and fuck?" I finally suggested.

So we went out to the alley behind the bar and proceeded to do the deed. And it would have been fine as alley fucks go, except that out there among all the trash they'd also dumped the body of the man who'd been shot.

"He dead?" I asked, stepping over him.

"He's dead," she answered after kicking the corpse in the ribs.

We fucked standing up not three feet from the body— two hardened professionals banging away at our hopeless jobs while the eyes of a dead man looked on.

The next morning the entire Legion cohort was transferred off the Béret Bleu base. It seemed the big Tahitian had suffered a bit of brain damage in his fight with the Englishman and the generals figured they better separate our two forces before things between us turned to all-out war.

For the rest of our stay in Chad we pulled round-the-clock guard duty on the far corners of the air force base. I didn't know if the Legion brass was trying to punish us or if they'd just forgotten that we were men and not dogs. But, then, maybe we were dogs. Maybe somewhere along the way we'd become dogs without our even knowing. Maybe that's what the Legion training was all about. After all, only a dog would endure punches and kicks and still come running back to its master. Only a dog would spend its life tethered to a post without complaint. As long as there's food, water, and the occasional bitch a dog will do pretty much what it's told. Sit! Stay! Guard! Attack! There wasn't much in my life as a soldier that a dog couldn't do just as well. So I was a dog—an ill-tempered mongrel left to stand day and night in this faraway tower.

"*Awrooo . . .*" I howled at the moon, barked at the sand, then sniffed at the air like a madman. I clicked the safety off my FAMAS and set it for full automatic. A few days before another legionnaire in another lonely desert tower had done the same thing. Then he'd stripped himself naked, slipped the gun muzzle to his mouth, put his finger on the trigger and . . .

Nothing. I gazed out over the desert and saw nothing. Nothing that mattered. Nothing at all. I cradled my FAMAS in the crook of my arm and felt the soft, comforting curve of her stock. We'd been a long time together, me and my FAMAS; till death do us part as they say. With my free hand I reached for my belt. My FAMAS would never betray me. I undid the belt, tugged at my zipper and let my pants fall to the floor. My FAMAS would always protect me. I ransacked my underwear till I found my dick. My

FAMAS would always be there. I pulled out my dick and gripped it in my palm. I gave it a short tug and then a few more before settling into a monotony of long even strokes.

They say that a stiff prick has no conscience and I certainly hoped they were right. I was in Chad and had been for nearly two months. My God, how much longer could I last?

Kawthoolei

The name the Karen have given to their guerrilla
state. It means "the Promised Land."

Stretched out naked on the hood of the car, her
eyes closed, her lips, like her legs, parted, she
looked beautiful. I stepped out of the car,
stripped off my shirt and jeans, and we made love, our
supple bodies rising and falling until finally they merged.
She was beautiful, I thought as she cupped my hands to
her breasts and guided me back inside the car where we
made love again. Beautiful. Even in this city of beautiful
women, even here in Paris, she was a standout, worth
every penny of the two thousand dollars I'd paid for the
pleasure of her company. "Come on, let's go up to the
room," she whispered in my ear. I gathered up my clothes
and followed blindly.

I'd been in Paris for five days. Five days spent shining
the torch of sex into every cavern of my bat-like soul, and I
still felt as smudged and dark as the day I'd arrived. I'd
had sex on strange floors with even stranger women; I'd

fucked in parks, in beds, on rooftops, in back rooms, bath-tubs, hallways, elevators, and now a backseat with one, two, three, and more. But the places didn't matter, or the numbers either, because all I really wanted was the one. The one whose touch would magically cure me; the one whose voice could erase the ugly screeching I heard inside my head, and whose image could burn away all the bloody snapshots of Africa that I carried deep within me.

As soon as we stepped into the hotel room the whore shrugged her coat to the floor. "Is this what you dreamed of?" she asked, raising a black-gloved finger to her unim-peachable mouth and beginning the slow spectacle of a silent strip tease. I answered her first with my body, which shivered with pleasure, then, as she straddled the bed and greeted me with her lips, I let go with a low, reedy sigh.

That night we made love over and over, and for the next day and night we never left the room. It doesn't come much better than this, I thought, tracing a finger across her sweat-dimpled back. We'd been at it so long I could almost forget that she was a whore and I a legionnaire. Almost for-get that I'd just come from Africa and was on my way to Burma to fight for a little-known guerrilla army. Almost forget, but not quite. As we lay intertwined on the sex-dampened sheets I tried to imagine how we must look from above, so naked, so silent, our arms and legs tangled, just like the bodies I'd seen heaped in mass graves in Africa. Immediately, I pushed the image from my mind, but the bits and pieces of mangled people would not go and the death scene played on with a life of its own. She was a fine woman, this whore, and she and I liked each other as much as we were able, but right then I knew that she wasn't the one.

The next day I boarded a jet bound for Bangkok. From Bangkok I planned to travel to Burma, where I would vol-unteer my services for the next eight weeks of my leave to

Wearing the paratrooper insignia.

the Karen National Liberation Army. I'd heard about the Karen from my Legion friend, Branko. Branko had been fighting alongside the Karen for years. Every time he took leave from the Legion he'd head straight for their territories. "You'll like it," he told me. "It's a place where you can really be yourself because every man, woman, and child there is a soldier."

I knew what Branko meant. One of the hardest things about leave in the Legion was having to go out and face the civilian population. As a legionnaire I'd been trained to kill and it showed. No matter how much I tried to pass myself off as a normal person, everywhere I went people would stop to stare or whisper. "Look at him," they would murmur. "What's his problem?" My problem, of course, was them. They were afraid of me. I could smell it on them like a sour perfume that left me feeling sick and sad. This wasn't the ring. This wasn't battle. These people had nothing to fear from me. All I wanted was to belong. For a few days or weeks I just wanted to pass myself off as one of them. But to them I was some kind of monster. I was Frankenstein's monster in the village, waving his arms and shouting out for a friend while they drove me off with torches and rakes.

With the Karen, my military bearing wouldn't be a problem; there I'd be in my element. Even though it was a completely different culture, I'd belong. No wonder Branko said he planned to settle there permanently after his Legion contract was up.

I started reading what I could about the Karen. There wasn't much. Hidden behind the curtain of silence that had been drawn around Burma, the Karen didn't figure significantly in the chessboard of modern politics. From what I could glean, however, I could see that I'd be fighting for a good cause. The Karen were struggling for independence from an oppressive central government. They wanted the freedom to practice democracy and live in peace with their neighbors. Their ultimate goal was a Burmese federation of all races, something a lot easier said than done.

I landed in Bangkok and headed straight for Marc's bar. Marc, Branko had told me, was the man to see in Thailand. His bar was a clearinghouse for all kinds of wandering mercenaries and local bad boys in search of work or battle.

I walked into the bar at midday and was immediately hit by that same sinking feeling you get when you accidentally catch sight of yourself in a mirror after a few days of hard drinking. The place was a dark, stinking barnyard of beer, tobacco, and pent-up animal rage. From four different TV sets placed high on the walls four different Asian porno tapes blared out a crowing fuck fest of grunts, sighs, whinnies, and groans. As I walked toward the bar, the half-dozen or so Americans that were in there, leftovers from the Vietnam War from the looks of them, eyed me from over their drinks. Dressed in their camouflage fatigues, they looked as if they'd fallen into their seats twenty years ago and hadn't gotten up since, except maybe to piss.

"*Légionnaire parachutiste?*" the man behind the bar said as soon as he saw me.

I nodded and put out a hand. "You sure know your soldiers."

"Radar," he answered, tapping his nose.

We shook hands and exchanged names.

"I'm Marc," he said.

So this was the famous Marc. Dressed in sandals and shorts, his huge belly bursting through the riot of a Hawaiian shirt, he didn't look at all like the ruthless fighter I was expecting.

"Branko sent me."

"Branko, eh?" he asked, not fully believing me. "And just how is Branko?"

When I finally satisfied him that Branko had indeed sent me, Marc finally eased up.

"So, what can I do for you, Dominiquie?"

When I told him that I wanted to hook up with the Karen army he motioned me into the back room. "Dump your shit in the corner; I'll watch it while you're up there. I don't suggest you take anything valuable with you. Just makes you more of a target than you already are." I dropped my duffel where he pointed and watched him rifle through some open shelves. "What size boot you take?" I told him. "Here," he said, throwing me a pair of jungle boots and a set of camouflage fatigues. "These ought to do ya."

I started stripping down to put the stuff on.

"No, over here first." He steered me toward a blank wall, and had me stand and smile for a couple of snapshots. "Come on, try and look like a tourist, would ya? It's for your passport," he explained.

"But I already have a passport."

"No, you don't want to go up there on your own passport. There could be trouble. So, what do you want to be? French? Canadian? American?" He opened a drawer and began pulling out passports. "I think French, don't you?"

"Marc, I appreciate what you're doing for me here, but shouldn't we talk money first? I mean, how much is this going to cost me?"

"Cost you? Hell, it ain't gonna cost you nothing. Any friend of Branko cuts carte blanche with me."

I wondered what Branko had done for Marc to earn me this kind of ride.

"In fact," Marc went on, "I'm even going to show you a way you can make a couple of thousand bucks on the side, help you cover expenses."

Now the free ride was starting to make sense. It was a setup, but for what?

It's easy. All you got to do is carry a package."

"What kind of package? Not drugs?"

"No, no, nothing like that."

I looked at him hard. He raised his hand in the air to swear.

"On my honor, it's only a letter, a dispatch to General Bo Mya."

"General Bo Mya?"

"Yeah, the leader of the Karen, a damn good man. The American who was supposed to run the delivery is sick."

"American? What's his angle in this?"

"Does it matter? All you need to know is you'd be doing him a favor; he'd pay you well."

And he did. A thousand dollars down and a thousand more if I made it back with a return letter from the general.

The next day I took a train to Chiang Mai. From there I traveled to a dilapidated frontier village on the bank of the Moei River. As I walked through the narrow dirt streets of the village, merchants standing in front of open-fronted jumble stalls beckoned for me to stop and buy. For such a backwater outpost, the profusion of goods was stunning. Watches, radios, children's toys, audiocassettes, camcorders, and other modern manufactured goods filled the stalls to overflowing. I even spotted an electric guitar or two, as well as tailor-made European suits being offered for sale. Who bought all this? I wondered as I wandered through the bizarre conglomeration of crap. Certainly not the locals, who looked as if they'd consider the simultaneous possession of a full bowl of rice and a fish head as a sign of sudden wealth.

As I stood by the river and watched a team of barefoot drovers work a herd of unbranded cattle into town it suddenly hit me. Smugglers. That's who all these Western goods were for. The Thai-Burmese black market was huge. From Burma poured a treasure trove of antiquities, gems, and drugs to be sold and traded at border towns like this one for the best the West had to offer. Opium for toilet paper. Emeralds for Aiwas. Statuary for cigarettes. It made you wonder which side was getting screwed worse.

While I waited for the tiny boat that would ferry me across the river I studied the far bank. Now I could see why the Burmese hadn't been able to extract the Karen from this territory. The whole far bank of the river was a dense jungle of huge trees and impassable undergrowth. Only one small pathway was visible through the foliage, and it was guarded by uniformed soldiers who would periodically disappear into camouflaged bunkers. Obviously this was a Karen customs gate, one of many that dotted their river frontier.

I crossed the river and passed through the gate without incident. The Karen settlement that Marc had told me to make for was a good ten miles in-country. I started down a narrow jungle trail, and a few hours later arrived on foot at the isolated village. The village, a collection of maybe fifteen or twenty straw and bamboo huts, was surrounded by a tall fence of pointed bamboo stakes. The fence, I would later learn, was a traditional feature of Karen villages. Originally built to protect against marauding bands of Burmese slavers, they now were used primarily as a corral to prevent livestock and young children from wandering into jungles seeded with landmines and booby traps.

Even if I hadn't known there was a war on, one look around the village would have told me so. Not because of anything I saw, but because of what I didn't see. There were no men. There were plenty of children, pregnant women, and grandmothers, and even a few wizened grandfathers, but on my first pass through the village I didn't spot a single man of fighting age.

I stepped up to an old men squatting in front of a hut and handed him a letter that had been written for me in the Karen's native language explaining why I was there and whom I needed to see. The old man read it slowly, then jumped up and began shouting for the other villagers. They crowded around me, cooing and ahing and reaching to get a look at the letter.

I watched the letter pass from one eager set of hands to another with surprise. I'd assumed that few of them would know how to read. I didn't yet know that the Karen had once been among the intellectual élite of Burma, and that even after forty years of jungle exile, the tradition of learning was still being passed on.

Suddenly, a soldier dressed in military fatigues appeared. The crowd parted to let him pass. After reading the note and consulting with the other villagers, the soldier spoke to me in broken English. "Tonight you stay here. Morning we go soldier camp."

That night, poor though they were, the villagers brought together what they could to make a feast. I felt embarrassed over all the attention, and even a bit ashamed that I'd brought nothing with me to offer in return for their generosity; nothing, that is, except my life, which any day I expected to be risking on their front line.

The next day, the Karen soldier and I, together with a half-dozen young boys leaving home for their first turn at military training, started out for the Karen base. For the next several days we hiked through picture-postcard-green jungles, across streams, and through cloud forests from whose heights I could see sunlit peaks rising in the distance. It was a magical landscape, as sublime as anything nature could present, and had I been born a painter or a poet I would have wanted to stop and express what I saw as art. But I wasn't a painter or a poet. I was a warrior, a man born to fight, and what I saw in that landscape was not art, but a canvas on which to kill and make war. Give me the men and the means and I would paint the whole jungle in blood. I would compose a symphony in screams, a poetry of devastation, and it would be beautiful, for violence makes its own kind of beauty, and war has an aesthetic every bit as compelling as the rapture that nature inspires.

We arrived at the Karen camp and I was immediately brought to see the general, a moon-faced man with eyes black as coal. He was busy inspecting a new series of fortifications when we were introduced. I handed him the package.

"Thank you for this," he said in perfect English. "I'll have a response drafted. You'll be able to leave with it first thing tomorrow morning." Then he turned and continued his inspection.

"Excuse me, General," I interrupted, "but I'd like to stay for a few weeks and fight. I'm a trained French Foreign Legion paratrooper. I'd be an asset to your forces in the field."

"You'd be even more of an asset right here. Major!" The

general addressed one of his aides, then issued what sounded in any language like orders.

"Crummy," the major said to me in an English so heavily accented that it took me a second before I realized that he was saying, "Come with me." I followed him. "How long you want stay with us?" the major asked.

"About a month," I answered after adjusting my ears to his lilt.

"A month is good. You train many new soldiers in month."

"But I came here to fight."

"No, you teach. Is better."

"I'd rather go out on patrol. I can snipe, you know." I imitated sighting a rifle and firing. "You must need snipers out there. I could kill Burmese officers. You'd like that, wouldn't you?"

"Kill Burmese officers? Yes, I like. You train new soldiers to kill Burmese officers. Then we kill even more. Much better that way. Yes?"

We arrived at a small hut built of mismatched planking and thatch.

"You sleep here." The major gestured toward the hut. "Tomorrow you start training."

I glanced around the camp. There looked to be about two hundred people based there, most of them boys between the ages of twelve and sixteen, but I spotted girls and women as well. A little way off, the six boys with whom I'd traveled in were squatting around a cook pot. As soon as they saw me, they held up balls of sticky rice, grinned the way young boys do, and gestured for me to come over and join them. A few months from now, I knew, those grins would be gone, wiped from their faces by the killing fields that started just beyond the camp wire.

"Okay," I told the major, "I'll help train your soldiers." At least it might give the boys a fighting chance. As I walked over to join them I wondered if any of them would live to see twenty.

For the next several weeks I trained my young recruits hard. Under my tutelage they learned how to assemble, maintain, and fire the AK-47s and M-16s that formed the bulk of their weapons stock. They also learned to set and detonate landmines, booby traps, and Bangalore torpedoes, all of which the Karen possessed in abundance.

Between the shooting and the explosives training I even found time to instruct the boys in hand-to-hand fighting. The kids seemed to love the rough-and-tumble of close combat drills, so I began to teach it more and more. One day, as we stood on the camp parade grounds practicing knife-fighting techniques, a Karen instructor walked up to us.

"What do you think you're doing?" he challenged me in English.

"I'm teaching them how to knife-fight. What the hell does it look like?"

"It looks like you're teaching them how to die, that's what it looks like to me. Who gave you permission to do this?"

"No one gave me permission."

"Well, then stop it."

"Why should I?"

"Because I'm the hand-to-hand combat instructor on this base and I'm telling you to. I don't want them learning what you teach. It's no good. It's for the white men, not us; we have our own way of fighting," he said and stormed off.

I watched him go then turned and picked up my instruction where I'd left off. A few minutes later he was back again, this time with a few of his Karen buddies.

"I told you to stop teaching them that foreign crap. They try to use any of that in the field and they'll get killed."

"Bullshit. If anything it'll keep 'em alive."

"No, it won't. In fact, it won't even keep you alive, foreigner." He pulled his knife and gripped the handle in an attack hold. "Come on, white man—you think you know so much, try me. Show me what you got!"

I stepped clear of the kids and raised my knife to go at him. I didn't particularly want to fight this guy, but he left me no choice; I couldn't back down from his challenge and still maintain honor.

We circled to engage, but before we could close the other Karen jumped between us. "No! No! You can't do this," they pleaded with their friend. "Big problems if the white man gets hurt. Bad for our people when his government finds out."

My opponent sheathed his blade in disgust. Even though he wanted desperately to go at me, he recognized that his duty to country came first. It was the mark of a real soldier, and I had to respect him for it. He'd shown a warrior's level of self-control. Now I would honor him for what he'd done, as only another warrior could.

"Don't worry about my government," I shouted out slowly so all would understand. "Nobody from my government knows I'm here. See! False passport," I said, pulling mine from my fatigues and waving it in the air. "If you and I fight," I said to the one who had challenged me, "whatever happens stays between us. No governments. No grudges. Just you and me. Understand?"

My opponent glanced toward his friends and they talked for a minute in their native tongue.

"All right, we fight," my opponent finally said. "But on one condition."

"What's that?"

"My friends are worried that you might try to run and I'd have to chase you all over the camp. Other people could get hurt. So if we're going to fight, we need to be tied together." He pointed to a coil of braided leather that one of his friends held looped in his hand. "You accept?"

Without saying a word I held out my left arm. He nodded and extended his own. While his friends bound us together we stared into each other's eyes. I liked what I saw there, the strength and the fire, and hoped I wouldn't have to kill him. Of course, there was always the chance that he might kill me. Initially, at least, he'd have the advantage, because he'd already seen my fighting style while I knew nothing of his. I put the thought out of my mind and focused instead on the dim and deep chamber within me where the fighting beast slavered and howled.

After his friends were through tying us off, they moved back and gave word to start. About two feet of leather was all that separated him from me. Two feet. Not much when it comes to dodging sharpened steel. My opponent opened with a slashing attack. I parried and stepped back as far as the leather cord would let me. Then, when my opponent lunged toward me, I sidestepped his knife and pulled him off balance by jerking hard on the cord. As he lifted his arm, I dropped underneath him and stuck him in the armpit with the point of my knife. He spun around to attack me, but before he could even step into position, his right arm fell, paralyzed, and I was able to kick the knife out of his useless hand. A moment later, I took him to the ground and set my own knife against his throat. I looked into his eyes. They were dark and blighted but they showed no fear. As he nodded his chin in surrender, I stood up and began untying the leather cord from my wrist.

The fight had taken less than a minute and had ended just as I hoped it would. The wound he received would be painful, but unless it got infected it shouldn't cause permanent damage. With luck, in a few days he'd be good as new.

"Than! Than!" A woman dressed in battle fatigues rushed in shouting.

So that was his name—Than. The girl kneeled down next to Than and began applying first aid. As she helped Than sit up and then get to his feet, she shot an angry look over at me, and for the first time I got a clear view of her magnificent face.

"Sorry," I heard myself saying to her in spite of myself.

"You're sorry? He's my brother; how do you think I feel?" she said and then helped her brother off toward the infirmary. I watched her go and felt myself falling into a million love-struck pieces.

The next day I went to visit Than in the infirmary and found her there, not as angry this time, but every bit as magnificent. I marveled at the beauty of her face—the noble chin, the catlike eyes, the elegant eroticism of her lips—until I forget even the pretext under which I'd come. All my life I'd dreamed of such a warrior woman, and now there she was, smiling like a burst of light while her brother talked and talked. Unfortunately, I didn't hear a word he said, and it wasn't until after I'd left that I realized he'd apologized to me for suggesting that we fight a duel, and asked me if, when he returned to health, I would teach him some of what I knew about close combat knife fighting.

A few days later, Than was out of the infirmary and he invited me to come to his hut to have dinner with him and his sister, Waruny. Waruny—her name had been tracing circles in my head ever since I first learned it. Waruny, a name as exotic as the woman who bore it. The syllables had the sounds of sex and struggle in them, and of mystery as well. Waruny. My beautiful warrior queen.

That night we sat at a communal table. I ate little. I wasn't hungry for food, but for Waruny. Did she know that? I wondered, as I asked her all the common questions.

I learned that she was twenty-two, that she'd been a guerrilla fighter since she was thirteen and had fought in several major engagements at the front. Her father was dead, killed in battle. Her mother lived in a village a few days' march away.

Her brother watched us talk. I could tell that he knew how I felt. A man can always read another man's heart, but a woman's heart is like the sun, blinding to a lovesick man, equally impossible to know or live without.

That night I walked back to my hut like a beggar with an empty bowl. Most of the camp was already asleep when I lay down on my pallet. A slight breeze drifted in from the jungle smelling of rot. In the distance a small explosion sounded. An animal, most likely, had tripped off a mine. At least its suffering was over. Not mine. If I didn't tell Waruny how I felt, and soon, I was sure that I'd go mad.

"Dominiquie." I heard my name being called from outside.

"Waruny?"

"Yes. Can I come in?"

I got up and showed her in.

"I noticed your arm when you were over tonight," she said, gently touching and turning my wrist to expose a powder burn that ran up the length of my forearm. "That's a very bad burn. It must hurt."

I stared at her, unable to speak a word for fear it might break whatever spell had brought her to me.

"I have something to put on it," she said, uncovering a bowl of unguent. "It's what we use here. It really helps. Here, sit down. I'll show you."

I sat and offered her my arm, and she reached out with hands warm as the sun to heal me. That night we made a kind of love I've never known before or since, and from that day on we were inseparable. We ate, trained, lived, and slept together. We shared everything. Secrets. Bodies. Souls.

"Do you love me, Waruny?"

"I do."

"You know, I'm still bound by my contract with the Legion."

"I know."

"And I have to fulfill it. I have to go back."

"I know."

"It'll be at least eight months before I can return. Will you wait?"

"For you? Forever."

"And when I come back, Waruny, will you marry me? Will you spend the rest of your life with me?"

"I will, Dominiquie. Gladly."

"God, I love you, Waruny. I swear I do."

"Then come, take me. Give me something to dream on while you're gone."

She was the finest woman I'd ever met, but there was no dodging what I had to do. A week later I packed my things to leave. Waruny sat watching me in the early morning light.

"Are you really coming back?"

I looked into her large full face and felt the contours of her naked body as she rose up to embrace me.

"I'll always be coming back to you, Waruny. Every step I take from now on will be a step on the road back to you."

Huisvader

Flemish for "family man."

I stood at the door. How long had it been? Two years? Three? Oh, God. Maybe I should just leave rather than sunder whatever routine their lives had fallen into. I could send them a letter. I could drop them a line. Yeah, right. I was already standing on their front porch. Why not just knock? What was I so afraid of? Their judgment? Their disappointment? The fact that I had abandoned them? Just what kind of warrior was I anyway? Afraid to face my own mom and dad.

A cold wind blew as I lifted my hand to knock. I was doing this for Waruny. "Peace in the family, peace in the heart," she had said. For her I would try to make that peace, as long as it didn't come at the expense of my honor. On that I wouldn't compromise. I would never be the small-town man that my parents wanted, slaving five days a week at some off-the-shelf job, drinking on Saturday, and then, come Sunday, trailing off after the Holy Ghost for a quick fix of priestly redemption.

I knocked quietly, and then again louder. Maybe they wouldn't be home. Then the dog started barking. I could hear him on the other side of the door, sniffing and scratching, then yelping like he always did when he got excited.

A hand parted the curtain, and my dad's face appeared in the window. "Oh, my God!" he mouthed. Then his face disappeared, and I heard him running back through the house, the dog at his heels. "Mother, Mother, come quick! You're not going to believe it!"

"What? What's wrong?"

"It's Dominiquie! He's here!"

"Dominiquie? Here?"

"At the front door. Come and see. Hurry."

The dog bolted out when she opened the door, and Mom and Dad after him in a rush of love and pleasure that caught me head on. After the initial burst of laughter and tears we moved inside to chat over little things—the new front rug, did I want coffee or tea?—because the real issues before us were so large that none of us knew how to broach them.

My mom sat down next to me. Auschwitz, I thought; that's what she looked like, Auschwitz. Radiation and chemotherapy had desecrated her body. Her hair was gone. Her skin was gray. But there was still a clear light in her eyes. At least there was that. She reached out a black-veined arm and took my hand.

"We missed you, Dominiquie. We missed you a lot. With all our hearts and all our souls we missed you. We've done a lot of praying for you."

I sat there, ashamed and appalled over the suffering I must have caused them. "Forgive me," I heard my voice gurgle up from some bottomless well. My mother heard it too and went on.

"I know that we tried too hard to keep you here. That's why you had to leave us the way you did. I guess it was just too difficult for us to admit that you have your own calling, different from ours. But now that your father and I see that, I hope we can all start over. With whatever time's left, I want us to be a family again."

I nodded, and for a moment every other issue fell away and there was only our love. The next day I left for the Legion with a promise to write that I never once honored. How could I when every time I sat down to put pen to paper my mind was seized with the certainty of my mother's condition and the pain that I had caused her? She was dying and I had abandoned her, and no matter how hard I tried I couldn't break free of the cycle; I hadn't any words strong enough to shatter the chain to which a lifetime of habit had bound me. For that I needed Waruny. But it would be another eight months before I could bring her to Europe, and I doubted my mother would make it.

I returned to Calvi to serve out those eight months. I knew that in order to marry Waruny I was supposed to get the permission of my colonel. But I also knew that, if the colonel said no, I wouldn't be allowed to ask about marriage for the rest of my contract, and there was no way I could bear that. Better to say nothing, marry Waruny in Thailand, and present our marriage to the colonel as an accomplished fact. That way I could claim love at first sight; I could plead that it was impossible for me to live without her. Being French, the colonel might just understand.

While I was mulling over my options, the Legion asked me if I wanted to take the F-2 course that would qualify me as a *caporal chef de groupe.* I agreed at once. The corporal stripes would not only mean more money in my pay envelope, but they would also show the colonel that I was a responsible soldier who could be trusted to take care of a wife.

The training course as taught at Calvi was an all-out, balls-to-the-wall affair. About half the soldiers who enrolled didn't finish. As in most Legion training courses, you barely slept, you never stopped running, and everything you did was timed by men with stopwatches who were forever shouting at you to do it over again, this time faster. If you failed you were beaten, then punished with extra work. If you quit you went to jail. If you kept up, well, sometimes just surviving is its own reward.

The course was so hard that after three weeks even two of the instructors dropped out. That really amazed me, because next to us the instructors had it easy. They got to sleep. They got to take breaks and rotate out every few days while fresh officers were brought in to drive us. After six weeks the twenty-five of us that had made it this far had been transformed. We weren't paratroopers anymore; we weren't even men. To survive, we'd gone primitive. Prehistoric. We'd become Stone Age men. We lived in the moment, in a blind urge to endure. We knew we were suffering, but we no longer cared, because somehow all that pain had driven us back into our own deepest selves.

For me it was wonderful. Stripped to the root of my being, I felt indestructible. Invincible. A man in my own right. Ready to fight. Ready to lead. Ready to die if need be to demonstrate what it was I had become.

Once again the Legion's crude magic had worked. I graduated from the course and took charge of eight men. Now it was my turn to give like I'd gotten, to forge men through punishment and pain into the most stubborn, dogged soldiers on earth.

To make myself into a better leader I started boning up on Legion lore. I read about a captain in Sidi-bel-Abbès. When the captain heard that one of his legionnaires was drunk and boasting that he was going to shoot his commanding officer, the captain strapped on a revolver, went to the bar, and sat down next to the braggart. After downing a drink or two, the captain announced that he was returning to the post and needed an escort. Drawing his revolver, he handed it to the braggart and ordered him to be the escort. After a long walk through darkened city quarters, they arrived back at the base. The captain reached out for his revolver, and, when the legionnaire passed it back, the Captain spoke:

"Legionnaire, you just earned yourself ten days in jail for boasting that you would kill me. And ten more days for not doing it when you damn well had the chance. Now get going. And remember, a legionnaire always keeps his word."

Sometimes, it was the enlisted man who had the last word. In Algeria, a conspiracy was hatched to murder a cruel sergeant, but, before the deed could be done, news of the conspiracy leaked out. The next morning at *appel* the sergeant was conspicuously absent. Instead, a lieutenant walked the line.

"I want to know which one of you was chosen to kill the sergeant?" the lieutenant asked the assembled men.

A man stepped forward from the ranks.

"So you were going to kill the sergeant?"

"Yes, my lieutenant."

"And you intend to do it still?"

"Yes, my lieutenant."

"Perhaps you would like to use this, then?" The lieutenant unholstered his side arm and offered it to the man.

"Thank you, my lieutenant, I will," the legionnaire answered, taking the pistol.

That same morning the sergeant was shipped out, never to be seen again.

Things might have changed some in the Legion since the days in which those stories were set, but not much. To lead, you still had to prove to the men that you were a man of your word and worthy of being followed. Sadly, most of the new group leaders did their proving with fists.

Blowing off steam with the guys.

Instilling fear was all they knew. Not me. I was after respect, and I figured the best way to get it was by showing
respect for my men.

"I don't care if you drink all night and chase pussy till
dawn. As long as you're back at your post in time for
appel, can stand on your own two feet, and don't puke on
my shoes when I walk by, you'll be okay in my book and
I'll back you up all the way."

And I did. I even went so far as to break my own rule
after their first weekend pass and run into town to person-
ally retrieve those men who'd gotten too drunk to make it
back on their own. After that, they were mine, and I
watched with pride as their initial fear of me turned, first
to respect, and then to feelings of camaraderie. In just a
few short weeks we'd become a highly functional team.
The men did everything expected of them without me ever
once having to yell, hit, or kick them into line, and, when
word came down that I was being transferred to Africa, I
could tell that the men were genuinely sad to see me go.

I landed in Arta and was assigned to the Second Section of the Fourth Company. By now, word of my skills as a martial artist had spread through the regiment, and when I was introduced to the eight soldiers who'd be serving under me they presented themselves like frightened mice. I decided the faster I could disabuse them of their fear of me the better. In Africa you never knew when war might break out; if we were suddenly called into another Chad or Rwanda, I didn't want mice at my back—I wanted men.

That night, right before lights out, I called my men together. "Legionnaires, I want to see your sorry asses up and ready for action, because I'm taking you out on maneuvers. You and I are going down to Arta tonight."

The men stared at me like I was crazy. No orders had been issued to leave the base. None of us had passes to go into town. But if I wanted to get these boys to trust me, to turn them into fighting men, I knew the fastest way to do it was to *faire la bombe,* as they say in the Legion—to do something slightly mad.

"You hear me, legionnaires? Tonight, you're going to learn to take a town, Legion style. In my book that means two things. First, I expect every one of you to get as drunk as possible. Second, I want every one of you horny sons of bitches to score some pussy tonight, and if anybody gets in your way I don't want you to hesitate; I want you to kick ass. You think you can handle all that, legionnaires?"

"Oui, mon caporal!" they shouted back.

"Good, then follow me."

We timed the guard's movements and snuck out behind their backs. Over the wall, through the wire, and down a deep gully we went. It was easy enough getting out. Coming back would be a different story. It would be hell sneaking eight dick-drained and drunken men back up over the wall. I figured the only thing I had going for me was that every man knew that if any one of them got caught they would all lose the best damn group leader they could ask for.

Ali's Bar looked just like the hellhole I remembered, but to the eight sex-starved legionnaires of my group it was pussy heaven. Each of them had a little money in their pocket—I'd made sure of that before we left—and since we were the only legionnaires out that night my men had their pick of the whores.

"I'll meet you all back here at 3 A.M. sharp," I told the men. Then I grabbed a bottle and walked out into the night. I knew if I stayed there among all those whores that I'd break down and fuck one of them. It had been almost four months since I'd seen Waruny and I was pretty damn horny. I didn't know too many soldiers who could make it through a whole tour without getting laid, but I was determined to try, because I knew that as soon as I saw her again Waruny would ask, and I didn't want to have to lie, not to Waruny.

I went out and wandered past the outskirts of town into the empty expanse of the desert. I thought of my mother and how she used to speak to me about the transforming power of Christ. Usually, I ignored her. All that talk about sin and redemption was completely lost on me. But that night, under the vault of the desert sky, I began to understand what it might mean to love so completely, so deeply, that you felt yourself washed forever clean, because Waruny had done that for me. Before I'd met her I'd been a dead man, sunk deep in the wound of the world. But now, by her grace, I'd been saved, and, if not quite a saint, at least I was less of a sinner.

Back in town I could hear the men laughing. It was coming on 3 A.M. Might as well let them enjoy themselves a little longer. The poor souls had no idea what they were in for. They'd joined the Legion expecting something live and magnificent, but it wouldn't be long before they realized that all they'd ever get would be a numbing exile that would go on and on and on.

At about 3:30 A.M., I returned to the bar to gather up the men. They were good and drunk, and they greeted me with raised glasses and the thieving grins of men who'd just gotten away with murder. I made a quick count. Two were missing; they'd gone off with whores and hadn't returned. I figured I'd find them in time, but first I wanted to get the rest of the men back to camp, a task I thought was going to be hard, but actually turned out to be easy, as even the drunkest did what was required to steal through the lines of the camp.

After I made sure that the men were bunked down, I snuck back into town and started a door-to-door search. Anywhere else I'd get killed or arrested for kicking down doors in the night, but the locals were used to it. Legion MPs thought nothing of barging into native huts at all hours to search for missing men, and now, as I went from hut to hut shouting for my men and shining a flashlight into sleeping faces, most of the natives just cursed and rolled over in their beds. After almost two hours of searching I found both my soldiers, passed out in the arms of their whores. When I kicked them out of bed, one stumbled to his feet, but the other was too drunk to stand and I had to toss him over my shoulder and carry him back to base.

That morning, my men stood for roll call stinking of whiskey and looking pathetic. The lieutenant walked our ragged line.

"Had a late night with your men, Corporal Vandenberg?"

"Oui, mon lieutenant."

He nodded and moved on. As long as our wild nights didn't get in the way of our training, the lieutenant didn't care. Like any good Legion officer, he knew that a bit of indiscipline was good for the men, that *des actes fantaisistes* were absolutely essential to an army whose *métier* was to fight like the mad dogs of hell.

When the first telegram arrived, begging for me to come home because my mother was sick, I ignored it. When another arrived a week later I put it aside. Instead, I went off on a five-day forced march with my men. By the second day out I knew something was wrong. My vision was blurred. My head ached, and I started sweating and shaking. I put it off to fatigue, to the heat, the bad food, the constant stress and lack of water.

I marched on. By the third day I wasn't quite sure who I was anymore. I felt like a speck under the lens of a giant microscope. Above me, the sun glared down like an annihilating eye. Then the world tipped away and I found myself standing naked and alone in a desolate place. I must be mad, I thought, as I watched Waruny and my mother rise straight up out of the sand in front of me. I tried to scream, but my mouth had become a soundless tomb in which my tongue lay dead and heavy. My mother moved to comfort me, but as soon as she stepped from the spot where she'd risen, she began to parch and wither. After one step, she was dry as a mummy. After two, she was coming apart, and as she reached out her hand to touch my face her body crumbled to dust.

I woke up in the infirmary. According to the doctor I was lucky to be alive. The nonrecurrent strain of malaria I'd contracted could kill a man in a day. For me, though, the worst was over. I'd burned through the initial fever, and according to the doctor I'd be ready to roll in a week. That sounded just fine to me. In another two weeks my tour would be up. The Legion would ship me back to Calvi, where I'd be granted a sixteen-day leave, and from there I'd fly straight to Waruny.

As soon as I was well enough to stand the captain called me in.

"At ease," he said, and handed me a telegram.

I opened it and read: "Dominiquie, Come home. Mama is dead. Signed, Papa."

"I'm sorry, legionnaire," the captain offered. "If you want, I'll see to it that you're aboard the next flight out."

"No, my lieutenant, that won't be necessary."

"But it's your mother's funeral, legionnaire."

How could I tell him that there was no need for me to attend my mother's funeral, that I'd already witnessed her passing, that in an unknown place in the African desert we'd made our final peace and said goodbye.

Marié à Mort

"Married to death."

Waruny was dead. What was left of her body had been ashed on a pyre, weeks ago. Now I was alone, squatting on the ruined bank of the muddy river that had taken her life. How long I'd been squatting there I didn't know. The passage of time didn't matter any more. Nothing did. Except death.

I took a long pull off my bottle of Mekong whiskey and thought back to the moment I'd shown up in the Karen camp. I'd practically run the whole way through the jungle to get there. Waruny and I had planned a big marriage feast. Her mother would come in for the ceremony. Her brother Than would give her away. Then it would be on to Bangkok, where Marc would forge the Thai passport and the papers that would get her to Europe.

But everything had come undone in a moment. I tipped at the bottle and every sight, sound, and smell of that moment came back to me. Everything. In every detail. And not just from my point of view, but from every point of view. From the point of view of every man, woman, and child in the camp. Every bird, bug, and animal. Every tree. Every plant. Even the dust in the air I became when Than told me that Waruny was dead.

"Dead? No! She can't be."

"I'm sorry, Dominiquie, but she's gone."

And all at once I felt the part of me that wasn't flesh leave the part of me that was as my soul, in its mad hopeless rush to be with her, abandoned me. And I found myself looking down on my body, standing fast and empty, feeling nothing, because I, its owner, had left.

"How? How did it happen?"

"You don't want to know. Believe me, you don't."

"Tell me!"

"Her head was cut off, okay, and stuck up on a pole. And her body . . ." Than dropped his face into his hands. "You don't want to know."

"Who did it?"

"We don't know."

"What do you mean, you don't know?"

"She was near the river when it happened."

"Was it the Burmese?"

"No, there's no Burmese that way."

"Then who?"

"We think it might have been pirates."

"Pirates?"

"Thai bandits that live on the river. They rob traders mostly, and tourists, but they've never attacked us before."

"So what makes you think it was them?"

"Because whoever it was came off the river. That could only mean bandits or Thai military."

"You go after them?"

"After who, Dominiquie? We can't go to war against the whole river."

"Why the fuck not?"

"Because our fight is the other way. We can't start making enemies at our backs; that would be suicide."

I asked Than to outfit me with whatever weapons he could spare. I'd find who did it. I'd kill every rotten fuck on the river if I had to.

"No, I can't allow you to do that. Orders. I'm sorry."

I nodded. If the Karen wouldn't help me there were always other ways.

"Why don't you go home, Dominiquie? That's what she would have wanted. There's no need for both of you to die. Go home. It's not your fight anymore."

I left that same day, taking the only road home I knew. It led me to every backwater bar and grimy riverfront village for miles around, searching for Waruny's killers.

In the gathering twilight an old, Vietnam-era patrol boat rounded a bend in the river. On board, a half-dozen soot-streaked Thai stared at me from their perches. Were these the ones who'd killed Waruny? Just give me one clue that they were and I would tear the life out of each of them. But that clue never came, and after a week of fruitless searching I'd had enough.

As the patrol boat disappeared around the next bend, I slipped Waruny's wedding ring from my pocket and threw it into the deep of the river.

Fuite en Avant

Literally "forward flight." In military circles it means
to willingly retreat into the face of the enemy.

I staggered toward the table, falling into, then off of, my
chair.

"You asshole," Jim cursed when I puked near his
boots. Though he hadn't seen action for years, Jim still
kept his boots spit-shined and polished, a habit left over
from his years of service with the Katanga Tigers in Zaire.

"Sorry, man, next round is on me," I sputtered from
under the table right before another wave rose from my
belly, scalding my throat as it passed.

"Whatsa matter, legionnaire, can't hack it?" There was
no mistaking that sneer; it belonged to Fabrice, a mercenary who'd fought in Rhodesia until it became Zimbabwe,
at which point he'd hightailed it for the greener pastures of
Thailand.

I put up a hand and grabbed for the edge of the table.

"Come on, soldier, cut the shit and belly up." Oscar issued the order, then rapped at the table with the remaining

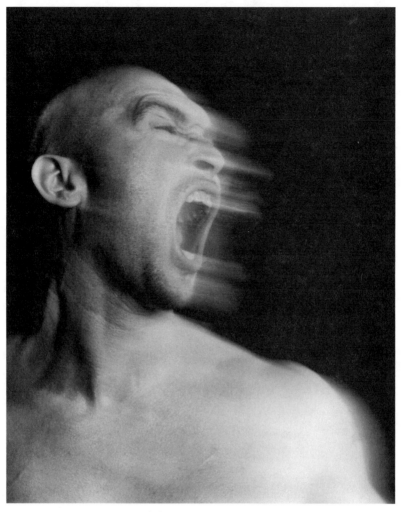

(Copyright 2004 by Kevin Lynch)

fingers of his left hand. "Shrapnel," he'd explained when
he first caught me eyeing his mangled hand. "Angola."

I pulled my ass into the chair, gave my lips a quick
swipe, and scanned the faces of my drinking mates. If I had
any doubt as to how low I had sunk, the stubborn chins,
sloping foreheads, whacked-out insomniac eyes, ruined
skin, scars, and broken noses gathered around that table

dispelled it. I'd gone straight to the bottom. All the way down, slumped in the mud next to all the old tires, the rusty cans, the lost boots, and, somewhere among all that trash, the unrecoverable treasure of Waruny's unworn ring, its diamond forever flashing a hopeless SOS.

I favored my mates with a smile that barely hid my desire to kill them. I knew that, except for the small matter of the epicanthic fold, these men were no different from whoever had killed my Waruny. They all came from the same race of scumbag. Of course, the misery these men left in their wake hadn't been mine, at least not yet. But it was still early.

I'd only met these three five hours ago in a bar on the other side of town. Like dogs we'd sniffed each other out, formed ourselves into a pack, and then run howling into the night—four brutal ex-soldiers, out to have a good time, which for us meant that someone else wouldn't be, unless of course we turned on each other first. It was a distinct possibility. The top dog in our pack hadn't yet been decided. So far, Oscar was in the lead. His age and his predisposition to bark orders gave him an instant leg up. But sooner or later I knew that Jim would try to break that leg, and when he did Fabrice would side with him, and then there'd be no telling which way it would go.

Not that I cared. I hadn't thrown in with these louts to make myself their leader. I just wanted a little company on my trip into hell, and I knew these three would get me there, fast.

"Fuck all!" I hollered as I threw back another shot. Then I slammed my glass down and shook my head like a dog wrestling with a rat, only in this struggle I was the rat.

"Come on, it stinks in here. Let's get out of this shit hole," Jim roared in a play for command.

I stood up to an astronomy lesson of spinning black

holes and comets, and leaned into Jim for support. He pushed me away.

"You puke on me again, you bastard, and I'll rip out your fucking tongue and sew up your lips with your dick."

I stared him blankly. Then, when his threat finally cut through the fog of my drunk, I laughed. Rip out my tongue? Why the fuck not? What did I care if I lost another piece of myself? I imagined myself being whittled away: first a tongue, then a foot, then an arm, then a leg, until all that was left was a spasmodic torso, twitching away in the dirt—just like Waruny. I tried to bury the horror that my mind's eye had created as I followed the rest out the door.

The next thing I remember, I was climbing out of a cab and stumbling down a dark, stinking, rat infested alley.

"There's treats in store, gentlemen," Oscar promised as he raised his hand to knock at a heavy iron door.

"Hey, you okay?" Fabrice asked me as Oscar rapped out a code on the door. "Here, try some of this. Perk you right up."

Fabrice held out a bag filled three inches deep with some kind of white powder. I licked two fingers, jabbed them into the bag and shoveled the stuff up my nose.

"Whoa!" was all I could say as the stuff vectored its way through my sinuses. "What is this shit?"

"Cocaine, cut with speed, and a pinch of heroin to take the edge off. You like?"

I nodded. Who wouldn't? The stuff worked like rocket fuel. I felt like an astronaut on his way to the moon.

When the iron door opened and a pair of Thai bouncers gestured us in, I flashed past the rest and bounded down the stairs. I had no idea where I was going. I was simply following the breakneck pounding in my head, down a long, narrow hallway, straight into two men who were dragging a limp body behind them. Must be tossing out a drunk, I thought as I flattened myself against the wall to let them pass. But then I saw that the man they were dragging behind them was dead, and when I followed the trail of his blood down the hall and discovered three more bodies, neatly stacked in an alcove, I stopped and bent down to examine them. Each one had been shot in the temple. All at close range, and not long ago either. The repulsive black goo that oozed from their skulls and matted their hair hadn't even begun to crust over yet. The wounds were still warm.

I stood up. In the dim light, I noticed a man, or at least what looked like it had once been a man, crouching with his face to the wall. "Hey, you! You speak English? French?" I asked the huddled man. "What is this place?" He turned and looked up at me. A half-empty syringe dangled from the white of one of his eyes. Ropes of snot hung from his nose. When I stepped back in horror he started laughing, then choking on the thick clots of foam that bubbled from his toothless mouth.

"Jesus Christ!" I jumped when Fabrice laid a hand on my shoulder.

"Hey, looks like that shit really reset your clock."

"Where the fuck are we?"

"You'll see," Fabrice said as he continued down the hall.

I followed Fabrice and the others into a large subterranean room that was part Asian bar, part Aztec torture chamber. Against a bare stone wall a long wooden bar had been set up. Against another, dozens of chains had been hammered and hung, and I could hear them rattling above the din of the place as man after man stepped up to have his way with the naked Thai women who were manacled there.

"Nice, huh?" Fabrice spread his arms wide.

I nodded. I'd wanted hell and I'd gotten it.

Oscar led us to an empty table, one of the last in the

place. We sat down and ordered whiskey—a bottle for each of us—from a completely naked hostess who stopped and impassively spread her legs when Fabrice slipped a hand up her thigh.

"Whiskey and cunt, no finer combination," Fabrice said after savoring the scent she'd imparted to his fingers.

Just then, a shot rang out from across the room and I glanced over just in time to see a man fall dead.

"What the fuck? Did I just see what I think I saw?" To me, it looked like the man had just blown out his own brains.

Fabrice arched an eyebrow. "It's an all-or-nothing game, my friend."

"Game?"

"Russian roulette."

"Yeah, right."

"Go see for yourself, you don't believe me. It's how the junkies around here make their money."

I walked over to get a better look. From the edge of the crowd I watched a fat Thai fuck pry the revolver from the dead man's hand. I saw him load the revolver with four bullets and spin the chamber. When he handed the gun to the remaining player, I shot a quick look back at Fabrice who smiled, pushed a finger to his temple and squeezed off an imaginary round. After a quick rush of betting, the whole place went silent as the player lifted the gun to his temple. Because I was on the outside, and the crowd had closed ranks in front of me, I heard rather than saw the metallic click of the hammer dropping on an empty chamber. As the player stood and collected his cash, I returned to my seat at the table.

"So, you wanna play a round?" Fabrice joked as I sat down.

"Him? He ain't got the balls for it," Jim said.

I stared at Jim for a second, surprised by his sudden

rush of venom. There was no way I could let the remark pass. It was a challenge plain and simple, so I matched it with one of my own:

"I got the balls to whip your sorry ass, you don't get outta my face."

Jim flipped me the bird.

"Show me that finger again, I'll break it off," I said, fully prepared to do just that.

I watched Jim slowly raise his fists. He was about to take me up on the offer when Oscar reached out and grabbed his hand.

"Mellow out. None of you losers got the balls to play that game."

"Oh yeah, wanna try me?" Jim shot back.

Now it was Jim and Oscar's turn to get into a pissing match.

"How many bullets, Jim?"

Jim's eyes narrowed as he performed an angry arithmetic in his head. "All six, Oscar, and you can go first."

And suddenly, Oscar was laughing, "Six bullets, eh? That's a good one."

Jim leaned back in his chair, apparently satisfied that he'd come out on top. The victory must've put a little leeway in his mood, because when he noticed that I was still looking angry, he reached out with words meant to appease.

"I know you got balls, man. I was just razzing you. You got big, hairy monster balls, so what do you say we go over and drain 'em on some of those bitches over there?"

I nodded no thanks.

"Suit yourself, man, I'm gonna go lay some pipe on those girls."

"I'm with you, brother," Fabrice said, standing and gripping his crotch.

"Fuck a bunch of cunt. I'm hungry," Oscar said to the

air after Jim and Fabrice disappeared in the tangle of bodies on the far side of the room.

I watched Oscar get up and wander over to a heavy
groaning board where plucked chickens, whole gutted
pigs, fish, and an immense fly-covered side of beef sat in
their own blood and ichor. Oscar gestured toward the beef
and an ancient Thai grandfather, himself more bone than
flesh, stood up and began hacking away. Oblivious to the
buzzing cloud of flies his work had raised, the old man ex-
pertly swung his machete, separating a large joint of meat
from the rest. Our whiskey arrived, and as Oscar returned
to the table, I watched the old man toss the joint onto a red
hot brazier which smoked and spat at the intrusion.

A while later, Jim and Fabrice returned and the finished roast was delivered to our table by a woman whose
pubic hair was flecked with bits of charcoaled fat and gris-
tle. By now, Fabrice's rocket fuel was wearing off and the
whiskey was coming on strong. Too strong, because it loosened my tongue with a vengeance, and before long I found
myself helplessly spewing out shit that only a moron
would say.

To Jim: "What the fuck makes you think the Katanga
Tigers are so great? What'd they ever do except maybe lose
a whole country to that piss-ant rebel—what's his name?"

To Fabrice: "You're nothing but a fuckin' rookie, man.
They'd eat your ass for breakfast in the 2REP."

To Oscar: "Your whole army couldn't coordinate an attack against my goddamned grandmother. You got whipped
by a bunch of Zulus, man, that's why your sorry ass is
here."

Of course, after a bombing run like that, the boys had to
retaliate with a few strikes of their own:

"You Legion cocksuckers are all the same—you're living on fuckin' dreams, man. You're nothing since Algeria."

"Oh, I don't know about that. I hear those Legion

assholes can build a road. Isn't that what you legionnaires do now? Build shit? 'Cause you sure as fuck can't fight."

"Fucking army ants is what they are. They know how to march and that's all." Oscar lifted his bad hand in the air and wiggled his two remaining fingers like a walking wind up doll. "Look, a legionnaire," he said and the others laughed.

With that, our battle turned into an ugly land war that quickly got completely out of hand:

"Fuck you."

"No, fuck you, boy. You think the 2REP's so tough? You think you're so fuckin' brave?"

"Damn straight, asshole."

"Prove it, then!" Oscar stood up, knocking over his chair. "I wanna see you fucking prove it."

"Come on, let's teach this bag of shit a lesson," he said to Jim and Fabrice.

I figured this was it; I was going to have to fight them all.

"What the fuck are you doing?" Oscar said when he saw me stand up and slip into a martial arts pose.

I stared at him, expecting some kind of trick.

"I don't want to fight you, asshole. I want you over there," he said, pointing toward the Russian roulette table. "Come on, all of you; let's see if this legionnaire is as tough as he talks."

With that he turned and strode toward the table. I watched him go, and all at once it struck me what I'd just gotten into.

"Let's go, tough guy." Jim slapped me on the back as he passed.

I took a step forward and laughed ruefully to myself. For the past two days, all I'd wanted was die. I'd prayed for it, drank to it, and chased it deep into the night. Without Waruny life was too hard; it was so goddamned hard that I didn't want to live. But now that all my mad acts were about to be rewarded, my prayers answered, my secret toasts fulfilled, I wasn't so sure anymore. I was scared.

"You really fucked us, man," Fabrice said as he walked by.

Yes, I really had. After all the drunken boasts, the threats and challenges, there was no way I could back down. I walked toward the roulette table like a mourner at his own funeral.

Oscar was talking to the fat fuck with the revolver when I arrived.

"Give me your money," Oscar demanded. "All of it."

I fished it out and gave it to him. After counting out some for the fat fuck, he threw what was left on the table.

"Who wants to go first?"

"I will," Fabrice volunteered.

Then Jim nodded for the next spot.

"You go after me, boy," Oscar said. "Now stand back and watch how the real men do it."

Fabrice and Jim sat down at the table. By now a crowd had gathered and they pushed and hollered to get in on the action. The fat fuck loaded a bullet into the revolver, spun the chamber and set the gun down on the table.

In a rabbit-like flash Fabrice grabbed the pistol, squinted, aimed, and clicked down on an empty chamber. Then it was Jim's turn. He picked up the weapon, spun the chamber, and calmly laid the muzzle to his head. Click. The whole go around had taken about thirty seconds, but to me it seemed faster than starlight.

I slid into the chair Fabrice had just vacated. From across the table, Oscar smiled at me and then reached for the pistol as naturally as if he were going for the salt. A quick climb to his temple with the gun, a squeeze of his finger and *Click!* The hammer fell on an empty chamber.

Now it was my turn to suffer the gun. I picked it up and

felt its dead weight. "Man lives in the fruit of his deeds. He is the harvest of his thoughts, so that, without even knowing it, he is already everything he desires to be." The words sounded slow and easy in my mind, calming me, the same as they had the first time I'd heard them spoken by the old wise man who'd spent half his life with the Pygmies. Strange what the mind will pull out of its hat when it has to. Even stranger what it hides there, forever under the brim.

"Let's go, boy. End of the line."

I spun the chamber and settled the muzzle in a tender bone hollow about an inch back from my right eye. From behind me came the murmur of the imbecilic crowd. Before me sat Oscar, his face crazy with delight. What an image to go out on, but it was all I had, so I tried with all my might to preserve it in memory, as if by doing so I might somehow preserve myself. If I could just make the things around me as real in my mind as they were in the world then there was no way I could die, for I would be the world. I would be the heft and the hold of the gun. I would be the bullet. I would be the twitch that had possessed my right eye. The sweat stains in the armpits of Oscar's shirt. The smells of rotten meat and men and incense. The distant sounds of the chain artists banging away at their captives. I would be any or all of them. All I had to do was complete one pure and perfect act of memory and I would be saved.

I squeezed down on the trigger and suddenly found myself remembering: Waruny. She appeared in my mind, solid as rock crystal. Then *Click!* The hammer fell on an empty chamber and I lowered the gun to the table.

I broke out in a broad smile as money was thrown down to match the cash that we'd bet. In what seemed like a miracle, we'd all come out winners. I was reaching for the cash when Oscar spoke.

"Again. This time two bullets."

"What?"

"You heard me."

"Oscar, are you nuts, man? What the fuck for?"

"Whatsa matter legionnaire? Can't you *faire Camerone*?"

Camerone. Of all the sagas, myths, and legends about the Legion, this was the most sacred of all. For a hundred years, the image of Captain Danjou and his heroic band of soldiers had inspired countless legionnaires to acts of supreme sacrifice. Death! Death with full honor. Death in the field. Death under fire. Death chosen willingly as an act of creation. Double-barreled and ferocious, death was the legacy of Camerone that every legionnaire lugged in his heart.

I stared at Oscar for a blind moment. There was no fear in me now. Only rage. I could taste it at the back of my throat, could feel it rising inside me like a geyser.

"You want to *faire Camerone,* asshole? I'll show you how to *faire Camerone*! Three bullets. Three!" I said, rais-ing three fingers at the fat fuck.

The fat fuck stared at Oscar, and when he nodded okay, the fuck commenced loading the gun. Looking back on it, I still wonder why Oscar agreed. Maybe he wanted to die. Maybe he and the others had spent so long balanced on the lip of death's pool that they never thought they'd fall in. Or maybe, like me, they were so tyrannized by certain principles that they feared dishonoring them even more than they feared dying.

I guess I'll never know, because the instant Fabrice squeezed down on the trigger there was a blast that set my ears to ringing as Fabrice dropped backwards, his head half gone, blood spewing everywhere, and hit the floor.

The fat fuck called for some gnomes. While he reloaded

the gun, the gnomes pushed their way through the crowd, grabbed Fabrice by the feet and dragged him off.

With the stink of gunpowder still in the air, Jim reached for the gun and laid it to his temple. The dead spots in his eyes grew even deader as he slipped a crooked finger to the trigger. *Die,* I shouted in my head, and when no blast came, and Jim stood from the table triumphant, I didn't even try to hide my disappointment.

Oscar smiled when he read my bitter face. It was the last expression he'd ever show, because as soon as he sat down and set the gun to his head he was dead. As the gnomes returned to carry him off, I stared at the gun in the fat fuck's bloody hands. The chamber was open, and, as I watched him replace the spent cartridge with a fresh one, the ghosts of all the ruined men who'd ever died around this table rose up to scream a single word into my ear. "Camerone!" they shouted, hovering so close to me that I could smell their breath and feel their rotten luck as they passed back through the wringer of eternity.

"Give it here," I shouted, grabbing the revolver from the fat fuck. I spun the chamber and listened to it whine. Then I jammed the gun to my head and waited for the bettors to quiet. Three bullets. Six chambers. One try. A fifty-fifty chance. Hardly Camerone. I squeezed the trigger and heard the hammer fall. *Click!* And then again, *Click!* as I squeezed off another round just to show the ghosts that I could do it, that I wasn't afraid, that death didn't mean shit to this far-gone legionnaire. With a look of disgust, I threw the bloody gun onto the table, gathered up my winnings and walked away.

The next morning I came to in an alley. My money was gone, and so were my boots. In their place I'd been left with a lump. It rose from the back of my head like a mountain—a Kilimanjaro of pain. I stood up, massaged the awful lump, and tried, without luck, to remember how I'd gotten it.

I spent the better part of that day making my way back to Marc's.

"You look like shit," Marc said when I finally showed up.

"I need money. Set me up with a fight."

"I'll see what I can do."

A few hours later I was standing inside a broken-down warehouse, watching a cockfight while waiting for my turn in the ring.

"A Kali stick fight is the best I can get for you," Marc had apologized. "Not a lot of money. It's strictly amateur, but in your condition maybe that's for the best."

"How much is not a lot?"

"Oh, about fifteen hundred."

"I'll take it."

"You're up," Marc said after the cockfight had ended.

I stepped into a ring full of cock blood and feathers. From the other side of the bar a squat Thai came over and stepped in after me. He didn't look like much of a fighter, and when he started jabbering to me in Thai, I realized that he wasn't a fighter; he was the ref.

A man disentangled himself from the bar and walked toward us. This one looked more like a fighter. He had the dead eyes of a fish, the immense lolling head of a pig, the body of a skinned chimpanzee, and the hopeless bowed gait of a creature only recently evolved to two legs. He stepped up and locked his filmy eyes on mine. Drugs, I thought, when I saw him up close; drugs were what kept this man fighting.

From outside the ring, the ref retrieved four hollow iron pipes, each about two feet long.

"Sticks!" the ref said to me in English as he handed us each a pair of pipes.

The ends of the pipes were knuckled with screws and rusty metal bolts. A single brass ring as big around as four fingers hung from a bolt on each of the pipes. I stared at the lengths of pipe in my hands and then over at Marc, thinking it must be some kind of joke that Marc had put them up to. This was supposed to be a Kali stick fight, not an iron pipe fight. But before I could even catch Marc's eye, the ref stepped away and shouted, "Fight!"

The Thai charged me, pipes wailing. I dropped sideways and held up one of my pipes to block his attack. With the other, I swung hard as I could into his leading leg, catching him square in the knee. He fell forward and hit the floor face first, and before he could move, I rolled over and cracked the back of his neck with an elbow strike. Then I jumped to my feet and flashed one of the pipes down. It connected with his ankle like a wrecking ball, and when the sickening snap of broken bones and torn tendons gave way to the sound of him screaming I knew the fight was over.

Two days later, the fifteen hundred dollars was gone on drink, whores, opium, and cocaine.

"Set me up for another fight," I told Marc.

"You hang around here, the only thing I'll be setting you up for is a body bag. You're in free fall, man. Don't you see that?"

"I got plans," I lied.

"What plans?"

I threw him a shrug and turned back to my beer.

"Weren't you supposed to be going back to the Legion? Wasn't that supposed to be the plan?"

"That was before."

"When's your flight leave?"

"Tonight, but I ain't gonna be on it."

"Here, have a chaser then," Marc said, pouring me a big tumbler of whiskey.

Even if I'd known what he was up to I probably couldn't have resisted that drink. By nightfall I was so fucked up on the combination of booze and pills Marc fed me that I didn't know where we were going when we climbed in that cab. In fact, I was barely even aware of the cab, or the airport, or of most of the long flight back to Europe. To me it was all a big blur, a haze of disconnected images and sense impressions that in themselves meant nothing, but taken together meant another chance at life. Not that I cared. For me, there was no magic in the world anymore. No love. And that I lived at all from that day to this I can only ascribe to the keeping power of memory.

Baroud d'Honneur

A military compromise that allows one side to surrender with honor after a largely symbolic struggle.

I lived on remains. On memories of evenings spent stretched out beside her, watching her sleep, her face so alluringly tranquil that I dreamed once of swimming through her closed eyes, like a diver, never to emerge. Of those same eyes opening to pool the moonlight and gaze at me in love, of her rising to mount me, her passion ransacking my body of its pleasure and making it her own.

I felt myself quickening as the crazy tug of war going on beneath my sheets struggled towards its finale. I came in a cold shudder. Then I was alone again, lying in my Legion bunk, back among my fellows, like a corpse.

Outside, a sharp wind rose to rattle the windows and rake at the trees. Inside, a man rolled over and farted contentedly in his sleep. And suddenly I hated her, this dead girl whom I could not let go and who tortured and polluted all my dreams, and I was glad that I'd returned to the Legion. They would beat Waruny out of me, with ax handles and boot heels if they had to, until I no longer saw her picture-perfect eyes every time I lay down to close my own.

A week later I was transferred to French Guyana, to the jungle, to the rocket base there, to guard the lonely missiles that they fired into space. The Ariane Rocket base at Kourou was supposedly the pride of France. The site had been carefully chosen, I was told, because of its proximity to the equator. There followed a long explanation about foot pounds, fuel consumption, and rocket trajectory of which I remember nothing, because to me Guyana was a place I'd been sent in order to practice forgetting, and from the moment I arrived there I was determined to do just that.

For two months I stood guard like a statue, my eyes knitted tight against the flare of the rockets as they rose screaming into the sky. Around blind curves, down lonely spurs, and out to the very edge of the trackless jungle I patrolled, not only the ground, but also the most desolate parts of myself. What I found there frightened me: failure as a son and as a husband, a life out of control, a killing rage, a love of violence, and for every victory in the ring a loss outside it. No wonder I was only happy when I fought. Inside that iron circle I could not lose, I never failed; my mind was free. But, outside, my entire life was subject to the cold logic of the billiard table or the slaughterhouse and I was forever being racked or sunk or gutted.

When a friend asked if I wanted to go with him to the camp-run whorehouse to get laid, I shrugged and raised my palms. Life had gotten so damned confusing that every decision, no matter how small, felt like the wrong one, and I was content just to follow Legion orders.

When the order was given to march into the jungle, I grabbed a machete and started hacking. Jungle survival school, the Legion called it. A month and a half of green hell. Forty-five days of mosquitoes, bad water, heat, slime, spiders, poisoned frogs, mud, swamp gas, parasites, monkey shrieks, snakes, ants, black flies, jungle rot, millipedes, ticks, birds, boils, blood, worms, leeches, bats, leaf hoppers, earwigs, and Seals. That's right, Seals—U.S. Navy Seals, to be precise. About twenty-five of them had flown in to join us on maneuvers.

As a legionnaire I'd trained with a Seal team before. In the mountains of Corsica we'd run circles around them, and had even been able to match them quite often in swimming. But next to this team the group of Seals we'd trained with in Corsica was nothing. I knew it as soon as I saw them sweep into our base on a flood tide of muscle, maleness, and pride. They wore no uniform, but dressed as they pleased in sneakers, running suits, T-shirts, black pajamas, and red bandannas. For weapons, they carried all kinds of pistols, pump guns, and specialty knives. No question, these were the bad boys of the United States military, a handpicked élite given the run of the armory and set lose to scour the world. I liked them immediately and found myself wondering, as our two forces stood sizing each other up, which of us was tougher—us, or this group of cold-eyed, cocksure killers that called itself Seal Team Six.

After slogging for a week through the jungle I had my answer. Seal Team Six was tough, all right; there was no doubt about that. They were hard-trained, independent, and at sea they could probably kick our Legion asses—but on land, in the jungle, they were hopeless. When we told them that they should cover up as much as possible because of the jungle was full of parasites that could eat holes the size of dinner plates into their skin, they laughed instead of listening. When we suggested that they stop wearing socks because their feet would get jungle rot, they ignored us. When we warned them that their backpacks were stuffed with junk that they wouldn't need and shouldn't bring into the jungle they brought it anyway.

Now they were paying for their mistakes. Already, five of them were so sick that we had to stop and chop a landing zone out of the jungle so that a rescue helicopter could come in and pick them up. Working around the clock, hand-cutting the clearing took two days. That put us way behind schedule and pissed our men off. If the fucking Seals had only listened, this would never have happened.

To make up for lost time, the rest of us started sleeping less and moving more, which was just fine with me. In the jungle, sleeping was more of a chore than it was worth. Come nightfall, first we'd have to tie our hang nets up in the trees, then we'd spray our ropes with shaving cream to keep away snakes, pull on our ponchos, knot the hoods around our chins, coat our faces with more shaving cream, climb into the nets, and try to sleep. I say try because at night the shrieks, screams, and howls that came out of the jungle were so loud that it was like trying to sleep with a murder in progress. Plus, inside our ponchos it was hot, boiling hot, and even if you did manage to fall asleep, if you parted your lips to snore or to breathe, you'd instantly wake to a mouthful of bugs.

After the loss of five men, the remaining Navy Seals smartened up, and as we traveled deeper into the trembling jungle they began to show more respect for it and for us. Not that it mattered; after more than a month on the trail, our tempers, like our bellies, had grown thin. And if not for the fact that we were allies I'm sure each of our teams would have been more than willing to try their luck at kicking the shit out of the other. Instead, we slogged on, sometimes on our bellies along tunnels cut through the creepers, other times in single file through jungle so thick that it took us the better part of a day just to hack through a hundred feet of it.

By now our rations had been exhausted and we lived on what we could find. We ate the back meat of spiders and the entrails of bats. Insects plucked from the forest floor became a crunchy delicacy in our desperate mouths, and edible lizards a feast. Best of all, though, were snakes, and when the lead man in our group walked headlong into a boa the whole column came to a halt.

"Don't move! Stay still!" the soldier behind the lead man whispered. Then he and the next man in the column began the slow process of flanking the giant snake. I moved up in the column. Now another soldier and I were directly behind the lead man and could see the boa hanging from a tree, its head at eye level with ours. In training they'd warned us that a boa often opens its attack with a head butt. The force of its blow is so strong, they'd told us, that with one strike it could cave in a cow's skull.

"Hurry," I heard the man in front of us plead through clenched teeth as the snake began to raise and dip its head in a series of hypnotic undulations. But the path was narrow, just wide enough for one man, and the jungle thick, and the men were having a hell of a time getting clear behind the snake. Then, just as the snake rose to attack, the machete men closed and began hacking away. At the same time, we yanked the lead man backwards and the three of us tumbled to the ground just in time to be covered in a spray of fresh blood from the headless but still writhing snake.

That night, we gorged ourselves on boa meat. Of course, we offered the lead man first pick. More than any of us, he'd stared into the black reptilian eyes of the jungle and lived to tell the tale.

About a week later, we came out of the jungle. The next day, Seal Team Six packed and left. A few weeks after that we were sent back out again, this time for jungle combat training—a course that turned out to be even tougher than the survival course we'd just finished.

I returned to Calvi with six months left on my contract. My time as a legionnaire was tilting towards a close, and I was called to see the lieutenant.

"At ease, Master Corporal Vandenberg. So, tell me: do you plan to reenlist?"

"No, my lieutenant, I do not."

I was sent to see the captain, and then the colonel. They offered me officer's training, my pick of any of the Legion's top commando courses, sports school in France, the posting of my choice, permission to own a car or motorcycle, or even a shortened contract if I agreed to reenlist.

I turned it all down. I wanted out, and not because I missed the world outside the Legion gates. After all I'd been through, that world and I were strangers and always would be. No, I wanted out because after almost five years in the Legion the time had come for me to live or die as I was destined, and for me that meant Thailand and the bloody fighting ring. I was a single-combat warrior. Always had been, always would be.

And so I shook the colonel's hand and said goodbye. Like Waruny, the Legion would soon become a memory that would come upon me sometimes sweetly, and other times like a sword cutting through and through.

Kran

"Let's go. Get your ass out of bed." I opened my eyes to Daniel looming over me like a teth- ered zeppelin, a cold beer gripped in each hand.

I sat up, whipped and weary, and reached for one of the beers. Daniel tossed it over and I held the cold bottle to my cheek. The icy glass felt good against my ravaged face.

"How bad do I look?"

"What's the difference how you look? How do you feel?"

"Like shit," I answered. Last night's fights had been hard ones.

"Well, you got two months to get yourself right."

"Two months? Why two months."

"Because in two months you fight Kran."

"Kran?" And then it came wheeling back to me. Last night, in the truck, on the way back from the fights, Daniel had told me that he made the deal to fight Kran. Christ, Chiao Pran and that mercenary must've fucked me up worse than I thought if I had to search to remember that bit of news.

"Two months, huh? Not much time."

Daniel nodded and took a pull off his beer. "You're the one that wanted it, cowboy, not me."

I stood up and staggered. One of my legs had knotted up during the night. Like I always did the morning after a big fight, I started checking my body for damage: broken bones, bruises, joint injuries that I might not have noticed before.

Daniel stood watching me abstractedly. "Everything check out?" he asked after a while.

I wiggled my fingers and toes one more time, then did a couple more stretches. "Yeah. Got my money?"

Daniel gestured towards the bed. "Paid in full." I turned to where he pointed and saw the cash stacked up at the foot of the bed.

"Here, how much I owe you?" I said, bending down to snatch up the pile. "For room and board and all?"

"Forget it. I made plenty extra off what you did to that merc."

What I'd done to the merc had been a shame, a real shame, but he'd brought it on himself.

"You ask around who he was?"

"No, why? You need to know?"

"Just curious why he jumped me like that."

"Yeah, well I think the answer to that one went down with him."

I looked away and was about to toss the money back on the bed but thought better of it. "Here," I said holding the full thirty grand out to Daniel. "Hold it for me, and, when the time comes, bet it all."

"You got it, man. Now come on, pack up; we're heading out."

"Where to?"

"Laos."

"Laos? What for?"

"A freestyle training camp."

"Why the hell we going all the way there when there's plenty of good camps right here?"

"Not like this one."

"What's so special about it?"

"Kran is. He used to train there. They know his tricks and his style. You go out there, train with those boys, you're gonna know Kran's tricks too. Now get packed."

I popped my beer and raised it up. "To Laos."

"To whipping Kran's ass!" We clinked bottles and drained them off.

We drove to Laos in Daniel's truck, down bumpy roads, through fallow fields, under a cruel and climbing sun, the whole time talking of victory and the good times we'd have once the fight with Kran was through. We both wanted to believe—I desperately so—that I was going to be the one who'd beat Kran. After all, it wasn't just money I was betting here; it was my life, for Kran didn't suffer losers well. With him, there'd be no tapping out. If he didn't kill you outright, he'd leave you twisted and incapable of ever fighting again. I'd heard tales of men sprawled in the dirt with no fight left in them having their arms, knees, and ankles shattered for no good reason by Kran, of unconscious men being roused with a slap just so Kran could hear their death screams as he tore out their bowels with his hands.

"*Farang*, you must be crazy. Why you want to do this?" the Laotian teacher asked after Daniel explained why I'd come.

I stared at the teacher. He was old, past sixty, thin and pokerfaced. As he waited for me to answer he lifted the stump of his right arm, gone from the elbow down.

"You want this happen to you?" he asked. "'Cause this is what Kran will do. Believe me, I know, because I taught him."

"No, it won't happen to me. Not if you teach me how to fight him."

"Me, teach you? No. Go home, *farang.* You don't want to fight Kran. Go home and live," he said and turned to leave.

"Hey," I shouted and he spun back around. "You want me to leave, fine, but first you got to give me a fair chance to stay. Show me your best man. Let me fight him, any style. You don't like what you see, then I'll go."

The old man eyed me. I guess he liked my fire, because after a few seconds he nodded that we had a deal.

I was led to a boxing ring, thrown some gloves, and told to put them on. As I slipped on the gloves I watched the old man go over and talk to a few of his fighters who were working on some of the heavy bags. One of them, the largest one, broke off his training and came over to join me in the ring.

"You fight him. Muay Thai style. Three rounds. No breaks," the old man said.

"All right, just give me a minute to warm up here."

"This is your warmup. Now go!"

With that, the Thai fighter came at me, fists and feet blazing. I fought him defensively, blocking his low kicks and clinching when I could. There was no question he was trying for the quick kill. The old man must have told him to go in and humble the foreigner, but after two rounds I was still standing, and after three the fight had settled into a stalemate with neither of us able to effectively penetrate the defenses of the other.

At the end of the third round the old man called for a break. I knew I hadn't shown him my best stuff, but I'd done well enough, I figured, to ask him again if he'd train me. I was headed back to my corner to ask Daniel how we should proceed when the old man cut me off with a shout.

"Hey, *farang,* where you going? You're not through."

I turned just as the old man gestured a second fighter into the ring. Three rounds later, with blood running from my nose, and a cut opened above my left eye, the second fighter left the ring and was replaced by a third. By now, almost everyone in the camp had gathered around to jeer and shout every time I threw a punch or kick. It was humiliating and at the same time infuriating because I knew that had we been fighting freestyle instead of Muay Thai style I would have wasted my opponents long ago.

When the third fighter charged me I fought back with everything I had, but by now I was so tired that most of my kicks and punches barely touched him, while most of his scored direct hits. By the end of the seventh round he was smiling broadly. Halfway through the eighth we fell into a clinch and he caught me hard in the ribs. I fell to one knee, panting like a spent dog, the slick taste of blood on my lips. I looked up and for an instant saw the perfect opening to bring my opponent to the mat and choke him out, but since that wasn't allowed in Muay Thai, I stood up and fought on. For the next round and a half I took innumerable punches, kicks, knees, and elbows. The punishment was terrible, and when it was over, and the third fighter bowed and left the ring, I didn't even care if they sent in another because I already knew that I was lost. Everyone else in the gym knew it too, and as I walked back to my corner of the ring a silence fell over the place.

I glanced over at Daniel, who averted his eyes, and then towards the old man, who stared back at me for what seemed like forever. I knew he would never consent to train me now. Why bother? If it took all I had just to hold my own for nine rounds against three of his fighters what possible chance did I have against Kran? True it had been Muay Thai rules and not freestyle fighting, but still . . .

"I have one question for you," the old man finally said.

"What?" I asked between great gulps of air.

"Why?"

"What do you mean, 'why?' Why what?'"

"Why do you want to fight Kran?"

What the hell kind of question was that? I wondered. Was he going to tell me again to give up on a dream that was sure to get me killed?

"I'm a fighter, that's why," I answered. "The same as all the other men here."

"No, not the same," he said sounding indignant that I'd made the comparison. "You come from a rich country. It's different for you than for us. A man like you can do anything with your life, anything you want. But these men, they have to fight. For every man here, it's either fight or starve. You understand? These men don't fight, their families don't eat, their children go hungry. That's why they fight. Now why do you?"

Why did I fight? It was a question I'd wondered my whole life—how to explain my desire. "Because I want to be the best," I answered after a troubled pause.

"The best? But you already are—at least you're the best white fighter I've ever seen. You know how many Westerners have come here and tried to go nine rounds with my fighters?"

"No."

"Many. And do you know how many have?"

"No."

"One. You." He paused to let what he'd said sink in. Then, as soon as he saw the first flush of pride well in my face, he went on. "Not that there isn't a lot of room for improvement in your fighting. Your knee and elbow techniques, they're terrible; they need lots of work. And that's just for starters."

"So you'll teach me?"

"Yes, but that's the wrong question."

"Wrong question?"

Getting ready for Kran—a Muay Thai tune-up fight.

"Yes, what we want to know is not whether or not I will teach you, but whether or not you will learn."

The next day Daniel left the camp and I got busy learning: knee and elbow techniques, new kinds of takedowns, ways to attack various joints from in front and behind, and ways to defend against those same attacks. After I'd learned all the basics we began our study of Kran, his offense and defense, his strengths, and his weaknesses—which, according to the old man, were few.

"He's smart and he's fearless, and he usually makes it clear early who is going to be doing the losing in a fight. He can't be upset or distracted, because fighting is all he knows. You can't wear him down because fighting is all he does. You can't trick him or surprise him either because he's seen it all before."

"Great. Anything else I can't do?"

"Yes, you can't fear him, because fear is Kran's best ally. It's why he's gone undefeated for six solid years."

That night I slept to the sounds of beating wings and

horse's hooves, and the smudging horror of what I took to be Krans' face: his skin burnt black, his eyes exploded holes, his mouth an open pit, inferno red and screaming for my soul. I woke in a sweat, and that day, during training, everything I did was slightly off.

"What's the matter with you today?" the old man kept shouting, and when, finally, I got sick of making excuses, I broke down and told him about the dream and how the image of Kran's face had been throwing me all day.

"Go back to bed, then," he said.

I laughed, thinking he was joking, but he wasn't, and then he told me why.

"Understand that every time you fight a flesh and blood man, you fight his spirit too, and if you can beat his spirit, you can beat his flesh. They are two sides of the same being and it doesn't matter which you take on first. Crush one and you crush the other. So go back to bed, seek out Kran's spirit, and when you find it, crush it with your own."

Armed with the old man's words, I baited my hooks and went to sleep. All through that night, and for every night thereafter, I fished patiently for Kran, and when, finally, I pulled him from the black lake of my dreams, instead of trying to run or wake from the horror, I fought him spirit to spirit, man to man, because in sleep there is no difference between the two.

A few weeks later I was ready to draw real blood.

"Just remember," the old man said to me on our last day of training. "Kran will not hesitate, and he'll do whatever he needs to do to win. If that means biting the nose off your face or tearing the bones from your body, Kran will do it. To fight him, you have to be willing to do the same, without thought or hesitation. You have to be ready to kill."

I nodded that I understood and then asked him the question I'd been harboring for weeks.

"Why?"

"Why what?"

"Why me instead of Kran? Why aren't you training him?"

The old man shook his head. "You see this arm?" he said raising his stump. "I lost this arm fighting in Vietnam for the Americans. It's hard for a man to lose his right arm, but it's even harder for a man to lose his son. I lost my son to Kran."

"I'm sorry. I didn't know."

"No, you didn't, but now you should. You see, I trained Kran for almost two years, and when he left here and started speaking lies about me and the camp, my son challenged him to an honor match. I begged him not to. I knew what Kran could do, even then, but my son wouldn't listen. He fought him and was killed."

I bowed my head to spare the old man another witness to his shame.

"I tell you, if I was a younger man and had my arm, it would be me going out to face Kran, not you." The old man set his hand on my shoulder and squeezed. "Crush him. Do it. I know you can."

The next day, Daniel arrived.

"Ready?"

I nodded.

"Bring us honor," the old man said.

"Aren't you coming?" I gestured towards the back of the truck where others from the camp were already ensconced.

"I'll be there, Dominiquie, but not in flesh."

I bowed, climbed into the cab and watched the figure of the old man recede as we made our way to Kran.

A few hours later I stepped out of the truck, blinking in

the painful sunlight, scanning the empty dirt-brown fields that stretched in all directions.

"This is it?" I said to Daniel, looking puzzled.

"This is it," he answered, gesturing to the crude circle that someone had traced in the dirt with a stick.

I stood there staring. I didn't know why, but somehow I'd expected more. For the fight of my life, I figured a barn or warehouse, or at least a sheltering roof. Anything would be better than this nothingness. I turned away, annoyed. A little ways off, a bleak village squatted near a tangled growth of trees. I gestured towards it. "I'll be there," I said to Daniel, who twitched his head in answer. "In the temple. Come get me when it's time."

I walked towards the Buddhist temple. As I drew closer, a few villagers appeared, and then, as always, more, until I was surrounded by a gauntlet of wrinkled brown and yellow people waving fresh-plucked chickens, squealing baby pigs, and bony teenage girls under my nose. I shouted to drive them off, and when they didn't budge I raised my arm and pushed one to the ground. Seeing that, the rest backed off, their faces showing fear and disappointment. Immediately, I regretted what I'd done. These people's lives were hard enough without me adding to their pain, especially when I could just as easily give pleasure. Bending down, I rifled through my gym bag, searching for cash. It wasn't much, a few hundred at most, and I went through it quickly, pressing twenties and fifties into the hands of those who looked like they could use it most.

When the money was gone, I bowed and left them for the temple where I spent the rest of the day recumbent under the dream-struck face of Buddha.

"It's time." Daniel's voice cut through the temple silence.

I stood and stripped down to my fighting clothes.

While Daniel waited in the gathering shadows, I did my stretch and warmup drills. My last coherent memory was of leaving the temple and seeing baskets of fresh fruits, bowls of rice, and plates of eggs laid as offerings on the steps. Then came a maddening walk through darkened fields while inside me raged a terror so vast and pure that it left no room for anything other than itself. Then I remember cars and lights and the welter of the crowd that had gathered for the fight.

I stepped into the ring and waited. One minute. Two minutes. Five minutes and still no Kran. The bastard was playing a mind game on me and there was nothing I could do. Without an object to vent against, my mad, killing rut would soon exhaust itself. My angry terror would turn to common fear, and even my scent would change. After almost ten minutes of waiting I would be a different, lesser man than the one who had entered the ring.

And that's when Kran appeared. Bathed in an annulus of truck-mounted floodlights, he promenaded towards the ring like a prize fighting bull, scarred and muscled from head to haunches, his eyes blazing, his arms raised to acknowledge the crowd. He stepped into the ring and surveyed me with a snort. He likes it here, I thought; to him this is home.

I watched him perform the Thai ritual that's supposed to drive the evil spirits from the fight ring. As he stomped and spun and wagged his beefy legs, I searched within myself for some new reserve of power. I found none. Nothing. Not even a spark to fling into the face of the raging bull before me.

The ref gave the signal to start and Kran bent and charged in low. I met his attack as I'd been trained—by bracing my legs to absorb the impact and immediately throwing a modified guillotine chokehold around his neck. But Kran tucked his chin, and no matter how hard I squeezed I couldn't get him to lift it. The next thing I knew I was being pushed backwards, my boots furrowing dirt as Kran drove me before him. I redoubled my effort to close my hold on his neck, squeezing for all I was worth until my forearm felt like it would snap against the fulcrum of Kran's chin. It didn't even faze him. Instead, Kran broke out of my hold as if it was nothing and threw me into one of his own.

I didn't even have time to scream before I was face up on the ground with Kran sitting on top of me, raining down blow after blow. I tried to cover up and block his punches but had about as much luck doing that as I'd had in trying to catch him in the guard position—none.

Unable to lock Kran up, throw him over, or endure his short-armed punches much longer, I made what any fighter will tell you is just about the worst move you can make: I turned over on my belly and tried to slip away. Then, with Kran riding my back and bashing away at the back of my head I used what strength I had left to rise up onto my hands and knees. Of course, I kept my chin tucked to prevent Kran from throwing a chokehold around my neck, but that only made things worse when Kran reached down and yanked my wrists out from under me and I fell face first to the ground.

Now I was stuck face down in the dirt, a human worm doing a hopeless squirm-and-wiggle as Kran worked me to a pulp. Head butts, punches, knee and elbow stomps; I couldn't take much more, and soon my chin was giving way as Kran went for the chokehold. As he slipped his right arm in front of me and tried to close the hold on my neck, I reacted as only a freestyle fighter can. I grabbed his forearm, tugged it towards my teeth and bit him. I bore down with so much force that when he tried to tug his arm away I could hear the cheeping scrape of my teeth against his bone. He yanked his arm once, and then again, pulling so hard that I felt my teeth start to wrench free of their sockets. Rather than lose them, I unclamped my jaw just long enough to let my teeth find a new purchase, this time around the knuckles of his first two fingers, which I bit with all my might.

With his free hand, Kran began to punch the back of my head as he tried in vain to loosen my grip on his fingers. And when that didn't work he started kneeing me, and then he started screaming, and that's when I knew that the tide had finally turned.

As he ripped his mangled hand from my mouth, I rolled over and elbowed him full blast in the face, and when he fell backwards, blood gushing from his nose, I scrambled to my feet. My face was ugly, but Kran looked even worse: his nose was gone, his right hand useless, and as he rose up off his knees I added to his miseries with a front kick that left him spitting teeth. Then I really went to work, mauling his face and body with kick after kick until there was nothing left in me and Kran lay on the ground in a heap.

I turned around to face the anonymous crowd, too tired now to care either way how they felt about me or the outcome. I thought it was over, and was about to leave the ring, when all of a sudden Kran attacked me from behind. I couldn't believe it; I'd left Kran lying in the dirt with a face that in places showed clear through to bone, yet here he was again, his left hand clamping hard on my testicles, while his bloody right sought to pluck out my eyes.

We tumbled to the ground. I landed on my back with him astride. During the fall I'd managed to twist free of his viselike left hand, but not before he'd all but crushed one of my balls. With the pain of it ripping through my body, I fought him now from pure rage, all technique gone. Rolling in the dirt, we thrashed and threw punches, each one strong enough to kill a lesser man. Back and forth the fight went, first with him on top, then me. When I connected with an eye-gouge that jellied his left eye, and followed with a jaw-shattering right cross, I remember hearing the crowd howl in utter delirium. The fight had raised them to a fever pitch; now they wanted the cure.

I came to my feet and looked at Kran. He lay coiled on the ground, conscious, but without even the strength left to resist the killing blow that he surely knew was coming. He used his final moments to mumble what might have been a curse or a prayer. Around me, a hundred tongues began to scream their need for blood. "Kill him! Kill him!" And that's when I knew I that I wouldn't. Not tonight or any night would I kill for the pleasure of a crowd. The cunning hustlers, whores, cops, soldiers, and other rats who stood watching me would have to find their release elsewhere. I was going home; my bloody work here was through.

As I stepped past Kran's broken body and left the ring, I could feel his one good eye following me, and could tell that he too thought I was a fool for leaving him alive. No doubt, he was already plotting his revenge. Well, let him. I was better than him. I was better than all of them. I was Dominiquie Vandenberg, the best freestyle fighter in the world.

Geen Goede Daad Gaat Ongestraft

Flemish for "No good deed goes unpunished."

I'd defeated Kran, and as soon as the word got around the offers poured in. Suddenly, fighters from all over Thailand wanted to face me, and their backers kept upping the ante. Forty thousand. Fifty thousand. Sixty thousand. The amounts they proposed kept increasing. I should have been jubilant, but I wasn't. Instead, I felt nothing but a cold, almost killing despair, and for the first couple days after the fight I drifted around Daniel's place like a burned-out meteor.

Daniel chalked it up to my injuries and let me be for a while, but, as soon as I stopped pissing blood and the swelling in my face lessened to the point that I looked almost human again, Daniel started pestering me to fight.

"I think the Burmese boxer would be a good match. He's got a syndicate behind him. We're talking really big money. Beat him and your name would be all over Asia."

I told Daniel I'd think about it and went back to my ennui. Finally, Daniel confronted me.

"What's your problem, man? You wanna fight again or what?"

"Yeah, I want to fight again, but come on—it hasn't even been a week."

"You don't get it, do ya?"

"Get what?"

"You're on Thai time now, buddy. Like it or not, since you beat Kran, the Thai expect you to keep up his kind of fight schedule. That means a freestyle fight every month. Twelve bouts a year."

"You got to be kidding me."

"Why? Kran did it."

"Yeah, and look what it got him."

"He rode it too long. I mean, six years, come on. I figure all you got to do is put in about a year and we'll both be millionaires."

I let out a bitter laugh. Money—it always came down to that. Well, I didn't fight for money. I hadn't come to Thailand to become a performing monkey for the local betting crowd, and I told Daniel as much.

"What the hell are you talking about? This is what you wanted, isn't it? You're a fighter. What the hell else do fighters do?"

"Look, I told you up front, when I fight I do it for adventure, for honor, when the need wells up in me, or when there's no other way." I ticked off the reasons on my fingers. "You clear on that? I don't do it 'cause I'm supposed to. I don't do it for the money. I only do it when it says to do it from here." I rapped on my chest with my fist.

"From here?" Daniel pointed to his own chest and then shot me a look of exasperation. "Dominiquie, what the hell's that supposed to mean?"

I didn't even try to answer. You can't explain a warrior's heart to a man who doesn't have one himself.

Daniel saw he was getting nowhere with me. "Look, why don't you just take some time off. Go to Pattaya. Get yourself laid or something,"

"Yeah, sure. Why not?" A little travel might be good for me, I thought, might even lift me out of the post-fight funk I'd fallen into.

I grabbed fifteen grand from the pile I'd made off the fight and hopped the next bus to Pattaya. I wasn't quite sure what I'd do once I got there. Since leaving the Legion I'd lost interest in drinking. If my face weren't so banged up, I might try my luck chasing girls, though I doubted there's be many girls traveling on their own around Thailand. Thailand wasn't like Calvi, where during the last six months of my Legion tour I'd done nothing but chase easy pussy on the island's topless beaches.

As the bus rolled south, I thought back on my Legion days. It had been, what, nine months since I'd walked out the gate at Camp Raffalli? Hard to believe. It seemed more like forever. Another lifetime. And I wondered if, nine months from now, I'd look back on this time the same way. Maybe so, because even though I wasn't ready to admit it to myself, I was growing bored with my life in Thailand, as bored as I'd gotten in Calvi; even with all the sex, neither one was enough.

I got into Pattaya and took a room. After two days of trawling the beaches, I even managed to pick up on a vacationing Danish girl who'd wandered off from her canned tour to go exploring on her own. On our first night together we made love in the ocean, and then again on the sand, where afterward we lay like mollusks, oozing sex and open to the night.

The next day she dumped out of her tour to spend the rest of her vacation with me. At first, we stayed in Pattaya, humping in the tropical heat, but, when she started to worry that maybe she ought to be seeing something more of Thailand than me, I took her up to Bangkok, where we did a turn as tourists, taking in the sights. But to me, and to every man who saw her, she was the sight, bouncing along in a tiny tank top, her nipples poking through like darts, her perfect ass riding high in a pair of shredded cut-offs. She looked like an image out of one of those Scandinavian stroke books come to life, and for all I knew maybe she was.

"Will you be requiring anything else, sir?" the waiter asked. I shook my head no, and after he left I reached under the table for a friendly after-dinner grope.

"Can't you think of anything but sex?" she said, prying my hand off her thigh.

I looked at her, surprised, thinking maybe she was joking. But she wasn't, and that's when I knew that we were through, because the truth is, she was right. I couldn't think of anything but sex. I didn't want to. I plain refused, and with good reason. Like the drinking I'd given up, and the fighting and the training I still did, sex gave a cover to my boredom and blotted out most of my despair. The poor girl. I hadn't meant to use her, but I had, and there was no way in the short time we had left together that I could ever make it right, even if I wanted to, which I didn't.

"What is it? What's wrong?" she said as I stood up and tossed a couple hundred on the table as well as the keys to our hotel room.

"It's over," I said and walked away. She could keep the room and everything in it. If I needed to I could always rent another room. I could buy new clothes, even find another girl. I had the cash. Tucked in my money belt I had thousands and thousands, with plenty more waiting in the wings. I had so much money, in fact, that I could throw it away by the fistful if I wanted, because I knew that as long as I could make a fist I could always earn more.

I went out and walked the streets of Bangkok. Me and my fists and my money, and none of it enough to heal the pain inside me, or fill the empty architecture of my soul. Perhaps this was how Kran had been able to bring himself to fight every month for all those years. To get away from the dread that hides within us, a man will do just about anything. He'll bury himself in any hole, take any job, and gladly fight all comers. He'll even kill if he has to, and learn to love it if it means he doesn't have to face the terror of himself for one more day.

I walked for hours, lost in thought, until the sound of a young girl crying forced my awareness to the street. Looking up, I saw a Thai girl, maybe twelve or thirteen years old, being dragged along by a middle-aged white guy.

"Come on, bitch, move your skinny ass," he shouted at the girl in German, and then he kicked her.

Fucking Nazi scum, I thought, as I walked past him. And suddenly I remembered the rows of helpless children I'd seen quartered in that warehouse in Northern Thailand. All those innocents on their way to Bangkok to be raped, tortured, and beaten, and I'd done nothing. I'd never lifted a finger. Well, not this time.

"Hey, you!" I shouted out in German to the Nazi.

He stopped and turned around as I approached. "What's your problem, man?"

"What are you doing? Why is this girl crying like that?"

"Look, I just paid a pimp a thousand dollars for two days with this bitch. She's supposed to be a virgin; I'm going to pop her, and I don't give a fuck if she likes it or not."

"Well, I do."

"Well, fuck you, then. Screw off," he shouted and turned to walk away.

I followed him at quick pace, fumbling for my money. "Hey," I shouted after him. "I'll pay you whatever you paid for her. I got a thousand right here, see."

I held out the money. But instead of taking the cash from my hand, he swung a fist at my face. I jerked back, dodging his punch. Then I caught him with a right to the stomach, and followed with a left to the chin. He fell on his ass, and as he tried to get up I kicked him in the face, knocking him cold.

"Let's go," I said to the girl after I stuffed the thousand dollars into the unconscious German's open mouth.

She was very afraid, and between her broken English and my useless Thai all I could get from her was her name: Nitai, she kept saying over and over while pointing to herself: Nitai, Nitai.

I brought Nitai to a small hotel where the innkeeper knew me and could translate.

"Tell Nitai I want to help her. Ask her what she needs?"

The innkeeper translated, and soon Nitai's story spilled out in a flood of tears. It turned out that she'd only left her village a few weeks ago, and that the German had been her first trick. She and two of her friends had been lured from their homes with promise of jobs waiting for them as waitresses. But when they got to Bangkok they were immediately pressed into prostitution, and when her girlfriends refused, and fought and cried rather than sleep with the customers, her pimp murdered them by injecting them both with an overdose of heroin.

"You believe her?" I asked the innkeeper as Nitai wept.

"It happens, Dominiquie. If a new girl keeps refusing customers, their pimp will overdose them, that way it looks like an accident and it's impossible to prove that it wasn't."

"Did she actually see the pimp overdosing her friends?"

"She says she did. She says he made her watch to teach her to fear him. He said she was going to be next if she didn't please the German."

"Ask her if she wants to go to the police."

"Dominiquie," the innkeeper said without even bothering to ask her, "the police won't do anything. They're all paid off by the pimps—especially hers. I've heard of him; he's a powerful man, like a Mafia chief in your country. If he finds her now, she's dead."

That night, I lay on the floor while Nitai slept curled in the bed. I hadn't planned to get involved in this little girl's rescue, and I still wasn't sure how to play it. If I took her back to Daniel's, she'd end up a whore. If I sent her back to her poor farming family they'd only sell her again. If I gave her money and left her alone, her pimp would track her down, and that would be the end of her. As far as I could figure, there really was only one thing to do.

The next day I bought the kind of clothes that Western tourists wear, a wig, and some makeup to cover the bruises still left on my face. That night I walked into the Go Go Dream Bar like any other horny guy, except that under my shirt was a loaded Beretta that I'd bought off an old contact out of Marc's bar.

After a few turns around the bar I sat down and ordered a drink, and when one of the bar girls came to sit in my lap I slipped her a hundred and told her I wanted to see the boss about his house specialties. A few minutes later a man led me upstairs to a small room lit by a red bulb.

"Wait here," he said.

I nodded, and when he stepped out of the room I poked my head out and watched him tramp down the hall, knock on a door and enter a room thick with smoke and the sounds of men drinking and gambling. I ducked back in the room and waited.

"Welcome, my friend." The pimp greeted me with

greedy black eyes and the flash of a gold-toothed smile. "So what is your special taste tonight? Young virgin girls? Boys? We have the best."

"No, I'm here to buy Nitai from you."

"Nitai? Where is she?"

"She's safe."

"Oh, you think so?"

"I'll give you five thousand dollars for her."

"She's not for sale, *farang.*"

"I'll give you ten thousand and that's my final offer."

"Your final offer? Ten thousand dollars?"

He shouted something in Thai and two men armed with pistols stepped into the room. "*Farang,* do you know what you're getting into here?"

"Hey, I'm not looking for trouble," I lied.

"But you have already found it, *farang.* You see, Nitai belongs to me, and I say she's not for sale. And what I say goes. Always!" he said, stepping up into my face.

"You're right. I must have been crazy to even try this. I'm sorry. I promise I'll bring her back right now. I just fell in love with her, you know. I lost my head and—"

"You fell in love with her?" He laughed and translated what I'd said into Thai, and then his men were laughing too over the foreigner who'd stupidly fallen in love with a whore. It was just what I expected, and before any of them could a move I had the pimp locked up in a chokehold and the Beretta pressed to his head.

"Tell them to get on the floor! Hands on their heads! Now!"

I loosened the chokehold just enough to let the pimp give the order, and when he had, and his lackeys were face down on the floor, I pumped a bullet into each of them, pistol whipped the pimp, let him drop, and shot him twice.

A second later I stepped into the hall and lost myself in

the crowd of johns and whores, all rushing to get away from the sound of gunfire. Later, I burned the shoes, wig, and clothes, threw the Beretta into the sea, and returned to the hotel where I had the innkeeper tell Nitai that she was free.

"How'd you manage it?" the innkeeper asked.

"I bought her," I answered.

"Must have really cost."

"It did." I said and slid him a few thousand bucks. "Here, get her enrolled in some kind of live-in school."

The innkeeper nodded.

"I'll be back to check up on her in a few months. If she's still in school, there'll be plenty more money for both of you."

Early the next morning I gave Nitai all the cash I had left, keeping just enough to pay for my return trip up north. "Don't let me down," I told the innkeeper, then I left.

Two months later I returned to the inn, but the innkeeper and Nitai were both gone, and I never knew if what I'd done had saved her or only ended up making her sad life even worse.

Koan

To learn to fly first you have to
forget to hit the ground.

I remember the scorched red dirt, the bone-white sky, and the hours and hours of blast-furnace sun that licked at the train, so hot it made the tracks appear to shimmer and the walls of my compartment sweat. So hot that even my rage, which had been rising like drawn water ever since I'd left Bangkok, could not stand against it and eventually was boiled away. I sat alone in a compartment meant for four, on a hard bench like a penitent. Headed north. And why not? To the south, Nitai had disappeared, and with her went all belief that anything in this world could ever be helped or healed by the likes of me. To the east, Waruny had been turned to ash by the cruelties of war. To the west lay my brother and my mother both defeated by a common foe, which you call cancer but I know as civilization. No, I would not be heading any of those ways again. For me, only the road north still lay open. North to where Kran and others like him slept in the blood of their own wounds, waiting for the call to rise and fight. North to war. North to battle. North to rage inside the iron circle, eventually passing like all things great and true into legend, into myth, and into the shrouded mists of death.

As I sat in bitter contemplation, a Buddhist monk entered the compartment.

"May I sit?" he asked

I nodded, surprised to see a Westerner—an American, judging by his accent—in the orange frock, shaved head, and bare feet of a Thai monk.

Placing his small kit bag and begging bowl on his lap, the monk surveyed me with a look of tenderness and wonder. "You're a martial artist, aren't you?" he asked, and when I nodded that I was he added, "You remind me of a pot about to boil."

"Who wouldn't boil in this heat?" I answered.

"But it's not the heat that's cooking you—it's your desire. You're a man in love with his own drama."

I couldn't believe the monk's audacity and I shot him my best Legion glare; usually that would be enough to make a normal man stand down. But this monk was not a normal man. Instead he met my gaze with a look at once so knowing and forgiving that it cut through my contempt like sun through fog. Then he launched into a tale.

"A warrior once came to see a great master to ask him what Heaven and Hell were like. 'Who are you?' the great master asked. 'I'm a samurai,' the warrior answered. 'No, you're too lazy to be a samurai. You're just a lowly soldier,' the master told him. Well, that made the samurai angry, and he drew his sword to kill the master. But the master remained calm. 'That sword,' he said, 'is probably too dull to hurt me anyway.' And as the samurai raised his sword in a killing rage, the master looked at him and said, 'Now you know for yourself what Hell is.' Hearing that, the samurai stopped, sheathed his sword, surrendered his rage, and bowed in shame before the master. 'Now you know what Heaven is too,' the master said."

"Nice story," I told him, "but I'm not looking for any master to bow down to."

"Maybe not, but the fact is, you are bowing down; we all are all the time, either to Heaven or to Hell."

"Maybe so, but I'd rather it be my choice how I live and what I bow to."

"You think it's your choice, do you?'

"That's right."

"Then tell me why you chose to bow in Hell when you could be living in Heaven?"

I stared at the monk, unable to answer, and he continued.

"You believe in your own power, in the supremacy of your martial arts techniques, but actually you're just a sheep in wolf's clothing, and you're leading yourself to the slaughter."

No one had ever spoken to me like this before and gotten away with it, but somehow this monk, with a few simple words, had reached a part of me that I'd long believed was dead. When I boarded this train I'd fully expected that this would be my final ride. I was headed north to fight in single combat until the earth reached out to swallow me up. But now I saw that there just might be another way, the monk's way. And as I listened to the flood of his ideas I found myself being carried to heights and just as quickly dropped to depths that I didn't know existed.

"Why are you telling me all this?" I remember asking him at one point.

"Because when you meet a master swordsman on the road you show him your sword," he said.

And what a sword he showed, sharp enough to cut through the most well-defended enemy; it was a sword that did not injure but enlightened as it struck. I asked him how he came to master such a weapon and he told me about his past as a United States Special Forces fighter in Vietnam.

"When I was in Vietnam, I killed more men than I care to count, but it wasn't until I finally killed myself—my old self, that is—that I was able to jump clear of death. Now I only use my sword to cut through illusion."

And right then I knew that I had to do the same. "Help me cut through my illusions."

"How can I? You still believe that your illusions belong to you. Did you ever consider that maybe you belong to them?"

"What if I pay you? Will you teach me what you know?"

"Look at me; do I look like I want money? I want nothing. I offer nothing. Nothing to learn. Nothing to do. Nothing to attain that you don't already possess."

And when I asked again for his help, he told me something even stranger. "You think I'm here by accident? Your life has asked the universe a question. I am only here to help it find its answer."

"Are you saying our meeting here was preordained or something?"

"Don't ask me. You're the one standing at the gate. All you have to do is walk through. Walk through and you'll have your answer."

"Walk through what gate, to where?"

"That I can't tell you. But I can tell you this: As long as you think you have something to gain, you'll never gain it. As long as you think there's something more you need to do, it won't be done."

"You're talking in riddles now."

"Because words are not the gateway to true knowing, and riddles open the mind to something more."

Then for the first time since he entered the

compartment he fell silent. It was as if a voice inside him had suddenly begun to speak and he had stopped to listen.

"Your problem is that you haven't given up yet," he said after a full five minutes of silence had ticked by.

"I haven't given up yet? Given up what?"

And then, like a shot, I remembered hearing those same words spoken years before by Master Takimuro: "Give up. Forget everything. That's when it will happen for you."

"Reality is created by your beliefs," the monk went on. "Give them up. Give up your beliefs. And when you've given up even the belief that reality is created through belief, what's left is what lies beyond the gate."

I didn't know what he meant, not yet. But, then, I don't think he expected me to. Even much later, after I'd been sitting in the jungle and meditating with him for months, I wasn't sure I if fully understood or ever would. All I knew was that I had been launched on a path that has no beginning and no end, and that this man, who was now my teacher, had opened the door to a way that can not be learned but only lived, and to a knowledge that the more you speak of it, the more evanescent it becomes.

"Then why am I sitting here listening to you talk about it all the time?" I once asked him in frustration.

"Then knock on the sky and listen to its sound," he answered before stepping into the darkness that was really only light.